The Way of Ignatius Loyola

The Way of Ignatius Loyola

CONTEMPORARY APPROACHES TO
THE SPIRITUAL EXERCISES

Edited by

Philip Sheldrake SJ

THE INSTITUTE OF JESUIT SOURCES

First United States Edition 1991

First published in Great Britain 1991

SPCK
Marylebone Road
London NW1 4DU

Compilation and Introduction © Philip Sheldrake, S.J.

Number 13 in Series IV: Studies on Jesuit Topics

© 1991 The Institute of Jesuit Sources
3700 West Pine Blvd.
St. Louis, MO 63108
Tel: 314-652-5737
Fax: 314-652-0810

All rights reserved

Library of Congress Catalog Card Number 91-73016
ISBN 0-912422-65-3

Contents

Contributors

PHILIP SHELDRAKE SJ is a British Jesuit. He is Co-Director of the Institute of Spirituality, Heythrop College, University of London, and an editor of *The Way*. He is the author of a number of articles and of *Images of Holiness* (London/Notre Dame 1987) and *Spirituality and History: Questions of Interpretation and Method* (London 1990).

LAVINIA BYRNE IBVM is a member of the Institute of the Blessed Virgin Mary. She is an editor of *The Way* and on the staff of the Institute of Spirituality, Heythrop College. She has written a number of articles and books including *Women before God* (London/Mystic, CT, 1988) and *Sharing the Vision: Creative Encounters between Religious and Lay Life* (London/Cambridge, MA, 1989).

GERARD W. HUGHES SJ is a British Jesuit based in Birmingham, England. There he works in developing the lay ministry of spiritual direction and retreat-giving especially among Christians of different traditions engaged in justice and peace work. He is the author of *God of Surprises* (London 1985), *In Search of a Way* (London 1985) and *Walk to Jerusalem* (London 1991).

BRIAN GROGAN SJ is an Irish Jesuit and was until recently director of the Jesuit Centre of Spirituality at Manresa House, Dublin. Currently he is novice master of the Irish Province. A regular contributor to *The Way* on Ignatian topics, he has co-authored with Una O'Connor IBVM two booklets, *Reflective Living* and *Love Beyond all Telling*.

JOSEPH VEALE SJ is a member of the Irish Jesuit Province. He has regularly given the Ignatian Spiritual Exercises at home and abroad. He also teaches in the Milltown Institute of Philosophy and Theology in Dublin.

PETER MCVERRY SJ is an Irish Jesuit and has worked in deprived city and suburban areas for fifteen years. He works for the Jesuit Centre for Faith and Justice which seeks to raise awareness of the structural causes of injustice in Ireland. He is resident director of a hostel for homeless children and his other concerns are youth unemployment and juvenile criminal justice structures.

MONIKA HELLWIG is a professor of systematic theology at Georgetown University, Washington D.C., a past president of the Catholic Theological Society of America and is active in ecumenism. She contributes frequently to spirituality and theology journals and is the author of a number of books, including *Jesus the Compassion of God* and *Gladness Their Escort* (Wilmington, DE).

Contributors

WILLIAM BRODERICK SJ is a British Jesuit. He has been involved in retreat work in Britain and the United States for some years and was until recently the Director of St Beuno's Spiritual Exercises Centre in North Wales.

DERMOT MANSFIELD SJ is a member of the Jesuit Centre of Spirituality, Manresa House, Dublin where, among other work, he has contributed to training programmes for spiritual directors. During the past five years he has been involved in the development of directed retreats at parish level in Ireland and Britain.

MARGOT O'DONOVAN RC is a member of the Congregation of Our Lady of the Cenacle. After many years in formation and administration, she is at present based at the Cenacle Retreat House, Killiney, Ireland where she is engaged in retreats, spiritual direction and workshops.

MARTHA SKINNIDER SND is a Sister of Notre Dame de Namur. For the last fourteen years she has lived in a deprived area in one of Glasgow's peripheral housing schemes and works with local residents' groups. From this work has grown an involvement in giving the Spiritual Exercises to local residents.

JOHN F. WICKHAM SJ is a Canadian Jesuit. He has been on the staff of the Ignatian Centre of Spirituality, Montreal, since 1977 and has been its Director since 1980. He is the author of *Prayer Companions' Handbook* (1984), *The Common Faith* and *The Communal Exercises* (both 1988), and *The Real Presence of the Future Kingdom* (1990), all published by Ignatian Centre Publications, Montreal.

DONALD ST LOUIS teaches graduate students in pastoral ministry and counselling psychology at Santa Clara University, California. He has extensive experience in spiritual direction, religious formation and pastoral counselling. He is also a psychotherapist.

DAVID LONSDALE SJ is a British Jesuit. He has been working in Ignatian spirituality and adult religious formation for ten years. He is co-Editor of *The Way* and author of *Eyes to See, Ears to Hear: an Introduction to Ignatian Spirituality* (London 1990).

ELINOR SHEA OSU is an Ursuline of the Roman Union. She is engaged in spiritual direction and retreat work and is also involved with the training of spiritual directors at the New York Archdiocesan Center for Spiritual Development.

MICHAEL J. BUCKLEY SJ recently served as the Executive Director of the Committee on Doctrine for the U.S. National Conference of Catholic Bishops. He has taught theology for many years and is now professor of systematic theology at the University of Notre Dame. He has written extensively in spirituality and philosophical theology. His latest book is *At the Origins of Modern Atheism* (New Haven, CT, 1987).

MICHAEL IVENS SJ has been for several years a director of the final year of Jesuit formation (tertianship) in various countries. He is on the staff of the St Beuno's Spiritual Exercises Centre, Wales. He has contributed to *The Way* and other journals and is currently engaged in a new translation of and commentary on the Spiritual Exercises.

Preface

The Spiritual Exercises of St Ignatius of Loyola used to be largely the preserve of those Roman Catholic religious communities whose spiritualities were in some way 'Ignatian'. In recent years the text of St Ignatius has reached a much wider public (no longer purely Roman Catholic) through the striking increase of retreats in the Ignatian tradition.

As an aid both to people who have experienced the Exercises for themselves and to those who wish to guide others through this experience, *The Way* journal of spirituality has regularly published *Supplements* on Ignatian spirituality. This book is a response to the suggestion by a number of people in the fields of retreat-giving and training that a collection of essays from the journal, some of which are out of print, should be made available in book form. It is especially appropriate that its publication should occur during the Ignatian Anniversary year which marks the 450th anniversary of the establishment of the Jesuit Order in 1540 and the 500th anniversary of the birth of St Ignatius in 1491.

As editor, I have had in mind two types of people. First, those who have had some exposure to the Exercises through retreats will hopefully find that the essays deepen their understanding of the spirituality of St Ignatius. Second, the essays are written by people who are experienced in giving the Exercises to others and will, I hope, be of assistance to potential guides. This focus implies two things. First, most of the essays presuppose a basic familiarity with the text of the Exercises, its structure and vocabulary. Second, the purpose of this book is practical rather than scholarly.

Finally, the writers represent five countries of the English-speaking world: England, Scotland, Ireland, Canada and the United States of America. The essays, apart from the Introduction and that by Lavinia Byrne, have been published previously in *The Way* or *The Way Supplements*. These have, however, been revised and abridged for this book with the agreement of the authors. The titles of some articles have been changed to fit better the structure of the book. At times, some technical language has been 'translated' into more everyday terms. The better-known word, 'retreatant', has been substituted for 'exercitant' except where quoted from other sources. Inclusive language has been introduced except in direct quotations or references to early sources.

Throughout the book, the abbreviation Exx refers to the text of *The Spiritual Exercises* and references are to the standard numeration for its sections. The abbreviation MHSJ refers to the *Monumenta Historica Societatis Jesu* (the series of foundational Ignatian texts).

Philip Sheldrake sj
The Way
Heythrop College, London

Acknowledgements

I am grateful, first of all, to those people who suggested that a wider readership would benefit from a collection of essays on the Exercises drawn from *The Way* and *The Way Supplements*. My gratitude is also due to the authors of the original articles for agreeing not only to republication but also to some revisions of titles and language.

Lavinia Byrne kindly agreed to contribute a new essay. She and David Lonsdale, my fellow editors at *The Way*, and Mary Critchley, the Editorial Assistant, have supported the project from the start and have helped in many ways by their advice and tolerance. Philip Law of SPCK encouraged me by his enthusiasm when I first suggested the project and provided sensible advice during its preparation for publication.

I am grateful to David Lonsdale, Philip Endean, Terence O'Reilly and Kate Stogden for reading a draft of my Introduction and for their helpful comments on its content and style.

Of the material in the book, only the Introduction and Chapter 1 have not been published previously. In their original form the other chapters appeared in *The Way Supplement* (*WS*) or *The Way* (*W*) as follows: Chapters 2, 3 and 20 appeared in *WS* 27, Spring 1976. Chapters 4 and 5 appeared in *WS* 48, Autumn 1983. Chapters 6, 7 and 14 appeared in *WS* 52, Spring 1985. Chapters 8 and 13 appeared in *WS* 55, Spring 1986. Chapter 9 appeared in *WS* 58, Spring 1987. Chapters 10 and 19 appeared in *WS* 46, Spring 1983. Chapter 11 appeared in *WS* 49, Spring 1984. Chapter 12 appeared in *WS* 34, Autumn 1978. Chapter 15 appeared in *WS* 38, Summer 1980. Chapter 16 appeared in *W*, October 1985. Chapter 17 appeared in *WS* 54, Autumn 1985. Finally, Chapter 18 appeared in *WS* 20, Autumn 1973.

Further information about Ignatian essays in *The Way* or *The Way Supplements* may be obtained from The Editors, *The Way*, Heythrop College, 11-13 Cavendish Square, London W1M 0AN, United Kingdom.

Introduction

Philip Sheldrake

The situation of Ignatian spirituality has changed radically in three important ways since the Second Vatican Council. First of all, exposure to the tradition, especially the Spiritual Exercises, has extended beyond religious communities and, most strikingly, beyond the Roman Catholic Church. Secondly, the presentation of the Exercises, particularly in English-speaking countries, has recovered its flexibility and concentrated more on the individual retreatant than on the group. Finally, the main focus of Ignatian spirituality has become practical and experiential rather than theoretical. This book predominantly reflects the practical concerns of the period of rediscovery.

Many people, nowadays, experience the Spiritual Exercises as a highly effective instrument for spiritual growth. For some, exposure to the Exercises has been akin to a conversion experience. There have been positive testimonies in the British media, including the popular press, and a recent outstanding religious bestseller in English is based on Ignatian themes.[1] Some people, both Roman Catholics and others, find this surprising. The rather austere theology and hell-fire sermons of Jesuits, dramatized in James Joyce's novels and experienced in parish missions, lingers on in the memories of some older Catholics. Some other Christians have inherited folk-memories of the Inquisition and a suspicion of 'Romish idolatry' of which Jesuit devotions seemed particularly potent symbols. These changes are certainly welcome. Many of the riches of the Ignatian tradition have re-emerged after a long period of obscurity or misunderstanding and more people can gain access to them. However, the changes also raise serious questions about how to use Ignatian spirituality effectively and validly in our own age. In the remainder of this introduction I seek to highlight some of the more crucial questions and then conclude with some remarks about the structure of the book and my choice of essays.

CAN WE ADAPT THE TEXT?

The presentation of the Spiritual Exercises has, in practice, been adapted to the needs of its new public. Several writers in this book wonder how far we can use the text as it stands. It is dangerous to assume that the use of a spiritual text from one age in another involves few difficulties. Whether we rely on the Exercises for our own spirituality, or seek to offer them to others, we need some theory of interpretation, or hermeneutics. Without this, we will tend to adopt one of two extremes. Either we select those elements of a text that immediately suit our needs or we present the text in a literal way because, for us, faithfulness implies adherence to every word on the page. Rather, what is needed is a receptive and, at the same time, critical dialogue with the text. This allows its wisdom to challenge us and yet gives us the freedom to discover new riches in the tradition that directly address our present values, and were never conceived by Ignatius in his contingent circumstances.[2]

We also need to be aware that agreement on an appropriate text for use has been contentious. There are a number of early versions of the Exercises and people have disagreed about whether the so-called Spanish Autograph or the Latin Vulgate is more 'authentically Ignatian'. The vulgate became the officially-approved version from the sixteenth to the nineteenth centuries but it is more usual nowadays to treat the Autograph as definitive. The translation of the Autograph by Louis Puhl has become the most popular text in English.[3] This is not merely an arcane question for dusty scholars. It overlaps with issues regarding the subsequent history of the Exercises and how they were used in the period up to the Official Directory of 1599 and beyond. Was there an attempt, in official circles, to respond to criticisms that Ignatian spirituality placed too great an emphasis on inner freedom and personal inspiration by adopting a safer and more methodical path? The final essay in this volume draws attention to some of these problems.[4] The point is that how we interpret the text will determine what we emphasise when giving the Exercises.

The Exercises is a text for use rather than for inspirational reading. Thus, interpretation-through-use is central. What are we to include or to ignore in our presentation of the text? In practice, most retreat-givers I know bypass the Rules for Thinking with the Church (Exx 352-70) when giving the Exercises. The Rules appear to be a typically unattractive example of Counter-Reformation paranoia. Without insisting on rigid textual integrity or suggesting that such judgements about the Rules are necessarily incorrect, it seems to me that this is largely an automatic rather than a carefully thought-out response. More variable, perhaps, are attitudes of retreat-givers to other elements such as the meditation on Hell in the First Week (Exx 65-71) or the (unscriptural) apparition of the Risen Jesus to his mother as a contemplation in the Fourth Week (Exx 218-25).

It is worth noting at this point that, in any adaptation of the text, historical precedent, whilst important, cannot solve all the questions provoked by contemporary needs. This is why a theory of interpretation, that allows us to be critical of the limitations of the text, as well as sensitive to its continued riches, is so important and liberating.

CAN WE CRITICIZE IGNATIUS?

Since Ignatius's perspectives were time-conditioned and contingent we need to accept that they can be criticized. Modern historians, such as John Bossy and Marjorie O'Rourke Boyle, have pointed out the danger, detected in some Jesuit writers, of removing spiritual experience to a realm above and beyond historical and psychological conditions.[5] Modern historians are aware that historical 'facts' are not value-free but, because they are *mediated* to the contemporary enquirer through our own questions and values, always involve critical interpretation.[6]

Ignatius's Exercises operate within particular theological horizons. This involves two issues. Positively, the deeper theological insights (for example, the doctrine of God and christology in the meditation on the Incarnation, Exx 101-109), implicit in the methodology and psychology of the Exercises, can still challenge us.[7] Critically, however, some of Ignatius's conventional theological formulations are open to question. In other words, we need to take into account that aspects of his language may provoke unhelpful reactions among retreatants. While it is not helpful to turn a retreat into an abstract theological discussion, it may be necessary nowadays, in presenting the text of the Exercises, to agree certain ground-rules at the start.

3

A lack of theological awareness on the part of directors affects the presentation of the Exercises in subtle, and unhelpful, ways. The problem of theology is highlighted by Ignatius's understanding of salvation, sin and hell in the exercises of the First Week. Other potential sources of theological culture-clash might be the language of good and evil spirits, who influence human beings, in the Rules for Discernment, and the relationship of God's will to each and every person assumed by the Rules. To retain their effectiveness in the present day, the Exercises often need to be 'translated' in terms of a renewed theology of grace and the human person.[8]

Two contemporary values in particular, social justice and feminism, seem to demand a 're-translation' of the text. In interpreting texts nowadays we are more aware of the hidden ideologies in our spiritual past. We need to pay attention to the concerns of people who have been marginalized in the past and who now seek a proper identity and a sense of history which liberates.[9] Although some people believe that the Rules for Thinking with the Church *may* be an attempt to remind people of the need for a collective dimension to spirituality, it seems fair to say that the Exercises have a strongly personal emphasis.[10] Certainly, the text does not have a social dimension in the modern sense. However, that does not mean that we have to adopt a completely individualistic standpoint in order to be faithful to Ignatius's wisdom. Sometimes it is possible to show that the text is not as individualistic as we have assumed but at other points it becomes necessary to reread the text in more social terms.[11] A number of the essays in this book address this issue. We should not, however, be naive. The Exercises, however presented and 'reread', cannot provoke a social conversion on their own. They are not a magic formula. Equally, we need to be careful about illegitimately manipulating people's reactions within the dynamic of the Exercises.

Traditional translations of the Exercises cause problems for people who are sensitive about inclusive language. What are we to make of the Three Classes of Men? The issue, however, is deeper than masculine nouns and pronouns. Some of the imagery of conflict, battle and victory, for example in the exercises called the Kingdom of Christ and The Two Standards (Exx 91-8 and 136-47), does not recommend itself to women (or indeed to many men). The understanding of spiritual development implicit in the text may need some reappraisal in the light of a feminist critique of traditional spiritual theology. It has been suggested that to image sin primarily in terms of riches, honour and pride (Exx 142) contrasts with many women's experience. As far as I know, there is only one inclusive-language version of the Exercises in print although I have heard of another in private circulation. A feminist reflection on and critique of the language, imagery and process of the Exercises is due to be published in *The Way Supplement*.[12]

THE THIRTY-DAY EXERCISES AND OTHER 'IGNATIAN RETREATS'

In recent years most people have come across Ignatian spirituality through short directed retreats of six to eight days. Should these be mini-versions of the month-long Exercises? There is nothing in the text of the Exercises or in its early history to support a practice of squeezing a 'summary' of the *full* Exercises into a short space of time. Two points are important. Firstly, the wisdom of the tradition indicates that the *dynamic* of the Exercises, in relationship to the inner process of the retreatant, needs an extended period of time to unfold (e.g. Exx 4). Secondly, the underlying principle of flexibility in response to the particular retreatant counters any attempt to force retreatants through spiritual hoops (e.g. Exx 17, 18 and the Additions). These two basic values seem to rule out any possibility of collapsing the dynamic of the full Exercises into a short period of time.

Historically, it is worth recording that the Jesuit practice of making annual eight-day retreats began in 1608, long after Ignatius's death. These undoubtedly developed into mini-versions of the Exercises but this was a time when retreats were *preached* and took little or no account of the subjective states of the retreatants. The Exercises were conceived 'objectively' as key meditations in the proper order or the correct sequence of the four 'Weeks' with the appropriate 'graces' to be prayed for. The inner spiritual dynamic of the *particular retreatant* was not really considered. The renewed practice of relying on individual guidance demands a sense of dynamic simultaneously in the Exercises and in the retreatant. Thus, the idea of 'giving the Exercises' in shortened form has given way, in most directors, to a more flexible attention and response to the

5

needs of individual retreatants based more on Scripture than on the text of the Exercises. This may, if appropriate, refer to elements of the Exercises but no more than that. The effectiveness of such retreats is well documented and it may be valid to consider these as 'Ignatian' or even as adaptations of the Exercises *in the broad sense*. However, the witness of Ignatius's own practice, reinforced by the experience of contemporary directors, suggests that we respect the nature of the *full* Exercises and not attempt to adapt this particular dynamic to shortened retreats.

A second practice, of adapting the full Spiritual Exercises to 'everyday life', has emerged in the last few years. Because Annotation 19 (Exx 19) refers to retreats for those 'engaged in public affairs or necessary business' the term often used is 'Nineteenth Annotation Retreat'. People's instincts are always to look for historical precedent. However, the evidence seems ambiguous. For example, two recent writers on the subject differed substantially on what the tradition actually offers to the present. Annotation 19 may not, in fact, refer to the *full* Exercises. In this case, contemporary interpretation-through-use would also be a new departure. The effectiveness of giving retreats 'in daily life' over the long-term will, in practice, provide the only real criterion for judging the appropriateness and legitimacy of this modern adaptation.[13]

IS IGNATIAN SPIRITUALITY FOR EVERYONE?

What kinds of people may benefit from the Exercises? The text itself (Exx 18-20) suggests that the *full* Exercises should only be given to a few outstanding persons. Yet we know that the early Jesuits gave retreats in varied forms to a wide range of people. The first Annotation (Exx 1) provides the key. There, a distinction is made between 'spiritual exercises', which cover a wide range of activities, and 'The Spiritual Exercises' which refer to the full dynamic of the complete text. So, 'making the Exercises' implied a spectrum of activity, based on the text but not always involving the whole of it. Positively, this freedom to adapt elements from the Exercises enables Ignatian spirituality to reach a wide variety of people. Many people these days are involved in group retreats 'in the Ignatian spirit'. Examples would be the Open Door Retreats or the 'A Way of

Life' series.[14] For some people, such group experiences may be preparatory to making the full Exercises.

Some contemporary spiritual directors also argue that the social and spiritual elitism implied in Annotations 18-20 is historically conditioned and inappropriate today. With patience and proper preparation, it is possible to offer the full Exercises 'in daily life' in an inner-city context where the traditional limitations of 'the more educated' and 'freedom from daily affairs' hardly apply. This of course does not contradict a perception that to invest the time and effort needed to make the *full* Exercises in any form is advisable only for a limited number of people at particular stages of their lives. A number of experienced directors have written of the importance of criteria for selection.[15]

The influence of the Ignatian tradition beyond the Roman Catholic Church has a long history.[16] The contemporary witness of many experienced directors is that denominational differences, as such, need not present insuperable difficulties in directed retreats and that we need to rethink our over-facile distinctions between the 'Catholic mind' and the 'Protestant mind'. Historically too, some monastic communities such as the Carthusians made the Exercises and members of contemplative communities such as Teresa of Avila managed to survive Jesuit spiritual directors! But are the Exercises really suitable for contemplatives? Many people have assumed them not to be. It is also the case that 'contemplation' was often understood in a restricted way in reference, primarily, to a particular interpretation of the Carmelite tradition, especially the teachings of John of the Cross. This is very reductionist. The Anglican commentator, W.H. Longridge, recognized that the Exercises need not be opposed to 'contemplative prayer' and modern scholarship is re-situating Ignatian styles of prayer within the late-medieval contemplative and monastic traditions.[17]

However, the current enthusiasm for Ignatian spirituality involves certain dangers. Firstly, there is a danger of dogmatism regarding the universal usefulness and applicability of this spiritual tradition which may, at times, amount to spiritual colonialism. This means that other spiritual traditions are underestimated. It may also mean that we begin to view the Exercises as suitable (if not advisable) for everyone. The Exercises were not conceived as something suited to anyone at any stage of their spiritual growth. We need to think hard about whether the *full* Spiritual Exercises, at least, are really a general means of spiritual deepening and a 'school of prayer', or whether they are more appropriate for moments of decision and points of life-transition. Secondly, those for whom an Ignatian retreat (whether the full Exercises or not) has been an experience of intense enlightenment sometimes forget that this moment, while privileged, was built on years of hidden growth. The Exercises are not a cure-all for every crisis or an automatic fillip for failures in enthusiasm. In fact all of us have absorbed insights from a variety of sources. In the current enthusiasm for matters Ignatian and for the contemporary potential of that particular, but limited tradition, we need to remember that our religious experience is pluriform. Enthusiasm must not blind us to this nor suggest that once we have discovered Ignatius Loyola we can afford to forget anything else we have ever learned or experienced.[18]

PRACTICE AND THEORY

A final question concerns how vital theory is for our appreciation of the Exercises. Many of the questions I have been highlighting, as well as some of the essays in this volume, reveal a link between practice and theory when presenting the Spiritual Exercises. The emphasis on the details of practice is relatively new. Prior to Vatican II there had been a period of serious historical, textual and theological work especially in France, Germany and Spain. These researches led to a rediscovery of long-forgotten elements of the Exercises, especially the individual dimension, and revealed that some of Ignatius's insights did not fit easily with conventional Roman Catholic scholastic theology. The three most significant theologians were the Germans, Erich Przywara and Karl Rahner and the Frenchman, Gaston Fessard.[19] The series, *Monumenta Historica Societatis Jesu*, founded in 1894, gradually made available the foundational documents of the Ignatian tradition. Some well-known examples of the textual and historical revision that resulted are the books of Hugo Rahner, Joseph de Guibert's work on the historical development of Ignatian spirituality and Ignacio Iparraguirre's three volumes on the history of giving the Exercises which established the primacy of the individually-given retreat.[20] We must remember that, while Ignatian scholars prior to Vatican II did not, on the whole, practise the results of their insights, their researches provided the renewed vision of the Exercises which lies at the heart of present practice and interest.

An experiential and practical emphasis involves dangers as well as gains. There is a tendency to overlook the dependence of good practice on sound theory. True, the kind of mystification that leads to elitism and de-skills the unlearned is unhelpful. People with only a minimum of theological or historical expertise give the Exercises very effectively. However, to ignore the theoretical questions entirely will cause difficulties for our implicit interpretation of a text as we use it. Serious work on the theology and exegesis of the Exercises is not an eccentric sideline but is highly relevant for what happens in retreat houses. Experts serve the practitioners. A musical image may be useful. A pianist will not do justice to Debussy without some awareness of the tradition of interpretation as well as the assurance that a generally reliable score is available. A pianist cannot do just anything at all and call it 'Clair de Lune'. Similarly, an anti-intellectual *naïveté* regarding spiritual texts does damage to their integrity and, consequently, to the people we are trying to help. Unfortunately, a reliable and accessible theological and historical commentary on the Exercises is lacking and this tends to perpetuate the problem.

To oppose theology and experience perpetuates a false dichotomy. Good theology is ultimately reflection on experience and, conversely, significant religious experiences involve some *theological* understanding, even if at the time unconsciously so. The distinction between 'dry theory' and 'living experience' in our approach to the Exercises is a destructive one. Either we end up with a sterile theory which effectively protects us from the pains of real growth, or we fall into the opposite trap of accepting uncritically any emotionally heightened experience that happens to come our way. As David Lonsdale reminds us in his essay on discernment, 'The brightness of a bright idea is no indication of its divine origin. . . . The same is true of the strength of feelings'. It is good to recall that Ignatius's own Rules for Discernment are a kind of hermeneutical framework, involving not merely psychological insight but a distinctive spiritual theology, to enable us to interpret our spiritual experience.

CONCLUSION: THE STRUCTURE OF THE BOOK

Some passing references have already been made to a number of essays in this book. To conclude, it seems helpful to explain in more detail how the book is structured and why particular essays were included. The selection of essays was not easy and many good ones have perforce been omitted for the sake of balance. My choices reflect the primary aim of the book which is to be a practical, rather than scholarly, guide to the process of the Exercises and thus to provide a broad treatment of its main elements rather than an exhaustive commentary on all its details.

The book generally assumes some knowledge of the Exercises. However, the two essays of Part One offer a gentle introduction: firstly, a straightforward exposition of the structure and vocabulary of the text, including contemporary problems with language and imagery, and, secondly, a helpful discussion of common misconceptions about the Exercises. The largest section of the book, Part Two, consists of nine essays by experienced retreat-guides on the actual process of the Exercises. I have suggested that flexibility is a central Ignatian value and so the first essay highlights this in relation to some of Ignatius's retreat guidelines (or 'Additions'). There follow essays on each of the four 'Weeks' of the classic retreat and on key meditations such as The Call of the King and The Two Standards. In line with my earlier comments about the importance of social justice concerns in contemporary spirituality, I have included two essays which discuss these in relationship to aspects of the Exercises. All of the essays assume the modern recovery of the practice of individual guidance. Finally, there is a contribution on the modern practice, which I have already mentioned, of adapting the full Exercises to a 'retreat in daily life' - in this case in a socially and educationally deprived area. Thus, it also addresses the issue I have raised concerning traditional limitations on the kind of people who make the Exercises.

This treatment of the overall process inevitably raises other subjects which demand more detailed attention. Therefore, the three essays of Part Three discuss the approach to prayer and discernment in the Exercises and Part Four, again with three essays, considers the spiritual direction relationship - which may be of particular help to present and potential retreat-guides. Each section has one essay with a specifically social perspective. The problem I raised earlier about the Exercises in relation to contemplative prayer is sensitively addressed in one of the essays in Part Four.

The relationship between theory and practice, particularly the dangers of detaching our contemporary interest in experience from theology, history and textual questions, has been mentioned throughout this introduction. Many essays show a general awareness of these issues. One essay, in Part Two, explicitly links our approach to the Fourth Week of the Exercises to reliable scripture scholarship. However, I felt it important to underline the relationship between good practice and sound theory in a structural way by concluding the book with Part Five on 'Interpretation and History'. The three essays, in turn, consider our need to grasp the importance of the structure of the Rules for Discernment; how Ignatius and other early Jesuits understood the possibilities and limitations of adaptation; and, finally, problems raised by changes in the understanding of the purpose of the Exercises in the period after Ignatius's death.

This book may prove to be a stimulus to further reading and reflection. In addition to footnote references provided by many of the authors, I have therefore included a selected reading list of other useful material, in English, on the Exercises.

NOTES

1. See Gerard W. Hughes, *God of Surprises* (London 1985).

2. For some basic guidelines to hermeneutics, or the theory of interpretation, in relation to spiritual texts, particularly the Exercises, see Philip Endean, 'Who do you say Ignatius is? Jesuit fundamentalism and beyond', *Studies in the Spirituality of Jesuits* 19, 5 (November 1987) and my forthcoming *Spirituality and History: interpretation and method* (London 1991), ch. 7, 'Interpreting spiritual texts'.

3. Louis J. Puhl, *The Spiritual Exercises of St Ignatius: based on studies in the language of the Autograph* (Chicago 1951).

4. See also John O'Malley, 'Early Jesuit spirituality: Spain and Italy', in Louis Dupré & Don E. Saliers (eds), *Christian Spirituality: Post-Reformation and Modern* (New York 1989/London 1990), especially pp. 12-17.

5. See John Bossy, 'Postscript' to H. Outram Evennett, *The Spirit of the Counter-Reformation* (Cambridge 1968), pp. 126–45, and Marjorie O'Rourke Boyle, 'Angels black and white: Loyola's spiritual discernment in historical perspective' in *Theological Studies* vol. 44 (1983), especially pp. 242–3. For a brief general introduction to the origins of Ignatian spirituality in the light of contemporary research, see O'Malley in Dupré and Saliers, pp. 3–27.

6. Although the penetrating essay by Philip Endean (see n. 2) on Jesuit fundamentalism is partly concerned with problems about the nature of Ignatian religious life, the points he makes are also applicable to the way in which we approach Ignatian spirituality in general and the Exercises in particular. On the general problem of historical knowledge in relation to our understanding and use of spiritual traditions, see my *Spirituality and History*, ch. 1, 'What is history?'

7. See the comment by Karl Rahner in *The Practice of Faith* (ET. London 1985), p. 103. See also Philip Endean, 'The Ignatian prayer of the senses', sec. III, in *The Heythrop Journal* XXXI, 4 (October 1990).

8. Roger Haight in his 'Foundational issues in Jesuit spirituality', *Studies in the Spirituality of Jesuits* 19, 4 (September 1987), highlights some of the major differences between Ignatius's theological horizons and our own. He also offers some suggestions for moving beyond these in our use of the Exercises today. See also Endean, 'Ignatian prayer', sec. III.

9. See Ottmar John, 'The tradition of the oppressed as the main topic of theological hermeneutics' in *Concilium* 200 (1988), pp. 143–55 and my forthcoming *Spirituality and History*, ch. 7.

10. See, e.g., O'Malley, 'Early Jesuit Spirituality', p. 5.

11. I have argued this, for example, in reference to the prayer of the Passion and the Third Week in my *Images of Holiness* (London/Notre Dame 1987), ch. 5, 'Discipleship and the Cross'. See also Michael O'Sullivan, 'Towards a social hermeneutics of the Spiritual Exercises: an application to the Annotations' in *The Spiritual Exercises of St Ignatius Loyola in present-day application* (Rome 1982).

12. For a brief treatment of masculine imagery in the Exercises, see L. Patrick Carroll, 'The Spiritual Exercises in everyday life', *Studies in the Spirituality of Jesuits* 22, 1 (January 1990), pp. 19–21. For a more general treatment of the issues, see the excellent book by Kathleen Fischer, *Women at the Well: feminist perspectives on spiritual direction* (New York 1988/London 1989). An inclusive language edition of the Exercises is Elisabeth Meier Tetlow, *The Spiritual Exercises of St Ignatius Loyola: a new translation* (Lanham, MD, 1987). Tetlow's 'An inclusive-language translation of the Ignatian Rules for discernment' also appears in Joann Wolski Conn (ed.), *Women's Spirituality: resources for Christian development* (New York 1986). A feminist reflection by Marie-Eloise Rosenblatt will be

published in Spring 1991 in *The Way Supplement* 70, a special commemorative issue for the Ignatian Anniversaries.

13. On the differing interpretations of Annotation 19, see Brian Grogan, 'A note on the history of Annotation 19' and Ian Tomlinson, 'Is the Nineteenth Annotation the full Exercises?' in *The Way Supplement* 49 (Spring 1984).

14. See, for example, Kathleen O'Sullivan, *A Way of Life: a human-spiritual growth series for lay groups* (Dublin 1987).

15. Brian O'Leary has some controversial views on the selection of retreatants for the full Spiritual Exercises in 'The retreatant: selection and preparation' in *The Way Supplement* 38 (Summer 1980). Warnings were also sounded by David Fleming fifteeen years ago in 'The danger of faddism and the thirty-day retreat' in *Review for Religious* 33 (1974), pp. 97-101.

16. See my article in *The Way Supplement* 68 (Summer 1990).

17. See W.H. Longridge, *The Spiritual Exercises of St Ignatius of Loyola: translated from the Spanish with a commentary and a translation of the Directorium in Exercitia* (London 1919). I am grateful to Dr Terence O'Reilly of the University of Cork, Ireland, for his comments on the late-medieval, and especially contemplative-monastic roots of the Spiritual Exercises.

18. See my article, 'Ignatian spirituality - the dangers of enthusiasm' in *Vision* 167 (1988).

19. See, for example, Przywara, *Deus semper maior: Theologie der Exerzitien* 3 vols (Freiburg 1938-40); K. Rahner, *The Dynamic Element in the Church* (ET. London 1964), pp. 84-170; Fessard, *La dialectique des Exercices Spirituels de Saint Ignace de Loyola* (Paris 1956 and two-volume expanded edition, 1966).

20. See for example, H. Rahner, *Ignatius the Theologian* (ET. London 1968), *The Spirituality of St Ignatius Loyola* (ET. Chicago 1953) and *St Ignatius Loyola: letters to women* (ET. Freiburg/London 1960); De Guibert, *The Jesuits: their spiritual doctrine and practice* (ET. St Louis 1972); Iparraguirre, *Historia de la práctica de los Ejercicios Espirituales de San Ignacio de Loyola*, 3 vols (Rome/Bilbao 1946, 1955, 1973).

PART ONE

Introducing the Text

CHAPTER ONE

The Spiritual Exercises: A Process and a Text

Lavinia Byrne

At a performance of the York Mystery Plays in the 1970s I was alarmed when the magic spell of live performance was broken during the interval. Onto the stage came a group of evangelizers holding stacks of Bibles. 'You've seen the show,' they said, 'now read the book'. 'Starring in a bookshop near you: the holy Bible.' I do not question the value of encouraging people to read the Scriptures; I question the timing. In the magical setting of St Mary's Abbey, the York cycle of Mystery Plays exposed us to a story familiar to all yet newly revealed and unfolded before us. The evening's performance and relationship between actors and audience on that particular July night had their own integrity and demanded neither commentator nor text.

Timing is all. Because of course text and commentary are needed and both have their place. At certain times this need will be acute. And then the individual Christian will want something to turn to in order to set up a conversation between personal experience and the story of the gospels. In a particularly gifted way Ignatius Loyola understood this need and gave it form and force in the book of his *Spiritual Exercises*. These Exercises exist to support and sustain experience, to enable it to be sieved and sorted so that the purpose and desire of God can be discovered in the life of an individual Christian in dialogue with the gospel story.

WHAT ARE THE SPIRITUAL EXERCISES AND WHERE DID THEY COME FROM?

The Latin vulgate text of the *Exercises* was published in 1548. The experience which preceded this text and out of which the Exercises emerged spanned a lifetime. They did not arrive from nowhere but have a long genesis in the life experience of Ignatius. The story of his

17

conversion is well known. As a man of thirty, Ignatius was wounded in a skirmish at Pamplona. The debonnaire and, if we are to believe his own account, somewhat profligate young soldier had been fighting for the Duke of Nájera against the French. Now he was taken home with a shattered leg to the family castle at Loyola in the Pyrenees. There he began a slow and painful recovery. He took to reading and found the gospels, the lives of Sts Dominic and Francis and romances or fiction. He read avidly. Time hung heavily on his hands and offered opportunity for reflection. At this moment the Spiritual Exercises began to be formed. For Ignatius noticed things about his reactions to what he was reading. Whereas the novels were enjoyable and entertaining while he read them, these effects did not last. True enduring consolation came and remained only when his imagination was triggered by the lives of the saints.

As his recovery progressed he set out to imitate the saints, to do deeds more striking than their own. He went on pilgrimage to Montserrat, lived as a hermit at Manresa and all the time noticed what was happening to him. He reflected constantly on the Scriptures and on the place of God within his own experience and listened to the resonances as the gospel story and his own story began to speak to each other. He began to realize the difference between consoling feelings such as joy and peace, shame for his sins and the grace of sorrow and anguish at the sufferings of Christ and feelings of desolation such as complacence and despair. Consolation and desolation as used by Ignatius come to be two technical terms which recur constantly in the text of the *Exercises*. It could be argued that, in the form in which he presents them there, they constitute his greatest contribution to the formation of adult Christian believers. By the time his insights were written into his text, they had become the Rules for the Discernment of Spirits which are given in two forms, one in terms of the First Week exercises and the other in terms of those of the Second Week.

At Pamplona, Loyola, Monserrat and Manresa - and beyond, for Ignatius's own journey was to take him on extensive travels - he gained other insights too. Central to his early experience was the gospel story, either in the Scriptures or as he read about it in the *Life of Christ* of Ludolph of Saxony. The events of the life of Jesus form the backbone of the Spiritual Exercises. The person who is making the Exercises is invited to share the same process as Ignatius had undergone and be exposed to the gospel story in the way he himself had found so beneficial. And so the Exercises follow a four-week pattern. During the First Week the one who is making them is invited to reflect upon the love and goodness of God our creator. During the Second Week the events of the incarnation, birth and public ministry of Jesus form the matter for prayer and reflection. The Third Week is spent considering the passion and death of Jesus while the Fourth opens with the resurrection narratives and moves onwards to consideration of God the giver of all things who is constantly giving us gifts from above and inviting us to seek and find the divine presence in all things.

The word Week is an ambiguous one. Ignatius envisaged a situation in which the one making the Exercises would retire from the circumstances of everyday life and spend some thirty days in solitude. These thirty days would divide roughly and with appropriate flexibility into four Weeks with transitional or repose days thrown in for good measure. But even in Ignatius's own time he began to realize that such a drastic withdrawal would not always be possible. For this reason in the explanatory pages at the beginning of the *Exercises* he lays out ground-rules – which he calls Annotations. Annotation 19 is the most well-known of these because in it he describes another way of making the Exercises. A busy person who cannot withdraw from everyday life and go off to make a thirty-day retreat is not debarred from the experience. Rather any individual is able to follow the same Exercises over a longer period, taking time each day to give to prayer and reflection. Nowadays this way of making the Exercises is called 'The Exercises in Daily Life' or, sometimes, a Nineteenth Annotation retreat. Many of the best handbooks for backing up the text of the *Exercises* envisage precisely this mode of following them.[1]

Annotation 22 deserves to be equally famous. Here Ignatius lays out what he calls the Presupposition upon which the relationship between the one making the Exercises and the one giving them is to be based. I quote his text in full.

> To assure better cooperation between the one who is giving the Exercises and the exercitant, and more beneficial results for both, it is necessary to suppose that every good Christian is more ready to put a good interpretation on another's statement than to condemn it as false. If an

orthodox construction cannot be put on a proposition, the one who has made it should be asked how he understands it. If he is in error, he should be corrected with all kindness. If this does not suffice, all appropriate means should be used to bring him to a correct interpretation, and so defend the proposition from error.[2]

The insight has an astonishingly contemporary ring. It is about mutuality and respect, affirmation and integrity. Yet there is a problem. The language is quaint and decidedly sexist. We have to remember where the *Exercises* began. Ignatius was a man; his Church was clerical like our own; Ignatius used them to help men who were attracted to join his nascent Society of Jesus to know if theirs was a genuine call. After all he saw 'the conquest of self and the regulation of one's life in such a way that no decision is made under the influence of any inordinate attachment' (Exx 21) as the purpose of the Exercises. Vocation to the religious life or priesthood ranked high among the Christian choices he intended the Exercises to facilitate.

While he had women friends,[3] he was cautious about interaction with women. In 1611, when Mary Ward the young Englishwoman was called by God to form an actively apostolic group for women, she heard the words 'Take the same of the Society. Father General will never permit it. Go to him'. In the event neither Ignatius's then successor as Jesuit General Superior nor the Church permitted it and Mary Ward's Institute had a chequered early history. Her own retreat notes are still preserved but these too bear no evidence of any attempt to put the Exercises into inclusive language. Yet she herself claimed great things of women, writing in 1615, for instance,

> There is no such difference between men and women; yet women may they not do great matters, as we have seen by example of many saints who have done great things? And I hope in God it will be seen that women in time will do much.[4]

The inclusive language debate is part of the same polemic. Where women seek to use inclusive language about themselves and about God, they are making a statement about their own status, about the way in which they image the divine and about the value both of their experience and of the way in which they experience it.

How are the *Exercises* to survive in a world in which this debate has so much force and edge to it? Firstly there is work to be done on translations of the text. Some excellent work has already been achieved to produce a version which sounds more up-to-date than the highly accurate translation by Louis J. Puhl which I have already used in the quotation given above. His version was produced in 1951 and it has served as the standard textbook ever since. David L. Fleming's *A Contemporary Reading of the Spiritual Exercises* in both its 1976 and its 1978 editions has done a remarkable job, largely because it has given individual directors permission to realize that no translation is monolithic.[5] In today's climate the need for an inclusive language version is rapidly becoming an imperative.

I have said that Fleming's contemporary reading has done a good job because of its effect on directors. This in turn raises a further question. Who are the *Spiritual Exercises* for? The actual text as it stands, the book containing the Exercises, is intended to be used by the one who gives the Exercises. It is a manual to be used by a practitioner. In retreat houses world-wide you will see retreat directors sloping off to interviews with their retreatants carrying a Bible, a copy of the *Exercises* and their own notes. In certain instances I have seen the spine of the book removed so that individual directors can use the text in loose-leaf form, interspersing it with their own *aide-mémoire* such as Scripture references or notes to give them helpful hints and jog their memories.

Ignatius himself does exactly the same thing during the course of the Exercises. He writes notes to explain special terms he uses or to give instructions. An example: at the end of the First Week exercises he gives a note to indicate the times of day at which it will be helpful to make these exercises. Sometimes he puts in notes which he considers even more important. These he calls 'Additional Directives'. Their status is similar to that of the Annotations. At the end of his presentation of the full four Weeks he gives some forty odd references to Scripture passages to be used during the retreat and then concludes the book with further rules he elaborated to help root the Exercises in the life of the Church and in Christian practice. These include the Rules for the Discernment of Spirits, referred to above, Rules for Thinking with the Church and for the Distribution of Alms.

THE PROCESS OF THE RETREAT

So much for the book containing the text of the *Exercises*. What about the Exercises themselves, not to mention individual exercises? These different spellings are not meant to create confusion. Their purpose is rather to clarify and so help the person who is giving the Exercises to bring them in their fulness to the individual retreatant. Ignatius is very particular. The text has its integrity but so too does the process which is unfurled in the life of the individual retreatant during the course of the four Weeks. For if these Weeks are about the love of God and acknowledgement of our own sins, about the person of Christ and his call for us to labour with him in the salvation of the world, about the cost of that salvation wrought in the deeds of the passion and death of Christ and about his rising from the dead and abiding presence in our midst, if this is the objective content of the four Weeks, what is our subjective response to be? For in our subjective response lies the actual making of the Exercises. This is what the director is listening to in the personal interviews which accompany the retreat. This is the movement the director is attempting to follow and discern by testing it or nudging it along with appropriate passages from Scripture.

Ignatius anticipates two kinds of response: the consoling one of receiving the grace which the exercise in question offers or the response of desolation, of shrinking from the gospel call. When I made the thirty-days retreat myself one of my fellow retreatants went to the bursar's office each morning and paid up just enough money for another twenty-four hours. Until she was ready to she just could not commit herself to more than one day at a time. Ignatius anticipated this kind of reluctance and was not dismissive about the depth of anxiety his First Week exercises might cause. I should add that another exercitant during that same retreat would stamp up and down raging against Ignatius's text. 'That red book should be burnt', he would say. Each of these reactions has its own integrity and should not frighten directors away. Ignatius anticipated them, hence the tight structure of the First Week exercises.

For here he has the retreatant pray for the consoling grace of 'a growing and intense sorrow and tears for my sins' (Exx 55). This exercise is intended to lead to a moment of liberation and joy, the moment in which the retreatant experiences the forgiving love of God with a 'cry of wonder accompanied by surging emotion' (Exx 60). But what if this does not happen? What if the consideration of my own sinfulness leads me to withdraw in despair? Ignatius provides a containing mechanism which can sustain those making the Exercises and bring them again to the moment of grace his exercise envisaged. The mechanism is a simple one and one which serves a two-fold purpose. Firstly, as I have said, it offers a fresh attempt at movement into the light. No one is left to rot within the experience of despair, even though in certain cases this experience may be a lengthy one as he himself learnt at Manresa. He calls this mechanism 'Repetition'. The exercise is repeated, approached again from a different angle or with a fresh set of Scripture texts. This is far removed from a didactic, 'Go on doing this until you get it right' approach, because it has a second purpose as well. When fear gives way to love, when guilt gives way to contrition, the individual is shown an insight which will have far-reaching effects. For this reason it is important to return again and again to the experience of insight where God's forgiveness was revealed and refresh oneself at this source.

Repetition is a device which Ignatius uses often during the course of the four Weeks. There are other devices which serve his purpose equally well. One of these is the Review which is to follow each period of prayer during the Ignatian day. During the retreat there will be four or five of these prayer periods each day and the hour Ignatius envisaged would be brought to completion by a short period of reflection. During this the exercitant goes over the experience of prayer noticing what happened and what it felt like, what helped and what hindered. Outside the retreat experience this practice becomes the 'Examen', daily reflection on the events and meetings of everyday life. Another of these mechanisms he calls the 'Application of the Senses'. Each day, as he realized, has its own internal rhythms. From the vigour of early morning we move into the calm of late afternoon. The entire four Weeks are marked by the same movement towards simplification. Those exercises which are to be done in the early hours or during the morning have new material in them; those which belong to the end of the day settle down and simplify. The last exercise of the day asks for something simpler still. We would recognize it as right-brain activity. The material which the retreatant has prayed with during the day is considered again, only this time the means are the organs of sense. I 'taste and see that the Lord is good' (Ps. 34.8) by allowing my eyes and ears and mouth and nostrils to linger over the gospel scene. I touch the textures and fabrics and pass them over in my mind's eye.

This Application of the Senses presupposes that I have a scene which I can recall. Ignatius had fantasized on his sick bed at Loyola. He had imagined the great feats and exploits he would achieve in the service of the Divine Majesty. Dangerous stuff. And somewhat frightening as well. Our dreams throw up vivid enough images anyway without any conscious release of the imagination during the daytime. So runs much of our conventional wisdom. How does Ignatius's insight fit in to all of this? We have all met people who, for whatever reason, say 'I have no imagination'. Try asking them to visualize the place where they ordinarily go to look for their post in the morning, to have a good old look at it and then to pick up the mail and check it for bills or personal letters. . . . At that moment their imagination will have been released – and Ignatius is asking no more than that. The triggers he uses for the imaginative contempla-tions in the text of the *Exercises* are usually gospel stories. He is concerned with detail, with having a good old look at the scene. My example is taken from his Contemplation on the Nativity from the beginning of the Second Week of the Exercises:

> This is a mental representation of the place. It will consist here in seeing in imagination the way from Nazareth to Bethlehem. Consider its length, its breadth; whether level, or through valleys and over hills. Observe also the place or cave where Christ is born; whether big or little; whether high or low; and how it is arranged (Exx 112).

Why this use of the imagination, why this preoccupation with detail? To the retreat director the answer is clear. When the imagination wanders freely into a scene such as this constraints fall away. In their place come an intimacy and immediacy which visit and heal our most distorted images and understandings. Jesus walks in our landscape, comes into our home, is our brother, our lover, our friend. The gospels are peopled with our own friends and enemies, we choose to follow the Lord and walk the way of Calvary. We stand at the foot of the cross and wait in the garden for resurrection.

For this reason many will speak of the experience of making the

Spiritual Exercises as a time of profound healing. The freedom they find as they follow the four Weeks releases them from false idealism and allows them to live authentically before God as their 'real selves' owning the past – whether it was level or it led them through valleys and hills – and to face a future which might be big or little, high or low. For others the experience of making the Exercises has its principal focus in the Second Week. Here they meet a Christ who calls them to serve under the standard of his cross, a Christ who draws us into colloquy or conversation 'exactly as one friend speaks to another' (Exx 54) and empowers us by giving us knowledge of the 'deceits of the rebel chief' (Exx 139). These retreatants will be especially attentive to the call of the King; they will be attracted to the idea of making an 'election' or definite choice – of vocation, state of life or state of mind. They will be helped by Ignatius's presentation of differing levels of response where he analyses how three differing 'classes of men' behave when they acquire 'ten thousand ducats' by somewhat dubious means. They will find that his 'Three Kinds of Humility' call forth new levels of generosity and integrity within them.

Is this language too triumphalistic to speak to our age? I know that for some people it causes alarm. In preparing an inclusive language version of the *Exercises* a translator might be tempted to go for something less militaristic because Ignatius's imagery is dated. Yet if proof were needed of the power of the imagination to compensate for the inadequacies of his text, the exercise on the Kingdom of Christ and Call of an Earthly King give it in abundance. Two brief examples: the retreatant who saw Jesus calling from a wheelchair. This image was inspired by the action of Rick Hansen who crossed Canada in his wheelchair to raise money for the 'Man in Action Legacy Fund'. This supports various initiatives controlled by disabled people themselves and reverses the historical pattern of charity-giving. And then the retreatant who saw Jesus as the French underground leader Jean Moulin. The mayor of Chartres, Moulin attempted suicide while first imprisoned by the Nazis and always had to wear a scarf to conceal his wound. He later went on to organize an entire underground network, was eventually re-captured, tortured and killed. Both these are images of courage and insight, of weakness and strength working together without invalidating each other. The Jesus revealed to these particular

25

retreatants was a Jesus who pointed up militarism and triumphalism as 'deceits of the rebel leader', as the mechanisms of sin and death.

THE EXERCISES AND IGNATIAN PRAYER

Is imaginative contemplation the only form of prayer to be used in the Exercises? The answer has to be 'no'. Ignatius himself accommodated many different prayer styles into his text. The quiet prayer that accompanies the Application of the Senses, the discursive and meditative prayer of the Colloquia give ample instances of this. A Colloquy comes at the end of most of his major exercises. Here the person praying the exercise speaks with Jesus or his mother or God the Father 'pondering what presents itself' (Exx 53) and asking for the grace the exercise was designed to inspire.

The Exercises are framed by two key texts which take this part of my discussion beyond the framework of the four-Week experience. The First Principle and Foundation upon which Ignatius bases his entire 'method of proceeding' is given in Exx 23. Here he reminds us that we were created 'to praise, reverence and serve God our Lord'. Here he reminds us that 'our one desire and choice should be what is more conducive to the end for which we are created'. Ignatius is a man of desires; his Exercises enable us to know our own desires and follow Jesus the liberator of our desires. How are we to do this? The text which closes the retreat experience, the Contemplation to Attain the Love of God, invites the retreatant to take its insights out into a world newly conceived.

Ignatian prayer, if there is such a thing, is revealed most compellingly in this text. Here contemplation is presented not as an activity but as a way of being in the world. The retreatant is enabled to look at the world and all its people contemplatively, to see all relationships and events and experiences with the eyes of God, as a place of desire and of blessing. If the Spiritual Exercises make any difference to a person's life this difference will be manifested as the individual in question gradually becomes a man or woman of the Contemplation. These are people who have indeed seen the show; if they read the book and share its insights with others then Ignatius's task will have been accomplished.[6]

NOTES

1. The Canadian Jesuit John A. Veltri's *Orientations vol. 1* and *vol. 2* (Loyola House, Guelph, Ontario, 1979 and 1981) are justly the most famous of these. Other examples would include Barbara Paleczny SSND and Michel Côté OP, *Becoming Followers of Jesus: A people's approach to wholistic spirituality, Facilitator's guide and participants' manual* (Ontario, Canada, 1983). A more recent version is prepared by Joseph Tetlow SJ. Entitled *Choosing Christ in the World*, it has been printed in a loose leaf binder by the Institute of Jesuit Sources (St Louis 1989).

2. cf. Hugo Rahner SJ, *Saint Ignatius Loyola: letters to women* (Freiburg London 1960). The general introduction to this book as well as the introductions to each of the six sub-sections make fascinating reading.

3. *The Spiritual Exercises of St Ignatius* trans. Louis J. Puhl SJ (Chicago 1951).

4. *Till God Will: Mary Ward through her writings* ed. M. Emmanuel Orchard IBVM (London 1985), p. 57.

5. David L. Fleming SJ, *A Contemporary Reading of the Spiritual Exercises* (St Louis 1976); and *The Spiritual Exercises of St Ignatius: a literal translation and a contemporary reading* (St Louis 1978).

6. An informative introduction to Ignatian spirituality is given in David Lonsdale, *Eyes to See, Ears to Hear* (London 1990).

CHAPTER TWO

Forgotten Truths

Gerard W. Hughes

'And then I have to fit in a retreat sometime.' So ends the sentence of many priests and religious as they try to work out their programme for the summer. For Jesuits, an annual eight-day retreat has been part of the rule since 1608, over fifty years after St Ignatius's death; and many other religious orders have adopted the same rule. Official documents of popes and Jesuit Generals recommend the Exercises of St Ignatius with enthusiastic praise for their wonderful effects. Those who have to make them do not always share that same enthusiasm, but keep their grumbles to themselves or to a select group of friends. This article takes a selection of these grumbles as a means of rediscovering truths about the Exercises which many of us had forgotten.

GRUMBLES

1. 'If I hear once again that "man" is created to praise, reverence and serve God, I'll scream': a sister's reaction after yet another Jesuit retreat. Others react less dramatically: 'I re-read old copies of the school magazine', said one Jesuit whom I knew. For him it was certainly true that 'it is not much knowledge that fills and satisfies the soul, but the intimate understanding and relish' of all that had ever happened at the school of his youth, where he always made his annual retreat. We may never have been driven to screaming or reading the old school magazine, but we know the boredom which repetition can induce.

2. Another reflection on the Exercises from the old-school-magazine friend: 'I never have understood all this consolation-desolation business; I suppose it is something which afflicts hot-blooded foreigners. I usually feel much-of-a-muchness myself, occasionally dropping into a mild depression at retreat times'.

3. As retreat-director I met a very unhappy and broken religious who, on being asked, 'Have you not spoken to anyone about this

before?', answered, 'Yes, many times, but I am always told to practise the third mode of humility'. This is one example among many of the damage that the Exercises can do. Far from liberating, they can often be given and made in such a way that they cripple the retreatant, imprison the spirit, and engender religious nausea, rather than the love of God.

4. The experience of many in making the Exercises may be compared to riding a bicycle which has no chain. One may pedal away vigorously at the meditations and additions, but somehow the Exercises do not engage with real life. One retreat-giver, after exhorting his retreatants to 'go in spirit with St Francis Xavier and lick those lepers' wounds', was later heard by one of them complaining loudly at breakfast about the quality of the marmalade. We can all identify with that retreat-giver.

5. Eulogies of the Exercises by popes, bishops, Jesuit Generals and retreat-givers can sometimes give the impression that they are a kind of magic. 'Are you worried, anxious, bewildered, confused, lukewarm? Try the Exercises and become a fully integrated, dynamic Christian, apostolic witness and eschatological sign.' The Exercises are enjoying a vogue at present. 'Solve your problems with a thirty-day retreat.' If the Exercises are treated as a magic panacea for the ills of our day, we shall reap a rich harvest of problems.

6. This last remark leads on to a final grumble. Recent writings, emphasizing the damage the Exercises can do, the skill required in a director etc., can lead the amateur to despair of ever being able to make or give them.

I think these are useful grumbles, because they can remind us of forgotten truths:

(i) In the time of St Ignatius, and for many years after his death, the Exercises were normally given to individuals, not to groups. In 1584, Fr Crusius, a master of novices in Germany, wrote to the Jesuit General, Fr Aquaviva, asking if he might give the Exercises to groups of three to six novices. Aquaviva's reply is interesting. He writes that group retreats are contrary to the tradition of giving the Exercises, because different people have different needs, and their individual needs cannot be answered in a group. If there are not enough directors then Fr Crusius should do what they do in Rome, namely cut down the length of each individual retreat.[1]

'Different people have different needs.' Therefore there is no one

29

form of the Exercises suitable for all. They must be adapted to the needs of each individual retreatant. The reason why we feel bored with retreats is because in the form in which we make them, or are given them, they no longer answer our needs. Jeronimo Nadal saw the purpose of the thirty-day retreat in the noviceship as an initiation into Jesuit spirituality, which would then become a way of life. Once the Exercises begin to 'take', the retreatant may well want to spend some time in prayer and quiet; but there should be a growing freedom in prayer and the manner of it. There is a false glorification of the Exercises which treats them as though they were magic. 'Keep on making them, and they will work, provided you have the right dispositions.' When they do not appear to work, the answer must be that we do not have the right dispositions; so we try again, until repeated dissatisfaction ensures that we never shall have the right dispositions. Boredom with the Exercises may well be a very healthy sign that we should no longer be making them in the form in which we are accustomed. We should pay more attention to our boredom.

(ii) In his preliminary observations to the book of the Exercises, St Ignatius writes (Exx 6):

> When the one who is giving the Exercises perceives that the exercitant is not affected by any spiritual experiences, such as consolations or desolations, and that he is not troubled by different spirits, he ought to ply him with questions about the Exercises. He should ask him whether he makes them at the appointed times and how he makes them.

Ignatius expects retreatants, even English ones, to have these experiences. Unless they have them, the retreat cannot continue, because it is through consolation and desolation that we come to discern what God's will is in our lives. The central importance of this experience is another commonly forgotten truth. Pelagianism, always a temptation for Anglo-Saxons, can creep into the Exercises, turning them into an endurance test: will-strengthening exercises designed to produce valiant men and women ready to advance under withering fire, heedless of life and limb and, consequently, of their own feelings. Desolation comes to be regarded as something to be snapped out of; and consolation is a feeling to be treated with circumspection, if not suspicion. Relying on the word of Ignatius, that 'love ought to manifest itself in deeds rather than in words', and adding 'or in feelings', we feel justified in paying scant attention to the consolation-desolation talk. Yet this was not the mind of St Ignatius, for whom feelings were of primary importance.

The Exercises are designed to help us discover the will of God in our lives, not by ignoring our feelings, but by listening to them, coming to know them and learning how to interpret them. The power of the Exercises, the need for skilled direction, lies precisely in this point. The Exercises, the Society of Jesus, began, in a sense, with Ignatius's own feelings, when he was lying wounded at Loyola. He read romances, he dreamed of courtly love and daring deeds. He also read the lives of the saints and Ludolph of Saxony's *Life of Christ*. He noticed that his day-dreams left him in a sad mood; whilst his thoughts on Christ and on the lives of the saints continued to attract him. These were not feelings he aroused in himself. They just happened. But he did not just snap out of them. He reflected on them, and this was the start of his discernment of spirits. He was uneducated in letters, in theology, in spirituality. He observed his moods in relation to his conscious activity, he came to know them, to be less naïve and more circumspect in discerning them, but he never stopped listening to them. It became a lifelong and continuous habit. Every decision, even the apparently most minute, was tested in this way. He tested his decisions, not against some external criterion, a practice which would have driven him insane, but on the criterion of the at-one-ness of his whole being which he had given over to Christ. He entrusted himself to Christ, an instrument in his hands, and therefore believed that if in some decision he was going against God's will, the disharmony would sooner or later manifest itself in his feelings of consolation and desolation.

Faber, whilst giving a retreat to Peter Canisius in 1543, wrote:

> I observe more clearly than ever certain evident signs for proceeding in the Exercises: how important it is for the discernment of spirits to see if we are attentive to ideas and reflections or rather to the Spirit itself, which appears through desires, motions, ardour or despondency, tranquillity or anxiety, joy or sorrow, and other analogous spiritual motions. For it is in these motions much more easily than in thoughts that one can pass judgment on the soul and its quests.[2]

Thus, the matter for discernment is the involuntary feelings and moods which arise in and from the meditations. This is the subject matter for discussion with the director. Through trying to articulate these feelings and moods, we become more aware of them. In one of his directories of the Exercises, St Ignatius says that retreatants may be encouraged to write down their reflections and feelings (*conceptus et motiones*).[3] If retreatants do not learn to discern for themselves, the Exercises will have no lasting effect.

Herein lie both the difficulty and the importance of the Exercises today. In western countries we have fostered the intellect and despised the emotions, thus becoming more cerebral than sensitive. We have developed a wonderful technology which threatens to extinguish human life either sooner, by nuclear war, or later, by pollution of the environment and exhaustion of vital resources. If we lose touch with our feelings, we become inhuman and capable of a terrifying callousness to the sufferings of others. In the promotion of social justice we need information, but unless the information touches our hearts as well as our heads, it will have no effect. That is why the Exercises have such a valuable contribution to make in the Church's mission of justice and peace.

The experience of consolation-desolation is not easy for us today, because the pace of life and our very conceptual education can so easily keep us out of touch with ourselves. Even in the sixteenth century, when the pace of life was so much slower, Peter Faber writes of pious retreatants who do not seem to experience any consolation-desolation:

> However, holy as they may be, lead them on to examine themselves in terms of a higher degree of perfection in their lives and conduct; then you will see two spirits appear, one a source of strength, the other of darkness, one of justice, the other of degradation.[4]

To become aware of our feelings, we need to articulate them in writing and in talking with a director. But we can only do this with a director who can treat us gently and not judge us. 'If the director observes that the exercitant is in desolation and tempted, let him not deal severely and harshly, but gently and kindly' (Exx 7). Because of the difficulty of experiencing consolation-desolation, an individual may require a long preparatory period before beginning the Exercises. Faber, for example, before he began the Exercises with Dr Cochlaeus, spent several hours daily for several weeks in conversation with him. Ignatius was four years with Faber himself before giving him the Exercises. There are other reasons too why retreatants may require a long preliminary period before beginning the Exercises: for example, their basic notion of God may be so tinged with unacknowledged fear, or resentment, or scrupulosity, that to plunge them into the Exercises may only accentuate their difficulties.

So far, the answers I have given are open to the charge that the Exercises encourage and foster a spiritual narcissism. There is one prayer in the Exercises, the only one which never varies in all the meditations: 'I will beg God our Lord for the grace that all my intentions, actions and operations may be directed purely to the service and praise of His Divine Majesty'. The Exercises are not centred on our feelings and emotions; they are centred on Christ. It is in the light of God's revelation in Christ, and in the faith that 'God is in all things and all things in him' that we consider ourselves. 'What have I done for him? What will I do for him?' The Exercises are designed to lead us gradually into this light. Too much light blinds, which is another way of expressing grumble no. 3 on the danger of the Exercises.

(iii) St Ignatius's own teaching on this point is given clearly in the preliminary observations or 'annotations':

> Let him (the director) adhere to the points and add only a short summary explanation. The reason for this is that when one in meditating takes the solid foundation of the facts and goes over it and reflects on it for himself, he may find something that makes them a little clearer or better understood. For it is not much knowledge that satisfies and fills the soul but the intimate understanding and relish of the truth. (Exx 2)

'It may happen that in the first week some are slower in attaining what is sought' (Exx 4). No one is to be hurried. Most of the retreats given by the early Jesuits did not go beyond the First Week; and this included retreats to bishops, abbots and vicar-generals. In Annotation 11, Ignatius writes:

> While the exercitant is engaged in the First Week of the Exercises, it will be helpful if he knows nothing of what is to be done in the Second Week. Rather, let him labour to attain what he is seeking in the First Week, as if he hoped to find no good in the Second.

The retreatant should go at his or her own pace. To be coerced or hurried on by an enthusiastic director can damage the retreatant. I am still grateful for two points in particular which we were given in an excellent preached retreat many years ago. One was that we should look on prayer time not as a duty, but as a gift: if you want to use the time in prayer, do so; but there is no compulsion. Somehow, when the pressure of 'duty' was removed, the desire to pray could grow. The other point was the director's preliminary observation on the third mode of humility. He said he was reluctant to talk about it in case he was waving us up a mountain which he had not climbed himself. His honesty was encouraging and helped us to see the third mode of humility as an invitation, not a command.

To conclude this answer to grumble no. 3 and a fuller answer to grumble no. 1: the retreatant must be allowed to go at his or her own pace. That is why there must be a great variety of ways in which one makes a retreat. Some people may be over-worked, over-tired, over-anxious. They may need a few days of quiet idleness without even attempting to pray. Others may feel that they are growing increasingly isolated, anti-social, dogmatic. They may need some form of community retreat. Others, whose work leaves them little time for reading, may need a 'preached retreat' which includes informative conferences. Others again may need solitude and withdrawal with plenty of time for prayer on their own, perhaps on only one part of one meditation of the Exercises. The director must never force the pace. We do damage not so much by our own ignorance, or failure to live up the ideals we profess, as by refusing to acknowledge our own ignorance and failures.

(iv) The fourth grumble was about the unreality of retreats: lepers' wounds and marmalade. The Exercises are designed to help the retreatant to become a contemplative in action. This cannot happen in eight days, or even in thirty. In a retreat we can withdraw for eight or thirty days to learn a method of prayer which can open us up to God and help us to begin to experience God in a new way in our lives; but this is only a beginning. The 'Contemplation for obtaining Love' (Exx 230-37), for example, is not an annual event to be fitted in with the packing on the eighth day. It is to become a permanent attitude, 'to find God in all things, and all things in him'. Ignatius the mystic was also Ignatius the practical administrator. He could weep at the sight of a flower and then give his whole attention to very mundane details of daily living. The Spanish Jesuits of his time were all for more prayer. Fr Oviedo, the rector of Gandia, was a three-hour-daily-prayer-man. Nadal, on his return from Spain, told Ignatius that he had agreed to the Spaniards' request for one and a half hour's prayer daily. Nadal describes Ignatius's reaction. 'He sharply denounced me in the presence of others and thereafter made no great use of my services.' Da Camara, in the *Memoriale*, reports that Ignatius said it was

> his opinion, from which no one would ever move him, that, for those who are studying, one hour of prayer was sufficient (two examens of conscience plus the divine office), it being supposed that they are practising mortification and self-denial.[5]

To use a later analogy, the Exercises are not a battery-charging operation, but a way of learning how to be self-charging in our ordinary occupations. It is a continuous process, which we only assimilate slowly and gradually. Those who do learn it, as Ignatius did, are capable of turning to prayer from the most exacting occupations. The work helps their prayer, and the prayer helps their work. This leads us back to an earlier point: the need for honesty in the Exercises, bringing our whole person into them, warts and all. Otherwise we cannot find God in all things, but only in that ideal image of ourselves which we bring out at retreat time and put away again on the eighth day.

(v) The answers given to the first four grumbles contain the answer to grumble no. 5, on the danger of considering the Exercises to be a magic remedy for our ills. If the retreatant is not ready to begin them, if they are not adapted to his or her needs, if there is not a careful discernment of consolation–desolation, and if the Exercises are not 'earthed' into the actual life experience of the retreatant, then they will not produce their effects. The Exercises are designed to help us to grow in the knowledge and love of God according to our talents, energies, abilities, and the grace God gives us. Any attempt to reach sanctity by a short cut, which ignores us as we really are, is like trying to jump a mountain: a useless expenditure of energy which can land us flat on our faces.

(vi) I hope the effect of these reflections has not been the opposite of what I intended, discouraging instead of encouraging the diffident amateur to make or give the Exercises. Ignatius says:

> We call Spiritual Exercises every way of preparing and disposing the soul to rid itself of all inordinate attachments, and, after their removal, of seeking and finding the will of God in the disposition of our life for the salvation of our soul. (Exx 1)

There are hundreds of ways of 'preparing'. But some people will feel the need for something more, and may want to make an eight-day, or thirty-day retreat. To direct someone in such a retreat does require skill and training. The greater the skill, the more we can help. Many of us know we are not skilled, but would like to be. If we try to be honest with ourselves and do not try to coerce the retreatant, then though we may not give them all the help they need, at least our willingness to be with them will be of some help, and we shall not damage them. Practice will make us more honest and less likely to force or coerce. In St Ignatius's own time, novices were giving the Exercises. If in Ignatius's time there had been a well-educated and talented body of laity, he would have had them giving the Exercises. After all, he was a layperson himself when he began giving them. It is good that the practice has been re-introduced.

Finally, to whom should the Exercises be given? According to Nadal, the Exercises can be given to every class of people, including heretics and 'pagans'. The Exercises may be given to 'pagans', according to Nadal, provided they can be brought to believe in one God and pray. Such exercises will include the Principle and Foundation, the meditations of the First Week (excluding confession and communion); whilst the exercises termed 'the Kingdom' and the 'Two Standards' can be given and referred to the one God. If all these exercises are completed, an election or choice of a way of life, adapted to the individual, is in order. With 'heretics', Nadal says that the director should prescind from those truths which are unacceptable to the heretic. During the Second Week meditations, simple contemplations and application of the senses are to be preferred to subtle intellectual speculations.[6]

In Ignatius's own lifetime, a time of rapid change, when old structures were falling and everything was being questioned, the Exercises, and the early Society of Jesus which grew out of them, were a most powerful instrument for renewal in the Church. After his death, later Jesuit General Congregations (similar to General Chapters) began to make changes, which the Jesuit Constitutions allowed for, as the need arose. These later Congregations began to determine by law universal norms for the spiritual life of Jesuits, for example one hour of meditation daily, daily Mass, an annual retreat. These regulations, opposed by Ignatius in his own lifetime, became the criteria for a Jesuit vocation. Retreats began to be made in groups, sometimes five hundred at a time. Different people were not allowed to have different needs: and the Exercises, consequently, no longer produced their extraordinary results. They began to be used to buttress whatever we happened to be doing. We are now living in a time of much more rapid change. Old structures, formerly accepted assumptions in the Church and in society, are being questioned, found wanting, and swept aside. The Exercises too have been questioned; but the questioning has uncovered forgotten truths, which speak to us in the confusion of our times.

NOTES

1. G.A. Hugh, 'The Exercises for individuals and groups' (Program to Adapt the Spiritual Exercises: New Jersey, no date).

2. MHSJ *Faber*, 639-9; and see Paul Robb, 'The retreatant in a directed retreat' (PASE).

3. MHSJ *Monumenta Ignatiana*, vol. 2, *Directoria*, Doc. 3, n. 8.

4. Robb, op.cit.

5. R.E. McNally, 'Prayer and the early Society of Jesus' (PASE).

6. F.T. Erhart, 'Nadal on the Exercises' (PASE, 1967).

PART TWO

The Experience of the Exercises

CHAPTER THREE

'To Make the Exercises Better': The Additions

Brian Grogan

This essay will refer to all the advice which Ignatius offers to the person who gives the Exercises, some of which is to be passed on to the retreatant. It is not restricted to the notes commonly called Additions,[1] but also includes the Annotations, preludes to prayer and various sets of rules. The Directory which Ignatius dictated to Father Vitoria supports this broader interpretation of the Additions:

> Also he can be told as a sort of annotation or counsel (*quasi como annotacion o aviso*) . . . that he should agree that he should be able to take so much greater fruit from the Exercises to the extent that he is resigned into the hands of the Lord. . . .[2]

The purpose of the Additions is to mobilize the whole person in the search for the divine will. Ignatius had a comprehensive view of humanity: body, imagination, mind, senses, feeling and will were all to be brought into play to reach the goal of the Exercises. The quest for God's will is not limited to formal periods of prayer, but extends throughout the day: there is an Addition to cover the moment of waking and another for the moment of going to sleep. All the human resources are harnessed to the work of the Exercises; obstacles to God's action are removed; peace, harmony, simplicity, unity of purpose are promoted. Ignatius states that the Additions are 'to help one to go through the Exercises better and find more readily what he desires' (Exx 73). He considers them important: 'All ten additions are to be observed with great care' (Exx 130). Throughout the four Weeks he expects the retreatant to use the Particular Examen to see whether he or she is being faithful to the Additions (Exx 90). If the retreatant is not experiencing God's action the director is to ask about the Additions (Exx 6). Observance of the Additions expresses the retreatant's seriousness of purpose and willingness to co-operate with God (Exx 5).

THE CONTEXT OF THE ADDITIONS

We can only understand the Additions by referring them to the purpose of the Exercises, which in turn must be placed within the context of God's initiative. It is first of all necessary to want to make the Exercises; to be eager and generous in seeking God's will (Exx 15). God must implant the decision to make the Exercises and the desire 'to make as much progress as possible' (Exx 20). It would be semi-Pelagian naturalism to think of the Additions as work done by the retreatant to prepare to receive God's grace.[3] The person giving the Exercises does not know in advance what is going to happen and what he or she is going to do. The director can only watch to see how God will guide this particular retreatant through the various Additions. The director has to recall repeatedly that God is the real director of the retreat: 'He knows our human nature infinitely better than we do and when we try various Additions he often grants to each one the grace to understand what is suitable for him' (Exx 89). Annotation eighteen is addressed to those who seek limited peace of soul. Annotation twenty is for those who want to find the perfect peace of living their whole lives according to God's will whatever the price of reform. This Annotation brings out clearly Ignatius's grasp of the delicate balance between God's work and human co-operation:

> The more the soul is in solitude and seclusion the more fit it renders itself to approach and be united with its Creator and Lord; and the more closely it is united with Him, the more it is disposed to receive grace and gifts from the infinite goodness of its God.

FLEXIBILITY AND ADAPTATION

Ignatius himself learnt by hard experience how God wanted him to use penances, food, cleanliness, periods of prayers, light and darkness. Each Addition is a distillation of the knowledge he himself gathered in his progressive search for the divine will - for himself and for others. The Additions are so well-tried that they should not be lightly discarded; but to be of real value they must be used creatively and flexibly. They are designed for a particular person making the Exercises. Ignatius's sense of each person's uniqueness became blunted when we began to give retreats to groups. He intended the Additions to respect the Principle and Foundation: to use things in so far as they help and to avoid them in so far as they hinder spiritual freedom. Director and retreatant must follow Ignatius and learn from their own experience, which presupposes continuous discernment. In the Rules for Food, for instance, the retreatant 'will often experience more abundantly within the soul, lights, consolations and divine inspirations by which the proper means will become evident to him' (Exx 213). In the notes on penance Ignatius tells us that when we experiment and make changes God our Lord 'often grants each one the grace to understand what is suitable' (Exx 89).

The Directories emphasize both the importance of the Additions and the need for creativity and adaptability. Father Vitoria's Directory states:

> (The one who gives the Exercises) should watch the order of (the various rules), which is very important. For my part when I was giving them this was recommended to me by our Father, because any other method will make many mistakes and the exercitant will not make the progress that he should, as it seems from experience.

The Directory goes on to affirm that the director should take into account differences in temperament.[4] Depressed people should not be driven too hard. Fragile people may need to be handled with care. Some may have to be summoned to greater austerity, tempered by gentleness and affability. Today's director must be as sensitive to individual needs.

ENVIRONMENT

Annotation twenty recommends the person who wants to make much progress to withdraw from the place of residence, from friends and acquaintances, from all those cares which absorb body, mind and heart and leave too little leisure for listening to God. Today it is more important than ever to give this advice and even more difficult to take it. If we want to keep normal preoccupations at a distance, incoming and outgoing correspondence and telephone calls have to be stopped. It is probably more important than in Ignatius's day for retreatants to have a good rest before they start. Many exercitants find that they bring with their baggage much of the untidiness of everyday life, where the day is shaped by impulse and pressure. To counteract these complex and confusing rhythms and to do justice to the set times of prayer (Exx 72), the retreatant should arrange with the director a suitable time-table to distribute over the day times of prayer, preparation beforehand and reflection afterwards, a meeting with the director, examens and the Eucharist. It is necessary to recognize that some retreatants are incapable, when they start, of a full hour's prayer. It may be better for them to begin with short periods of prayer spread over the day and to build up gradually to the full hour as they go on through the first week.

All the details concerning environment, including music at meals, should help to create a new pattern in the retreatant's life. Solitude brings a person into the presence of God; silence sharpens our listening to God; our senses are heightened to be more aware of the action of God; the sacrifices we have to make are a sign of the God-given magnanimity and generosity, essential conditions for seeking, finding and carrying out God's will. Failure to establish this order and peace can be traced back in the first instance to a half-hearted acceptance and application of the Additions, but ultimately the root of the trouble is likely to be the absence of those dispositions stressed in Annotations five and fifteen.

The Eucharist may be an even more important event for us than it was in the sixteenth century, and yet it presents greater problems. Some will want to express the communitarian nature of the Exercises. This may best be done by a shared homily and bidding prayers. Others may prefer to let the simplest possible liturgy underline the tremendous mystery of Christ's death and resurrection and obviate the possibility of discord between the Eucharist and the different paths of the retreatants on their way to God.

THE BODY

The bodily discipline required by the Additions does not come easily to many modern retreatants. Corporal penance is recommended (Exx 82-89); laughter must be restrained (Exx 80); the eyes controlled (Exx 81); silence observed (Exx 20); punctuality in rising is presumed (Exx 73). The retreatant must pray for a full hour several times a day and usually at midnight (Exx 12, 13 etc). He or she has to oppose natural appetites and temptations.[5] The determination to avoid venial and mortal sin (Exx 165-66), the willingness to accept poverty (Exx 98) and insults (Exx 167) can make frightening physical demands on people who do not come from an ascetically-minded world. The spirit can be willing, but the flesh can be decidedly weak. The director should know what is being asked of each individual and what is possible.

To prepare the body for prayer I am told to stand a pace or two away from the place of prayer and to 'make an act of profound reverence' (Exx 75). In Ignatius's opinion the whole of a person must show reverence for the Divine Majesty. The appropriateness of a bodily posture in prayer is to be determined by whether or not I find what I desire (Exx 76). I am to remain in one position not until I am tired, but rather until I am satisfied. Ignatius presumes a degree of physical control which many people today do not possess. For the Zen masters posture is all-important: the lotus position is recommended, but failing that some way of sitting which will keep the back perfectly straight, and secure complete immobility. This posture considerably reduces discursive reasoning and helps the mind to concentrate on a single point. Breath control is also important: deep rhythmic breathing lowers the pulse and heart rate, promotes interior calm and peace and develops a deep state of concentration.[6] I believe that our western methods of prayer can be much enriched by what the East can teach us about the control of body, breath and mind. But we must be discerning in our use of this knowledge. Zen lacks the flexibility of Ignatius, who recommends darkness in the First Week and light in the Fourth. Ignatius draws on feelings and imagination in the service of what I desire: Zen aims to quieten feelings and imagination, while what I desire is either to remain constant or to be suppressed as much as possible. For Zen, silence and tranquillity are ends in themselves, whereas for Ignatius they are steps on the way to the summit of his prayer, which is to be moved by God towards action and service. Fortunately there is a growing wealth of experience in the use of Zen to help us to make the Exercises.[7]

THE MIND

During the weeks of the Exercises the retreatant is asked to direct the mind according to the different graces that are being sought. Mind, imagination and will all focus together on one subject. In the First Week the retreatant should not think of pleasure, but of the pain and sorrow he or she wants to experience (Exx 78). In the Second Week the retreatant is encouraged to read the gospels, the *Imitation of Christ* and the lives of the saints and to fill the mind with their words and images.[8] Ignatius does not choose haphazardly such images as the knight who feels ashamed (Exx 74). He realizes his deep need for compunction and the image aptly expresses the need. This is far from being mind control; rather it is more akin to the scientist or the poet struggling to understand, and so calling up some images and rejecting others. As Bernard Lonergan has remarked:

> . . . the stream of sensitive experience can become the automatic instrument or rather the vitally adaptive collaborator of the spirit of inquiry.[9]

The images of the knight or of the prisoner loaded with chains need to be re-fashioned. Fresh images may occur spontaneously to the retreatant or they may be drawn from the Bible or the liturgy.

Our minds and wills can easily be influenced by our feelings. Everyday emotional life is at the mercy of conflicting currents beyond my control. Several Additions propose that I should marshal my feelings and bring them into harmony with what I desire: 'I will seek to rouse myself to shame for my sins' (Exx 74); 'I will make an effort to be sad and grieve . . .' (Exx 78); 'I will strive to feel joy and happiness' (Exx 229). Two difficulties spring to mind. The first is that Ignatius is expecting more emotional control than many retreatants possess. The second is that reactions are sometimes thought of in too one-sided a way; there is a place for humble and joyful gratitude in the face of God's mercy (Exx 61), which is found in many scriptural stories about repentant sinners.

Ignatius has no time for a casual approach to prayer. Before beginning to pray I am to 'recollect myself for a while, and either seated or walking up and down, as may seem better, I will consider where I am going and for what purpose' (Exx 239). This Addition restores the cutting edge of prayer which can so easily be blunted through weariness or monotony. When I get up, my mind is particularly apt to wander; and therefore the direction of my thoughts last thing at night and first thing in the morning will help me to concentrate on what I truly desire.[10]

It is worth noting that the greatest gifts are often given outside periods of formal prayer; hence the importance of a tranquil atmosphere throughout the day. Zen masters believe that *satori* or enlightenment may come at any time: at the fall of the almond blossom or the sound of the temple bell. In such relaxed moments, when we are off guard and suitably open, the Creator comes to us to say and to do whatever is needed (Exx 330).

THE PRELUDES: COMPOSITION

Fr W. Peters has made an important contribution to this subject and I can add little to what he has said.[11] The purpose of composition at the beginning of an exercise or period of prayer is to make the retreatant at one with the event that is being contemplated; it means both inner unity and harmony[12] and oneness with surrounding reality. It is rather a composition of *self* than of *place*. The retreatant must become composed to the fact that he or she is an exile among brute beasts (Exx 47) or to the fact that hell exists and that he or she has been preserved from it by God's mercy (Exx 61). Composition therefore means reconciling oneself with and being present to the reality in question. It is in fact God who composes me; I remain where God wants me to be, where God gives intimate understanding and relish of the truth (Exx 2, 76 etc). Composition is strengthened by listening to the story and seeing the place with the imagination (Exx 102–103). Gradually the depth and totality of my presence to God's action in each event are increased.

Composition presents the modern director and retreatant with an interesting set of challenges. It takes time and is unlikely to give up its secret to the person in an unreflective hurry. The Old Testament has been opened to us, and scholarship has immensely enriched our understanding of the scriptures as a whole. But the same scholars may tempt us down side-streets to ask arid, irrelevant and awkward questions. Fortunately it is not so very difficult to be at one with some of the Old and New Testament writers. It may help the modern director to become more familiar with the use of fantasy and imagination in prayer. In *God is more present than you think*,[13] R. Ochs suggests that it is much more concrete to follow one's own fantasy than to struggle to re-create a gospel scene, and when one has failed, to conclude that there has been yet another bad meditation. He describes a man who saw himself barred from the cave at Bethlehem. This went on for some days, and gave him a new appreciation of his unworthiness. One day he felt himself invited to go in, and this was a turning point in his life.

THE PRELUDES: THE PREPARATORY PRAYER

The preparatory prayer (Exx 46) is made before every hour of prayer (Exx 49). I ask for the disposition contained in the Principle and Foundation: to want and to do only that which God wants of me. What *God* wants; while 'desirous of making as much progress as possible' (Exx 20), I allow God to indicate the limits of possibility at this stage in my growth. I must not run ahead of the Holy Spirit in a 'hasty or inconsiderate' fashion (Exx 14). God must give me the desire and the power to carry it out. Joyous consolation is the sign that God is doing so. Joylessness and harshness in performance are the signs that I am forcing God's hand. It is possible to choose a course of action which is good in itself but not intended by God for this person at this moment. Ignatius constantly counteracts such Pelagian tendencies. I pray for actual poverty provided only that it is for God's greater service and praise and that God 'deign to choose and admit me to such a state and way of life' (Exx 98, 157). In the Annotations the director is warned not to interfere with God's action by persuading the retreatant to become poor or celibate. The director is told to let God dispose the retreatant to serve God better in future (Exx 15).

The general advice for each period of prayer tells me to consider *how* God beholds me (Exx 75). How does God behold me? While my relationship with God develops slowly over the weeks of the Exercises, God's relationship towards me remains constant. The best description of how God looks on me is found in the Contemplation to Attain Love. God loves me as a person, wishes to give me all possible gifts, God included. God sees me as a temple, 'since I am created in the likeness and image of the Divine Majesty' (Exx 235).

THE PRELUDES: ASKING FOR WHAT I WANT

There appears to be a double contradiction: between what God wants and what I want; and between what I really want and what I am told to want at a particular point in the Exercises. Almost the first step in the Exercises is to believe that God deals directly with creatures (Exx 15) and that God implants good desires in our hearts. My prevailing desire at this moment may well be my God-given response to the divine initiative. But it is often a feeble response, because my desire to collaborate with God and to love as I am loved has to grow, a growth which does not necessarily correspond to physical and psychological growth. These good, God-inspired, God-directed desires will no doubt be in conflict with evil desires. To be aware of contrasting desires and to know where they are leading is in itself a gift from God. Retreatant and director can detect degrees of growth and types of conflict. The resolution of the contradictions – what God wants, what I want, what I really want, what I am told to want – consists at this moment in wrestling with my divided heart and asking for help. Sometimes I shall have to decide whether I have the magnanimity and generosity to begin or to continue the Exercises (Exx 5, 15). Prayerful reflection on such passages as the sons of Zebedee (Matt. 20.20-23), the man who built a tower (Luke 14.28-33) or the woman at the well (John 4) teaches me to understand the stage I have reached in my growth towards God and the clashes between my various desires.

GOING AGAINST

Ignatius's advice about going against what I desire is often misunderstood. It is not a question of always preferring the less pleasant course of action. Ignatius knows that the good spirit makes all things easy (Exx 315). Pleasant thoughts, inclinations and actions may show that at this particular moment I am free to go to God, and that this harmony has been established in my life. At other times I may find pleasure in being excessively attracted and attached to a form of imprisonment (Exx 16), to a job, a person, a set of habits, which hinder my growth and movement towards God. Desolation is a tyranny which keeps me away from God and prevents me from loving service. Hence Ignatius urges me to use my limited freedom to pray longer, to resist the enemy (Exx 13), to intensify my activity against desolation (Exx 319), in the name of greater freedom and greater pleasure. This is what Ignatius means by 'the conquest of self' (Exx 21).

EXTERIOR PENANCE

Ignatius's comments on exterior penance must be placed in their historical context. The tradition of the flagellants was still strong; St Charles Borromeo had to make regulations about their processions. Monastic tradition and reformers within the Church regarded the use of the scourge or discipline as obligatory. Lives of the saints were full of physical mortifications. Even the gentle St Francis de Sales praises the marvellous power of the discipline to stir devotion. At the beginning of his conversion Ignatius was impressed by the penances of the saints,[14] which he regarded as a measure of their generosity. He began to discipline himself each night.[15] Slowly his powers of discernment developed and he began to break away from the traditions of his day. In the Jesuit Constitutions he makes the revolutionary statement that in the Society there are to be no customary penances and austerities obligatory on all.[16] In the Exercises, forms of penance exist to foster and to express interior dispositions such as repentance and satisfaction for past sins (Exx 87). Penances must be subordinated to the whole process of the Exercises, whose purpose is freedom for the greatest possible service of God. Moderation is therefore essential: too much is as bad as too little (Exx 89). God must teach us to choose what is suitable. Here, as in the Rules for Eating and throughout the Exercises, the retreatant is God's apprentice in the art of discernment. Ignatius set much store by exterior penance: it warms the spirit and regulates disordered passions;[17] it is a *means* to acquire interior freedom in the greater service of God. Today few of his followers would subscribe to the view that 'the more we deny ourselves something of what is suitable, provided we do no harm to ourselves, the better the penance' (Exx 83). Yet retreatants do experience the spontaneous desire for penance. Inflicting bodily pain is out of fashion, but fasting and watching are normal and can be salutary. Some retreatants are frightened when penance is mentioned, but when invited to cut down alcohol, coffee or smoking, they are pleased to find a new sense of freedom. Our senses put us in touch with the world; when they are dulled our grasp of the world is dull. Clarity of vision is often obscured in a polluted world. Many of us eat too much and would be healthier physically and spiritually if we ate less. But let God teach us the mean to be observed.

CONCLUSION

Let God teach us. . . . This is perhaps the best conclusion to a set of directions, which are so detailed, so concrete and so much in need of creative adaptation to the circumstances of each individual. The director must learn personally - or rather be taught by God - what advice to give in order to set the retreatant free.

NOTES

1. Exx 73-90, 127-31, 204-7, 226-9.

2. MHSJ *Directoria*, doc. 4 (Rome 1955), p. 97. See translation, quoted here, by Program to Adapt the Spiritual Exercises, New Jersey.

3. Gagliardi, *Commentarii in Exercitiis Spiritualibus* (Bruges 1882), p. 74. *Nec ullae reliquiae in nobis residuae sint illius pelagianismi spiritualis, in quam multi incidunt.* MHSJ *Directoria*, p. 660.

4. MHSJ *Directoria*, doc. 4, p. 104; PASE translation, p. 30. The 1599 *Directory* states: *Ex altera parte caveri etiam debet omnis excessus, et habenda est ratio personarum et complexionum.* MHSJ *Directoria*, p. 660.

5. Exx 13 and Rules for Eating.

6. Philip Kapleau, *The Three Pillars of Zen* (Boston 1967), pp. 3-24; W. Johnston, *Christian Zen* (New York 1971); *Silent Music: the science of meditation* (London 1974), Part I, 'Meditation', pp. 13-52, Part III, 'Healing', pp. 105-58.

7. Kakichi Kadowaki, *The Ignatian Exercises and Zen - An Attempt at Synthesis* (PASE edition).

8. Exx 100: this directive and the one concerning not reading ahead should be supplemented today with a warning not to spend too much time reading one's favourite spiritual author and not to indulge in scripture study. The addition about readiness to accept the director's point of view (Exx 22)

should now include an agreement not to speculate about the demythologization of the infancy and resurrection narratives, hell, angels and so on.

9. Bernard Lonergan, *Insight* (London 1957), p. 186.

10. K. Rahner, 'A Spiritual Dialogue at Evening: On Sleep, Prayer and Other Subjects', in *Theological Investigations III* (London 1967), pp. 220-36, recalls the common experience that when we sleep on a problem we sometimes find the solution ready to hand in the morning. A mechanism for selecting appropriate images seems to be at work in our minds. He notes that imagination and fantasy have also been redeemed, although the struggle against evil persists in this sphere as in others. He talks about consecrating the world of darkness and recalls Christian tradition: 'On Christ is our thought directed even in the midst of darkness' by Prudentius; 'Far from us may evil dreams and night fantoms withdraw' from the Ambrosian hymn at Compline; 'I sleep, but my heart is awake' in Song of Sol. 5. 2.

11. W.A.M. Peters, *The Spiritual Exercises of St Ignatius: exposition and interpretation* (PASE).

12. MHSJ, *Directoria*, doc. 4, says the exercitant is to set a good example *con la humildad y composición de su persona*.

13. R. Ochs, *God is More Present than You Think* (New York 1970).

14. *Autobiography* 9.

15. *Autobiography* 13.

16. *Constitutions* 552.

17. *Constitutions* 582.

CHAPTER FOUR

The First Week: Practical Questions

Joseph Veale

In answer to the basic question of what the director should do in the First Week, I imagine an experienced director would say 'I don't know', or 'I don't know what I am going to do until after the interview'. It is part of the incomprehensible dynamic of the Exercises that the Spirit works through the prayerful relationship of the director and the retreatant. What is said or not said is in function of the relationship and what emerges in the conversation.

In practice there are three kinds of retreatant: (a) those who have met their director fairly frequently over a long period and who have been prepared by prayer and spiritual direction to begin the enclosed thirty-day retreat; this is closer to St Ignatius's practice; (b) those who have been preparing themselves in the same way for the Exercises in daily life; (c) those whom the director meets for the first time on the evening the thirty-day retreat begins. In practice this last kind would seem to be more common. In that case the first few days of the retreat need to be given to getting to know the retreatant; to allaying feelings of apprehension and founding the possibility of trust; to establishing a prayerful atmosphere; and to discovering (as far as possible without asking questions) why the person wants to make the Exercises, what the person desires and is seeking, something of his or her situation in life, what are the pressures of work, whether he or she has come to the retreat bone-wearied, whether the person has been praying, and how important prayer is, what he or she cares about, whether this kind of retreat has been made before, and who God is for that person.

Fairly early in the first few days I suggest, firmly, that the retreatant begin each time of prayer as St Ignatius recommends (Exx 75), so that the time of prayer has a formal beginning; so that the body is brought into prayer; so that the perspective is right (*cómo Dios nuestro Señor me mira*, 'how God our Lord is beholding –

53

contemplating - me'); so that the focus is on God rather than on self; so that the person begins to feel reverence before the holiness and majesty of God. I will also try (often with limited success) to show how to make the review of prayer, since it is essential to the dynamic of the Exercises and without it the person will not begin to learn what is helpful in order to reply to, 'Well, what has been happening . . .?'

READINESS FOR THE FIRST WEEK

During these days I will try to pick up the signs that will show me whether the retreatant will be able to make the exercises of the First Week. Negative indications will be: a defective image of God (demanding tyrant or wholly indulgent Daddy or Mummy), a very defective self-image; a weakened faith; a weakened sense of God that makes a true sense of sin difficult; a weakened hope that has small expectations of God's power and desire to give the divine gifts (Exx 5: 'to enter upon them with magnanimity'); an absence of mature relationships in the person's life; a Pelagian tendency that may imagine the Exercises to be a technique.

I will want to encourage the retreatant to spend at least a day or two ruminating about (the term of the early Directories) or praying the Principle and Foundation; in these times probably longer than that.

> For modern men, who need to discover the meaning of God's sovereignty, the Foundation cannot remain a mere consideration, lofty and luminous as it may be. It must be turned into an exercise for acquiring awareness of the absolute primacy of God. An intellectual demonstration . . . would have little effect on many of our contemporaries.[1]

By this time I will be hoping that the retreatant has begun to pray, to experience something of God's goodness and love in prayer. Until that has begun to happen, I should be unwilling to go into the First Week.

The retreatant's response to the Foundation is something of a touchstone for a readiness to make the Exercises and especially for a readiness to begin the First Week. The closer the retreatant comes to the dispositions that Ignatius describes in Annotations 5 and 20, the more I will have hoped that something of the following has been discovered: (a) some growth in desire to give himself or herself wholly to God; (b) in the light that comes from God and in the light of some previous glimpse of what interior freedom is, to have grown in the desire to be 'indifferent', to experience the freedom of the Spirit (2 Cor 3.17), to participate in the freedom of Jesus before the Father and before all other things; (c) with some realistic sense of personal capacities to be aware, in response to St Ignatius's casual statement 'therefore it is necessary to make ourselves indifferent', that: 'I have it in my power to expand somewhat the area of my human freedom. But I cannot "make myself indifferent". Only the power of the Spirit can do that.' And, 'I do not know how to find God's particular and concrete will for me'. Finally, 'Were I to know it, I do not have the moral strength to do it'. The early Directories seem to be clear on this, that the retreatant should experience the difficulty of becoming that free.² The fourth of the 'autograph' Directories and a later one speak of the fruit of the Foundation as 'resignation':

> Indifference is a 'resignation'; a man places himself in the hands of his God and Lord. . . . When the whole heart does this really and in truth, it greatly disposes him for God's communication of himself, because it opens the door of the heart, so that the Lord can work great things in him.³

All this has something to do with readiness to begin the First Week. I believe that in the coming years the director of the enclosed thirty-day Exercises will have much to learn from the guide of the Exercises in daily life; indeed the latter may (in practice if not in principle) become the paradigm of our direction of the Exercises. Maurice Giuliani, in his *The Exercises in Daily Life* says:

> From this point of view, certain moments are more characteristic of the retreat (in daily life). For example, the moment when, after several weeks of the Exercises, a real attitude of 'indifference' shows that the retreatant is ready to enter into the mystery of mercy and salvation. . . . A distance develops between being and action, between the fundamental desire of his heart and the manifold desires which swarm around, to the point of paralysing him; between the vital attachment he feels for people and the invitation to break with all love that is possessive. Some sort of order begins to emerge among his feelings; superficial movements of sensitivity die down and give way to movements that the person sees to

have another origin . . . that, at the very heart of everyday living, a power is leading the person's consciousness, making him pass from selfishness to the gift of self . . . in the sense, so to speak, that his daily life is 'ruled' by Another. . . . Is this what we call 'indifference'? I think so. In the Exercises in daily life, this is a threshold, the very threshold which marks the beginning of the experience of the Exercises.[4]

ENTERING THE FIRST WEEK

A director knows that one cannot contrive or bring about these insights or dispositions. And since this is so, he or she should not try. All the director can do is to propose or to urge or to suggest those dispositions that open us to receiving the gifts of the Spirit; to be alert to signs of such dispositions that may as yet be obscure to the retreatant, to clarify them, it may be to suggest that he or she return to them in prayer and to point the way forward. The director prays for the retreatant and also tries to discern and to help the retreatant to discern what is happening as well as to encourage gratitude for what has been given.

The more the retreatant desires to have the necessary dispositions and the more he or she has entered into interior silence and has really begun to pray, the more I should expect the person to begin to be moved towards a sense of sinfulness. The other side of the Principle and Foundation is a sense that I am not free, that I cling to many things whether they are God's will for me or not, that my capacity to love is imprisoned in a thousand ways. Before moving into the meditations of the First Week, I should be waiting for some sign that the retreatant was being moved in that direction. If the Exercises seem to be less effective than we might hope, it may be that people are moved prematurely into the First Week, that the Spirit has not been given time to prepare them or to dispose them.

Of course, if in praying the Foundation a retreatant were clearly and markedly moved in an unexpectedly different direction, or moved to remain in consolation in an attitude of adoration or worship or surrender to the goodness of God, then a good director would not interfere (Exx 15).[5]

Ideally it is the retreatant who discerns and decides when he or she should move into the First Week exercises, as into any further stage of the Exercises. It is for this reason among many that the Exercises in daily life are beginning to look like a privileged way, since there is plenty of time in which to allow an insight or a grace to go deeper before moving ahead. Maurice Giuliani is insistent that it is the retreatant who must decide when it is time to go forward.[6]

THE DIRECTOR'S OWN UNDERSTANDING

Among the things I keep in mind in presenting the First Week are:

(a) The grace of the First Week is one of profound consolation.

(b) St Ignatius's way of putting it is given in Annotation (Exx) 4: 'contrition, sorrow and tears for sin'.

(c) What is customarily called the *id quod volo*, that is 'asking for what I desire', focusing on a particular grace to be begged for and desired in prayer and throughout the day, is essential to the dynamic of the Exercises.

(d) The terms 'shame and confusion' can easily be misunderstood by a contemporary person. I see no such problem with 'a growing and intense sorrow'.

(e) It is better that the retreatant come to his or her own expression of the grace to be desired. Time is not wasted if someone can come truthfully to answer the question 'What do I really want?'.

(f) The terms in which St Ignatius proposes the concluding prayer or Colloquy indicate the kind of grace he hopes will be given: to be deeply moved *de arriba* (from above) to wonder and gratitude before the mercy and goodness of God.

(g) The director will expect the path to the consolation of the First Week to be an experience of desolation.

(h) The director will not want, through mistaken kindness or because of personal discomfort, to try to move the retreatant prematurely away from it.

(i) Desolation is a turning in on oneself, a being imprisoned in isolation from others, from the world, from oneself, from God. The director will be alert to sense if such a state is in danger of taking hold, of becoming a settled and barren self-preoccupation. Then he or she will try gently to shift the retreatant's focus from self to Christ.

(j) 'Only God speaks well of God.' Only God speaks well of sin. Only God can reveal my sin to me. Apart from the light and presence of God my unworthy behaviour may remain only a sense of pervading guilt at breaking laws, of acting unethically, of betraying my self-respect and undermining my self-esteem. (We need a new word to help us to distinguish between guilt and guilt.) For many, nowadays, much prayer in the presence of God's goodness may be needed to liberate a retreatant from such substitutes for a realization of what his or her sinfulness really is. The grace of the First Week is a liberation from *ersatz* guilt.

(k) The grace of the First Week is a new knowledge of God. I do not see how we can come to know God without a deep sense of our sinfulness and our absolute need for salvation. The closer a person is drawn to God the more he or she will experience layer beyond layer of self, of the false self. In the continuing experience of finding God in all things, the further discovery of unexpected sinfulness can become, in the light of the First Week grace, a joyful means of entering into a deeper knowledge of God.

(l) The grace of the First Week leads to a realistic facing up to the reality of oneself. It undermines our sinful need of self-justification. It places us naked and unprotected before the goodness and the love of God.

The director will want to have a clear grasp of his or her own understanding of the dynamic of the Exercises. The more this is the case, the more one can sit easily to the letter of the Exercises. And the more one will be free to use the text unaccommodated, if that is what will help the retreatant more. The dynamic of the First Week is understood by grasping the movement within a period of prayer from the *id quod volo* to the colloquy. The points in between in the text are of secondary importance. The parts of the First Week text that I should tend to look on as essential are: (a) the second preludes; (b) the colloquy before Christ on the Cross; (c) the triple colloquy; (d) the additions that recommend a sober environment and interior climate, a calm urgency of desire; (e) the repetitions; (f) Exx 46: the prayer before every hour of prayer for the grace of the Principle and Foundation.

THE FIRST EXERCISE

Should one use the three points given in Ignatius's text or not? I do not know. A director has to consider whether these points about the sin of the angels, of Adam and Eve, and of the sinner in hell, will help or hinder this retreatant, whether they will help to find the fruit of 'shame and confusion' and open the person to an intimate and personal speaking with Christ on the Cross. Scripture passages will be more helpful to some. The Ignatian principle should always prevail: have a contemplative grasp of the end and be flexible in your use of the means. The points are only means.

There are some parts of the text that it may be helpful to keep in mind. St Ignatius does not at first ask the retreatant to look at his or her own sin or sins. He first presents the person with the pervading contagion of sin in the world. The retreatant meditates first on sin 'out there' as it were. It would not be un-Ignatian to have the person recall to memory and imagination the effects of sin in the world as he or she has experienced and observed them. This would, besides, be in keeping with the dynamic of the First Week, which looks towards the contemplation of the Incarnation. In these days one would want the retreatant to be livingly aware of evil in the contemporary world, lest the sense of sin be individualistic, or lest 'the angels' and 'Adam and Eve' be too detached from the reality of his or her experience. There is a sufficient hint of this in 'and the great corruption which came upon the human race' (Exx 51). We are more and more likely to meet with two types of retreatant. Those who, for whatever reason, are anaesthetized to the sin in human structures; and those who are deeply moved by injustice but imperfectly aware of it as sin. Of course those people who are deeply moved by injustice and feel their powerlessness are already disposed for the prayer of the First Week.

However, for all that, St Ignatius does move towards consideration of one's own sins. This he does by a series of comparisons: 'When I compare the one sin . . . with the many sins I have committed . . . for one sin, and the number of times I have deserved . . . because of my numerous sins'. His stress here is on frequency, as much as to say that the multitude and frequency of my sins, whether serious or not, ought to be a painful reminder of my heedlessness and ingratitude. We cannot grasp our solidarity in grace if we do not see our solidarity in sin. It is our antidote to the professional hazard of phariseeism.

He wants to help the retreatant to begin to realize the intrinsic 'gravity and malice of sin against our Creator and Lord'. Many retreatants may need much time to seek to be given a sense of this, given that our contemporary climate gives us many reasons for justifying ourselves in our own eyes (and hopefully in God's eyes) and for diluting our responsibility. It is a mode of thinking that can coexist with a need to cling to a sense of one's worthlessness. And, note, the colloquy with Christ on the Cross at the end of each period of prayer is indispensable.

Should one use what Ignatius terms the first prelude, the use of imagination, 'a composition, seeing the place'? Or how might one use it? How might one suggest it be used? For all our fastidiousness about possible dualism or about a dis-ordered sense of evil in the world, it seems to me that the images St Ignatius uses are scriptural. It may help some retreatants greatly to stay with, to steep themselves in, some of the scriptural images of imprisonment, of unfreedom, of constriction, of exile, of alienation, of the absence of light, of blindness, of falsity and untruth, of the felt absence of God, of hopelessness, of the weight of sin and its oppression. 'And a great famine arose . . . and he begain to be in want. . . . And he would gladly have fed on the pods that the swine ate; and no one gave him anything' (Luke 15.14-16).

THE SECOND EXERCISE (MY OWN SINS)

(a) The first prelude. It may be helpful to gloss St Thomas Aquinas to the effect that God is offended by our sins only in so far as they hurt ourselves and each other. *Non enim Deus a nobis offenditur, nisi ex eo quod contra nostrum bonum agimus.*[7]

(b) The second prelude: 'to ask for a growing and intense sorrow and tears for my sins'. Since the grace asked for here is foundational to the gospel ('Repent and believe . . .'), there is no need to apologize for or to transpose the words here into another idiom. However, it is good not to present this too rigidly or absolutely. It may help some retreatants more to suggest that they beg for a sense of God's eagerness to forgive, or for a sense of their need of the compassion of Christ. There are some who may need to spend much time in praying the parable of the two sons (Luke 15) before making the second exercise.

(c) The 'points'. The *first point: el processo de los pecados* (the record of my sins); the modern retreatant, now possibly becoming rapidly obsolete, will need to be told that this is not an examination of conscience in preparation for a general confession. One of the earliest Directories stresses this: 'To arouse sorrow, it does not help so much to go into details, but rather to picture the overall view of their gravity'.[8] At the same time St Ignatius would not be content with vagueness but would want us to be concrete and specific. The *second* and *third* points, on the gravity of my sins, are not for those who would depress themselves into a state of disordered self-abasement. The director needs to be alert to shift the focus from a barren self-preoccupation. Should we allow our contemporary nervousness at words like 'the corruption and loathsomeness of my body' to force us to be completely silent about these points? Clearly if such imagery will be an obstacle rather than a help to being open to the grace of 'growing and intense sorrow', or will prevent the retreatant from entering into a 'colloquy' 'extolling the mercy of God our Lord . . . giving thanks to him that up to this very moment he has granted me life', then it should not be suggested. But perhaps many retreatants are tougher than we think. It seems to me that a sense of sin is likely to remain superficial and, in these times, too privatized, if we are too squeamish to accept that as a sinner I am a 'source of corruption and contagion'. The *fourth* point is an invitation to contemplate God, to turn the focus firmly to God and God's wisdom, power, justice and goodness. Together with the *fifth* point (a 'cry of wonder') it is a repetition of the Principle and Foundation. The point of affective insight that St Ignatius seems to hope for here is something like: 'It could have been otherwise. It ought in all justice to have been otherwise. If the roots of serious sin in me have not taken control, that is not due to me but to Christ. I am loved. I am alive. And I am free'. The director knows that he or she is impotent to accomplish that. It is not the director's work.

THE THIRD AND FOURTH EXERCISES (REPETITIONS OF PREVIOUS EXERCISES)

This is not the place to expand upon the crucial importance of 'repetition' in the Exercises. Whether one presents the Ignatian points or equivalent passages from scripture for meditation is of secondary importance. The petitions of the *triple colloquy* are indispensable. The words may need some exegesis. There should be a sense of calm urgency about the asking.

In the dynamic of the Exercises St Ignatius is looking ahead towards the degree of freedom of the Spirit that is a prerequisite for finding God's will. Any act of discernment requires that I be aware of my particular disorder, my ill-ordered affectivity, my bias so that I may constantly take it into account in practical judgment and decision. (Exx 21: *sin determinarse por affección alguna que desordenada sea.*)

What is being sought here is what Ignatius calls an 'interior knowledge' (*para que sienta interno conocimiento*). What we are desiring is not something acquired by willing and thinking, or rather by simply willing and thinking, but a knowledge which is given and is the work of the Spirit. What is being asked for is a sense, at a deep level, of the particular sinfulness that is at the root of my sins. St Ignatius would not be content with a vague and generalized sense of sinfulness, but would want us to be particular and concrete. But the grace is sought and desired in the confidence expressed by Julian of Norwich:

> He, in his courtesy, limits the amount we see, for it is so vile and horrible that we could not bear to see it as it is. In his mercy our Lord shows us our sin and our weakness by the kindly light of himself.

The conjunction of 'the disorder of my actions' and 'a knowledge of the world' may find some affinity with a contemporary theology of sin that sees men and women as structuring their world by their choices and being made by the world they structure.

THE FIFTH EXERCISE (THE MEDITATION ON HELL)

If a person has been experiencing great dryness or desolation I should not feel compelled to suggest this exercise. If the person has experienced something of the consolation of true remorse, I should certainly suggest the prayer of thanksgiving 'that up to this very moment he has always shown himself so loving and merciful to me' (Exx 71). A director might legitimately add 'and that God will continue always mercifully to save me'. If a retreatant has had experience of real desolation and is willing to recall the taste of it, he or she will know what the possibility of separation from God is like. That, together with the authority of the Lord's words, 'Lord, Lord, did we not prophesy in your name? . . . I have never known you'

(Matt. 7.21-23) and 'I do not know where you come from' (Luke 13.25-27), together with the parable of the judgment in Matthew 25, may be sufficient as a preparation for the colloquy, or prayer, of thanksgiving.

All the 'colloquies' of the First Week exercises open to a realization of mercy and love and goodness, to a sense of the gift of life, to the opportunity that remains to serve God, to release, relief and freedom, to gratitude and praise.

The question is whether in the context of the first exercise or here, with St Ignatius's fiery imagery, I should refuse to be drawn into theological argumentation.

ALL FIVE EXERCISES ON ONE DAY

The text nowhere says that the massive First Week programme is to be repeated day after day. The second of the autograph Directories is clear: 'Father [Ignatius] does not think that the exercises of the First Week should be given him all together. He never did so, but gave them one at a time, until all five were given.'⁹ If a retreatant is subjected to an introduction to all five exercises at one sitting, the result for most people would be clutter. Clutter, a sense of being oppressed with too much matter, is to be avoided at all costs. Rather than that, it is better to simplify and to omit.

One assumes that a person will spend some days at least on the First Week. Of course, if the grace is given without all the Ignatian apparatus of 'preludes' and 'points', then there is no point in giving them; if the end is given, the means become unnecessary.

When the time has come to move forward from the Principle and Foundation, I should give the first exercise or its scriptural equivalent. If a retreatant has entered into prayer, that is quite enough material for one day's prayer. The second exercise can be given on the following day. I would want the retreatant to begin to make the repetitions and to pray the triple colloquy as soon as possible. Only then would I perhaps suggest spending a day going through the five, or four exercises in succession. By that time they will tend, in any case, to be repetitions. But I see no especial virtue in doing all five exercises on one day in the order given. The contemplative shape of each day in the Second Week is quite another matter.

THE FIRST WEEK – HOW LONG?

Another question to which there is no simple answer is, 'How long should the First Week last?' The director will be watching for a marked experience of the First Week consolation. As soon as that is present the director will know that it is possible to move forward.

Why, then, should a person delay at all? For two reasons: (a) So long as he or she is experiencing consolation, he or she is finding God and God is enlightening and strengthening the person. 'Where I find what I desire, there I will rest, without anxiety to go forward until I am satisfied' (Exx 76). (b) To remain a few days longer praying the prayer of the First Week will confirm and deepen the grace. I should expect, however, that with many people the strong experience of consolations will begin to fade. The beginning of a certain distaste or dryness or weariness would be a good sign that it is time to move on.

Naturally the somewhat artificial arrangement of an imminent 'repose day' (one of the traditional series of rest days in a closed thirty-day retreat) should not determine how long the retreatant remains in any of the weeks. But supposing that someone, as far as one can judge, is not entering into the experience of the First Week and is not experiencing consolation, should one keep that person there day after day for nine or ten or eleven days or more, until he or she is moved to sorrow and tears? I take it that experienced directors would say 'no'! It may be that a person has been entering sincerely into the prayer of the First Week and is, one may confidently hope, being given the grace needed at the moment and may be given a deep experience of conversion and contrition during the Third Week contemplation of the Passion. Or this may be the time to judge that the retreatant should not make the Exercises. Perhaps some people would be more helped by spending the remainder of the month simply praying and being helped by daily spiritual direction.

NOTES

1. See Louis Beirnaert, *Awareness of God and of Sin in the Spiritual Exercises*.

2. MHSJ 76, doc. 4, p. 420.

3. MHSJ 76, doc. 10, p. 148.

4. In *Progressio*, Supplement nos 18-19 (November 1981), pp. 36, 14.

5. See the article by William A. Barry, 'The experience of the First and Second Weeks of the Spiritual Exercises', in David Fleming (ed.), *Notes on the Spiritual Exercises* (St Louis 1981), pp. 96ff.

6. Guiliani, op. cit., especially chapters II and VIII.

7. Aquinas, St Thomas: *Contra Gentiles* III, c. 122.

8. MHSJ 76, doc. 3, p. 86.

9. MHSJ 76, doc. 2, p. 80.

CHAPTER FIVE

The First Week and Social Sin

Peter McVerry

In the last twenty years or so, two developments in the Spiritual Exercises stand out for me as especially important. One is the emphasis on a return to the original sources and the consequent appreciation of how our giving of the Exercises had been influenced by later, often unhelpful adaptations; the second is the growing appreciation of the contribution that psychology can make, with consequently a growing willingness and ability to watch for the unconscious at work within us, influencing our responses and even reducing our freedom to respond in particular areas. Today, we are faced with a third development of equal importance to the giving of the Exercises: the growing awareness of the reality and significance of structural sin.

THE RETREATANT'S AWARENESS OF THE REALITY OF STRUCTURAL SIN

The terms 'social sin', 'sinful structures' and 'institutionalized sin' are used with increasing frequency in theological discussion. What is implied in these terms, it seems to me, is a radical expansion of our consciousness of sin. We are used to applying the word 'sinful' to individual acts when such acts are (a) harmful to oneself or others (i.e. violate the law of God), and (b) done freely and with full knowledge. When we apply the word 'sinful' to structures, it is obvious that we are using it in a different sense.

The word 'structure' refers to 'a formal set of relationships which are somehow distinct from the individuals who are related in them'.[1] Sinful structures are those formal sets of relationships which result in the oppression of groups of people, while enabling other groups of people to benefit from that oppression, even without those benefiting fully knowing or freely consenting to the oppression.

For example, if I hit José on the head and take his money so that he and his family go hungry, such an act is a sinful act (there is a high probability that I am acting knowingly and willingly!). But if United Brands Inc. buy up José's land to pay off his debts to unscrupulous suppliers, and use it to grow high protein foods for export to USA, while José and his family go hungry, that is just as harmful – indeed even more so – to José than the first incident. Such a situation is therefore called 'sinful'. This is not to say that *every* aspect of United Brands's activities is sinful, or that its directors are acting in bad faith. But it does say that José's hunger is a situation displeasing to God, and that it is due, not just to the malevolent action of certain individuals but to actions that are the result of a set of relationships involving directors, employees, shareholders and consumers.

For a person today, the concept of sin as a deliberate transgression by an individual of the law of God, done with full knowledge and full consent, is too limited to be adequate. No doubt we all sin in this sense too, and I do not wish to minimize the importance of acknowledging and repenting of such acts. It is also true that structural sin is often founded and erected on such acts. But the reality of structural sin cannot be *reduced* to such acts: José's hunger *today* is due, not only to the original, perhaps malevolent, act that took his land, but also to the thousands of individual, uncoordinated acts of consumers, investors, employees and directors throughout the world. Consequently, a change in the situation will not be produced solely by identifying and converting those key personnel in United Brands who make the decisions that maintain the situation.

Again, the educational system in Ireland ensures privileged access to higher education – and consequently to a more secure, better paid higher status employment – for particular social groups. This necessarily results in limiting access for other social groups. This situation is maintained by the individual decisions of those in privileged social groups to secure the best possible education for their children (an excellent desire) in fee-paying schools which are necessarily socially restrictive, and by the decisions of those in government and in religious orders to provide and support such schools. A person's decision to send his or her son or daughter to such a school contributes to preserving the system which limits access to higher education for some groups, yet a decision not to send his or her son or daughter to such a school will change nothing (except the son's or daughter's opportunity for access to higher education). The decision of a Provincial of a religious order to retain such a school in such a form contributes to restricting access to higher education for some social groups, yet his or her decision to close the school or change its nature will probably change little (though it could well contribute to the conscientization of many, thereby leading in the future to significant change).

Again, a large multinational company may be considering closure of one of its plants in a small town, with devastating effects on the quality of life of the whole community. The managing director of the company may be faced with a situation where the competitors have re-located to Indonesia, where average wage levels are some thirty times below those in the U.K. or Ireland, and are dramatically undercutting the company's price. In such a situation, the managing director may also have to decide to re-locate abroad or go out of business altogether. No directed retreat can alter the situation – although he or she might elect to remain and perhaps reduce profit margins as much as possible, in which case he or she will, in all likelihood, be sacked by the board of directors, on the justification that they are responsible to the shareholders, who have invested with a view to likely (high) dividends. The pain and suffering in that township cannot be avoided by an appeal to the conscience of the person whose decision will be the direct cause of that pain. The most such a person can do is to make a prophetic gesture by resigning, knowing full well that such a decision will change nothing except the quality of his or her own life.

Unless our consciousness of sin has expanded to include an awareness of our participation in sinful structures, we would have little to say to the vast majority of those who are suffering injustice today, and little hope to offer them. Yet the limited concept of sin is what Ignatius presents in the Exercises. I cannot see how we can remain within that concept today. If the retreatant has not been deeply touched by some experience of the suffering of the poor, the unemployed, minorities, etc., and has not reflected on how their situation is maintained by the structures of society, then the experience of the First Week may well be unreal. If such an experience of injustice has been absent from the retreatant's life, then it will be impossible to converse adequately with the Lord about the sin of the world, or his or her own sin.

It may be argued that this should be part of the preparation of the retreatant for the Exercises, but in that event, the numbers of those to whom we could actually give the Exercises today would, in my opinion, be very limited and a new criterion for entry into the Exercises would be applied. But if the experience of the First Week is to recognize my sinfulness for what it is, to see it as it were from God's point of view, so that I am moved to grief and a desire to serve Christ better in the future, then I think it is legitimate to use the First Week to open the retreatant more to an appreciation of the reality of structural sin. (The fruit of the First Week may well be the resolution to seek later a fuller analysis of the situation as a prerequisite for action in the future.) In such a case, an essential element in the First Week would be a deeply moving experience of the suffering of others which is imposed on them by the way in which our society is organized – that is, some form of contact with the poorest would be, for many, an integral part of the First Week.

THE RETREATANT'S AWARENESS OF HIS OR HER COMPLICITY IN STRUCTURAL SIN

An essential aspect of the retreatant's meditation on structural sin is an awareness of his or her own complicity in that situation – his or her sinfulness.

Recognizing sinfulness means acknowledging responsibility for bringing about change, and a failure to exercise that responsbility sufficiently in the past. I may well have to work through feelings of guilt and feelings of powerlessness to come to recognize that, while I remain a sinner, I am yet forgiven and called to discipleship in the power of the Lord and not in my own power.

The retreatant's complicity in the structures which oppress others arises fundamentally from the fact that he or she has benefited from them. *Any structural change which relieves the suffering of the poor will necessarily involve a lowering of the standard of living and/or a reduction in the power, status and opportunities available to the rest of us,* including retreatants and directors. Any real structural change will have the two-edged thrust of the Magnificat: 'He has pulled down princes from their thrones and exalted the lowly; the hungry he has filled with good things, the rich sent empty away' (Luke 1.52-53). It is this that prevents the First Week from being a meditation on something 'out there'. To recognize my sinfulness for what it is, is to face this reality squarely: my participation in the struggle for change will adversely affect my own living standards, my own access to opportunity; the more successful that struggle, the more I will be affected.

This could well be the context for the meditation on the Two Standards in the Second Week. There we seek to become aware of how the attraction of possessions and worldy status can so easily lead us to aid the work of Satan, even while believing that we are really following Christ. A recognition of the root cause of our inertia, the material gain or increased social position or leverage that accrues to us from the *status quo*, could well be a valuable form of the Two Standards meditation for our day.

It also places the Principle and Foundation at the beginning of the Exercises in a new context: unless we are indifferent to all created things, we will be so defensive that we will not recognize the real nature of our complicity in the unjust structures of our society – we will fail even to recognize our sinfulness. To counter our defences and our rationalizations of our participation in such sinful structures, we must question ourselves in the light of the Three Classes of Men meditation, and actually beg the Lord to admit us to that state where the benefits of the *status quo* are removed from us.

But besides recognizing the root cause of their complicity in the structures of society, retreatants will recognize also those forces which encourage their complicity.

In the first place, they will recognize their isolation from the sufferings of others. The division of many of our British and Irish cities into private and local authority housing estates is a very efficient way of ensuring that our awareness of the problems that others have to face is kept to a minimum. It may be that the daily newspaper with its emphasis on crime, riots and social welfare abuse, helps to impress on us the contrary view that in fact *we* are the victims of a disordered society and not *they*. This housing policy is not accidental, it is planned – though not necessarily intended. It gives rise to and is supported by the objections raised by some community groups in well-off areas to the prospect of a local authority housing estate in the vicinity; the flight of white residents from an area where black people are increasingly settling; the growing pressure for removing from society not only those who represent a threat to society but even those petty criminals who could only be described as a nuisance to society. The desire to shield ourselves from the effects of the sinful situations in which we find ourselves is sometimes quite explicit.

This planned attempt to shield the reality of structural sin from our sight and mind is a problem the retreatant will have to face, to avoid the risk of being like the seed that fell on patches of rocks:

> The one who receives it on patches of rock is the man who hears the word and welcomes it with joy. But he has no root in him, he does not last; let some trial come, or some persecution on account of the word, and he falls away at once (Matt. 13.20-21).

In view of the inevitable conflict that faces anyone who is involved in the struggle for change, perhaps Matthew's parable is particularly appropriate in this context. That the retreatant should make an option for the poor, expressed in some on-going tangible way, perhaps even in a radical way if that is what he or she hears the Lord saying, is the issue that may arise in reflecting on isolation from their pain. The retreatant may have to work through the fear that he or she will almost certainly experience, at the prospect of having to leave, again and again, the comfort of his or her own social class and customs and conventions to encounter the poor directly and hear their cry.

A second force that seeks to co-opt the individual into complicity with unjust structures of his or her society is an ideological one. An ideological justification of the *status quo* can come either from the right or the left. On the right, the attempt to portray the present situation as a regretful but necessary stage in our progress towards a better life for all, removes the urgency for action from us. The need to concentrate wealth in the hands of the rich so that increased investment will ultimately provide full employment and end poverty even suggests that to work for a more equal society is itself a sinful act in that it will only postpone the alleviation of the suffering of the poor! The poverty of the Third World, often portrayed as due predominantly to under-development or over-population, seeks to remove the problem from the moral sphere to the purely technical one.

An even more insidious form of ideological conservatism is that which lays the blame for the effects of oppressive structures on the victims themselves. The distinction between the 'deserving poor'

71

and the 'undeserving poor' (sometimes meaning the 'poor who do not threaten our position' and 'the poor who do') falls into this category. The cause of their plight is portrayed as laziness, irresponsibility, lack of initiative; the poor are parasites in an otherwise healthy society. Again the call to action is defused at its source.

The ideological justification can also come from the left. The call for violence as necessary for achieving a more just society, the temporary but necessary repression of human rights in order to deal with reactionary forces in society, the aloof insistence that the situation in the Third World is entirely the responsibility of former colonial powers, do no service to the creation of a more just world.

Ideological positions are deep-rooted in us; they result from a long, slow assembly of experiences – necessarily limited experiences – into a world-view that holds all those experiences together in a rational way. To call into question my ideological justification for inaction, or at least for avoiding the urgency of action, can often be a profoundly disturbing experience. It requires a conversion that calls into question our deeply felt beliefs.

The First Week of the Exercises is an ideal opportunity for such a process to occur. There is no question of the retreatant meditating solely on 'structures-out-there'. There is a constant dynamic linking the retreatant's recognition of the sinfulness of the world with an unease at what has been going on in his or her deepest self.

> We must bear in mind, however, that our efforts on the social and structural level are not sufficient of themselves. Injustice must be attacked at its roots in the heart of man by eradicating those attitudes and habits which bring forth the structures of oppression.[2]

THE RETREATANT'S IMAGE OF CHRIST

The First Week, for Ignatius, was to be centred on Christ crucified. The expansion of our consciousness of sin raises the whole question of our image of Christ. An excessively privatized or spiritualized image of Christ has to be discarded. Such an image can allow us to avoid questioning the structure of the world and our own society. We are only just beginning to emerge from centuries of such privatized faith.

Certain false images of God which prop up and give an aura of legitimacy to unjust social structures are no longer acceptable. Neither can we admit those more ambiguous images of God which appear to release man from his inalienable responsibilities. . . . We must find a new language, a new set of symbols, that will enable us to leave our fallen idols behind us and rediscover the true God.[3]

Such images might include that of a God who is more interested in what we think than in what we do; or a God who is more interested in what we do in the bedroom than in the boardroom; or a God who requires submission in the face of (avoidable) suffering and not protest. Or the image of a Christ, who as peacemaker, wishes all conflict to be avoided; or a Christ who was interested only in people's souls and not in the economic, social and political realities within which they lived their lives. Each of us has an image of God and of Jesus, his Son. That image, while it derives in large part from our reading of the gospel, is nevertheless filtered through the different experiences and world-views which we bring to that reading, reflection and prayer. Our ideological lenses condition what we read and how we interpret it.

My image of Jesus is of a man full of *compassion*. His compassion for people's inner suffering and searching did not in any way diminish his compassion for their physical suffering and pain. The disabled, the sick, the lepers, the mother's grief for her dead son, the hunger of the crowd who followed him into the desert, these were the encounters that drew from Jesus his untiring compassion. There is no indication that meeting the 'spiritual needs' of those he encountered was considered by him to be more important than meeting their material needs; indeed he even got angry with the pharisees for precisely such an attitude (Mark 3.1-6).

Jesus's compassion for the total needs of those he met was matched by an *angry indignation* at all in the society of his time that failed to meet those needs or, worse still, that helped to perpetuate them. The law forbidding work on the Sabbath, when it sought to prevent him healing, he frequently broke and sometimes in the most provocative way (Luke 13.10-17). He denounced the existence of wealth in the midst of poverty (Luke 16.19-31); he publicly called the lawful religious authorities of his time hypocrites, because they used their power, not to serve those who depended on them, but to gain privileges for themselves (Matt. 23.5-7); because they were

73

more concerned with keeping the allegiance of the people (Matt. 21.23-7) than with being true shepherds of the flock. He did not want the way in which political authority was exercised to be the model for his followers (Matt. 20.24-8).

In his compassion for the sufferings of the poor and the sick, he did not flinch from *conflict* with those whose power and wealth were not being used to relieve that suffering; indeed, in exposing their hypocrisy he sometimes deliberately invited conflict (Luke 16.14-15). He knew all along that they would have to get rid of him (Luke 9.22), under the pretext that he was a threat to the security of the state (John 11.48-50). In reality he was only a threat to their own positions of power and wealth, undermining as he did on every possible occasion their justification for maintaining the *status quo*.

He was a man who *questioned everything* - the traditions of his faith (Matt. 15.1-9) as they had been handed down to him, the law he was expected to observe (Matt. 12.1-14), the actions and attitudes of the political and religious rulers of his time. He tested everything by the criteria of his own deepest human feelings and instincts, for these could not be in conflict with the will of God (Matt. 7.15-20). His critical questioning of what was the accepted wisdom and teaching of his time shocked many (Matt. 15.12). Even the apostles found him, at times, too radical (Matt. 19.25).

He was a man who constantly called others to conversion. The central core of that appeal consisted in asking for an attitude of the *most profound respect for every human being*, without exception. Indeed it was those who were least respected in this world who would have the places of honour at the banquet in the Kingdom of God (Luke 14.15-24). Those who look down on them will get a surprise on the last day (Matt. 21.31). Respect for all, especially the most despised, is a more basic element in Jesus's call for repentance than prayer or sacrifice (Mark 12.33; Matt. 5.23). Indeed he so identified with the deprived and despised that he will not accept from us any honour or tribute or gift that we offer, unless it is also offered to the most despised in society (Matt. 25.45). On our treatment of the deprived - and only on this - our salvation depends (Matt. 25.31-46).

Such would be part of my present (ideologically coloured) image of Jesus. Our image of Jesus will support or discourage certain directions of thought as we contemplate the crucified Lord and ask:

'What have I done for Christ? What am I doing for Christ? What will I do for Christ?'. If the retreatant has blocked out certain essential aspects of the life and teaching of Jesus that limit the area of response, then the director will have to help to unblock them. This could lead a retreatant into very radical decisions, suggestive of the Two Standards and the Third Degree of Humility. A businessperson may very well decide that he or she can no longer continue employment with a multinational firm, resulting in real personal and family hardship; such action would be a real martyrdom, a following of Jesus to the cross, in that, like the crucifixion, such an action will have no tangible results that can be foreseen (the multinational firm will simply replace him or her and continue as before) except the sacrifice that personally will be suffered. (The bishop of one of the dioceses in Texas, where the production facilities for nuclear weapons are located, offered the support of the Christian community to any employee in the nuclear factories who felt in conscience called to give up his or her job.) Or one may feel called to withhold a portion of one's taxes in response to one's decision to oppose military expenditure. Or one might decide, in conjunction with one's family, to live a much simpler lifestyle in a poorer part of the city. Or to campaign actively in favour of an itinerant site or Simon Hostel for the homeless in one's neighbourhood (which will lose you a few friends!). Such decisions, if one feels called to make them, arise not just from meditating on 'structures-out-there' and what one might do to change them; the intermediate step, of meditating on one's own values and attitudes which promote complicity in those structures, in the light of the gospel, is the critical one which gives depth to the experience of the First Week and gives roots to (difficult) decisions.

This implies a real following of the suffering Christ; for a person who decides to become involved in the struggle for change is guaranteed to bring trouble to self and family. Not only may decisions be required which affect (adversely) the standard of living, but they may also bring conflict and hostility from those who oppose change; even our best friends, while admiring perhaps our idealism, may feel that I am totally unrealistic. 'When his relatives heard of this, they set out to take charge of him, convinced that he was out of his mind' (Mark 3.21).

Finally, it would seem to me that if such a concept of sin were to replace the concept of privatized sin which we find in the Exercises, it would be essential that the director also be committed to it. This implies that he or she: (a) has already experienced, at gut level, anger at the structures which maintain the suffering of others, through *direct exposure* to their pain; (b) has some knowledge of *social analysis*, which allows him or her to understand the causes of that suffering better; (c) through meditation on personal values and attitudes that maintain the complicity with those structures, he or she has made some - probably radical - decisions in this area.[5]

NOTES

1. Robert Havanek, 'The reluctance to admit sin', in *Studies in the Spirituality of Jesuits* (May 1977).

2. 32nd General Congregation of the Society of Jesus; 'Our Mission today', 32.

3. 'Our Mission today', 26.

4. The author wishes to thank the other staff of the Centre for Faith and Justice in Dublin for help in writing this essay.

CHAPTER SIX

'The Call of the King' and Justice

Monika Hellwig

The urgent need for conversion of our world to justice and peace is evident. It is not only a matter of the conversion of individual hearts and minds. The task is more complex and the problem more intractable than that. Much of the suffering is not directly or deliberately inflicted though analysis shows that it may ultimately be traced to selfishness. The need is evidently for a reshaping of the structures, large and small, that govern our relationships with one another in the world and its history.

Unfortunately, there is a certain reluctance to recognize the problems of the world as theological and spiritual issues. Yet it is clear that our individual spirituality cannot be authentic if it deliberately excludes public issues that are a matter of conflict of interests in which self-seeking opposes itself to compassion and justice.

The age in which we live has offered us immense technical competence. From the technical point of view there are few problems we could not solve if we were willing to make the necessary dispositions of power and wealth. The problem is unwillingness to sacrifice some self-interest for the common good. Putting it very bluntly, in terms of the issues named in the Second Week of the Spiritual Exercises, the underlying problem for groups, as for individuals, is the inordinate human hunger for wealth, honour and power (pride). It is the task of Christian faith and life to recognize the destructive workings of that inordinate hunger in all its many disguises, and to reverse it in the power of Christ's grace.

Conversion of the world to justice and peace involves a thoroughly new vision of possibilities and actualities in political, economic, social and cultural affairs. Christians seek that new vision in the following of Jesus, guided by meditation on the gospel accounts of his life and teaching. It is by observing and reflecting upon the attitudes, responses, initiatives, judgements and decisions, stances and relationships of Jesus, that we come to discern what the basic issues were for him. To know what the basic issues were for him is in turn to come to a progressively clearer vision of the character and dynamics of the redemption, and therefore to be able to discern what it involves in our own times and situations.

In the Second Week of the Spiritual Exercises, Ignatius suggests a selection of incidents from the gospel stories (and offers a much larger selection in the appendix on the 'mysteries of Christ's life') which serve just this purpose. To follow Jesus through these scenes in one's meditations is certainly to become aware of a deep conflict of values: the restoration of the divine order in the world not through the powerful but through the humble or powerless; commitment to God's will not by imposing one's own perception of it on others, but by a continuous quest to understand in the obscurities of a sinful history; reversal of the distortions of the quest for wealth by chosen poverty; the recentring of the world on God's reign and not on self, in the acceptance of suffering in pursuit of that obedience to the will of God which is compassion and community. To follow Jesus through the gospels with the focus that Ignatius continually proposes is to see the issues that arise for Jesus himself as those of poverty, contempt and powerlessness.

The Jesus that we see in these meditations seeks solidarity with the poor by becoming poor among them. Ignatius emphasizes this from the meditation on the Incarnation, through the nativity scene, the presentation in the Temple, the flight into Egypt, the life of obedience at Nazareth and the finding in the Temple. And he picks up the same emphasis in the meditations on leaving home, on the baptism by John, the retreat into the desert and the temptations, the call of the first disciples, the focus on the beatitudes in the Sermon on the Mount, the walking on the water to come to the disciples, the preaching in the Temple, the raising of Lazarus and the 'Palm Sunday' entrance into Jerusalem.

However, his seeking of solidarity with the poor by becoming poor among them is certainly not the end of the matter in any of these meditations. In all of these scenes the stance of Jesus implies a criticism of the relationships, attitudes, fears and desires that oppress the poor. It is a criticism of the motivations both among the poor themselves and among those who oppress them from without. Indeed, as Ignatius sees it, the life and activity of Jesus all follow from that divine scrutiny mentioned in the reflections on the

Incarnation – a scrutiny which finds human affairs in the world terribly, tragically awry.

The solidarity with the poor in the gospel accounts of Jesus always has another dimension. It is that of radical dependence upon God in gratitude, simplicity and confidence. Indeed it is that of total abandonment to the will of God, the other aspect of which is total dedication to the reign of God in human affairs. It is this total confidence in the power of God rather than in technical or bullying power which liberates Jesus, and eventually his followers, for a vision of human reality so new, so different, that it appears as sheer folly in the affairs of the world. It implies that what is right will triumph ultimately because it is right. It implies that the Creator has not lost control of creation but works with redeeming power that transcends all tragedies. It implies that the possibility of conversion is in all human persons and in all human structures and institutions. It implies that total dedication to the cause of the redemption is justified because redemption by God is possible and is under way.

The gospels deal also with the issue of contempt. Jesus responds to those who suffer contempt, exclusion, discrimination, by the kind of solidarity with them which progressively brings upon him that same kind of contempt, exclusion, and discrimination. Ignatius anticipates this in the meditations on the infancy narratives, as indeed the gospel writers themselves did. It is unfolded further in the meditations on the public life and preaching. Here again, the matter does not end with the identification of Jesus with the despised. That very identification is a critique of the respectabilities and controlling forces of human society. What we learn is that the Word of God spoken into the world clearly and with simplicity and concreteness is held not in honour but in contempt, which suggests that what we usually know as honour is dishonour before God and not worth seeking. But we also see how ugly and how painful is the contempt that privileged and fortunate people heap upon the underprivileged on whom they trample in their quest for status and honour. Moreover, we find that this is more than the deliberate action of individuals; it has been institutionalized in political, economic and cultural structures of human society. The contempt which Jesus suffered is a revelation of what is really at stake in the quest for status in human society, and the attitude which he, as Word of God in history, took towards the exercise of privilege and the leverage of status and honour shows what these things mean in the sight of God.

Perhaps the most subtle of the issues for Jesus revealed in the Ignatian approach to the gospel meditations is that of powerlessness or humility. Unfortunately, we have trivialized the word 'humility' so that it carries connotations of self-denigration with a view to spiritual 'progress' – a strange variety of crypto-self-promotion. The meditations on the mysteries of the life of Jesus in the Second Week of the Spiritual Exercises offer a far more down-to-earth notion of humility. Humility is powerlessness. In the meditation on the Incarnation, Mary is described as humbling herself when she allows God's power to work in her, and in the Nativity meditation the Word of God is presented as made human in a humble condition.

The humility or powerlessness of Jesus is most meaningful when seen in the context of the history of sin, and especially of 'the first sin' as presented in the First Week of the Exercises. At the root of the whole order of sin is pride, understood in the basic sense of self-assertion in an independence that refuses to be held accountable. In human history such self-assertion necessarily means domination, injustice, oppression of others. Moreover, in human history such self-assertion tends to build alliances and to express itself in the structures of society, both large and small.

The humility of Jesus is his familiarity with the true human condition and his willing solidarity with the powerless in the social and political structures of the world. He chooses powerlessness according to the usual understanding that we have of power, that is to say in terms of being able to compel people to one's own desires and advantage. Like all folk of humble origin and humble condition, Jesus is stripped (though by his own choice) of the ability to compel others in ways that counter and deny the divine role in creation and providence. His power is that of dependence on the Father, which is also the power of community in human affairs. The humility of Jesus turns the course of human history around because it restructures human life in dependence upon and in accountability to the divine will. But this is concerned not only with the relationship of human persons individually to God. It is concerned also with the relationship of human persons to one another, respecting the order of creation in respecting the freedom and dignity and Godward meaning of other persons.

To share the vision is not enough to bring about conversion in one's own life and in the world. It also requires personal and social involvement. It involves choices which refer, of course, to one's immediate context in terms of family, career, life-style and so forth. But they also refer to the larger context of the social setting of our times. They refer to peace and justice, to solidarity with the poor and suffering of the city and the country and the world. They refer to a new kind of solidarity with the despised, with 'the enemy', with those who are socially invisible and 'don't count' because they are not 'our sort'. The choices also refer to basic solidarity with the human race and the human condition before God.

Ignatius takes no chances that the retreatant might miss the immediacy of the gospel call for personal involvement, for he frames the gospel meditations of the Second Week with meditations characteristically his own, which he places at the beginning and the middle and the end. By proposing the Kingdom meditation at the beginning, Ignatius places the entire week within the frame of reference of a worldwide crisis. The choices and decisions that we make in situations of crisis tend to be clean-cut and unqualified. The Kingdom meditation assumes that the world as it is can by no means be taken for granted, as divinely intended. It can only be seen as an immense battleground of opposing forces with different loyalties. Jesus is the King who calls for followers to share the hardships and burdens of the campaign, because there can be no standing still. It is war-time and there can be no 'business as usual', no room for partial engagement or for enlisting in the reserves. The crisis is upon us now.

There are many reasons to accept this view of the world in the present crisis of world hunger, armaments race, nuclear threat and racial violence, not to mention enormous imbalances in material resources which are enforced and maintained by brutal use of force. The world around us is certainly the world of Christ's campaign to reconquer.

Lest this call should lack concreteness, Ignatius follows it up with the meditations on the Two Standards and the Three Classes of Men, both placed in the middle of the Second Week. The meditation on the Two Standards continues the symbolism of the Call of the King and makes a contrast that might be seen as an interpretation of the gospel story of the temptations of Jesus in the desert. The issue of loyalty is the understanding of the interrelated and inseparable character of the three factors in each position, and the clear choice made on the basis of that understanding. Here the issues Ignatius has brought into focus in the gospel meditation become inescapably explicit. Lucifer's call is to the pursuit of riches, honour and pride and to the propagation of that pursuit among the peoples of the world, until they are horribly ensnared in the self-defeating destructiveness of it. Christ's call is to help all human beings, by a detachment that is prepared for actual poverty, by courting contempt rather than honour, and seeking humility rather than pride.

These choices are personal but they are not simply a matter of the private life of the individual. To choose either way is to implicate others also. To be committed either way is to seek alliances, co-operate in policies and structures, build systems that sustain the position. To be neutral is impossible. To opt for the standard of Christ in private while acquiescing in the standard of wealth, honour and pride in public is an idle fiction liable to be unmasked in tragic ways when a crucial choice presents itself (as in the time of the Hitler regime, or in times of racial tension).

In spite of this, most of us are adept at evading the issues and Ignatius proposes another meditation to reveal the 'games people play'. In the meditation on the Three Classes of Men, we meet the people who manage to avoid the real issues by chronic postponement, and the people who persuade themselves that they are committed to the cause while making sure no actual renunciation is involved. In both we meet ourselves, and never more clearly than in matters of social justice. In the third class we meet Jesus Christ, who acted with perfect detachment from self-interest because of his overwhelming commitment to the coming reign of God.

But in the third class we also meet our own potential in the grace of Christ - the potential to grow in grace to the full stature of Christ, completing the work of his 'body', his people, the Church. It is in the third class that we meet the real possibility of restructuring the world in peace and justice, because this is the class of martyrs – martyrs in blood, political martyrs (who are willing to subordinate their careers to their ideals without compromise), economic martyrs (who are willing to decide and act for the common good and the relief of the oppressed by sacrificing opportunities for self-enrichment), social martyrs (who will maintain solidarity with the oppressed, the despised, the 'enemy', at the cost of losing friends and respect and support).

For good measure, Ignatius confronts his retreatants once more at the end of the Second Week with the issues that he sees emerging from the life and teaching of Jesus. In the meditation on the Three Modes of Humility, the now well-established triad is again presented under a slightly different aspect. Ignatius invites retreatants to consider the three 'modes' or degrees of humility before choosing a way of life. By this he means a vocational choice, but the reflection is relevant also before casting one's vote in an election, before making choices of lifestyle and standard of living and before making policy decisions in business, professional or political matters.

What is at stake is a progression from minimal to maximal commitment to the cause of Christ. The minimum is never seriously or knowingly to act against the will of God in grave matters, no matter what profit is to be gained and no matter what disaster is to be averted. While many people accept this standard in their private lives, there is a tendency to set it aside as irrelevant in public matters in which the decision to act is not the responsibility of one individual but the outcome of complex corporate procedures. Perhaps we need to become more sharply aware that shared responsibility is nevertheless personal responsibility, and that the ethical demands of God do not end where our activity becomes public.

Perhaps if we were to accept this fully we would not be inclined to see such a large leap from Ignatius's first mode to his second. The second mode requires indifference to wealth, honour and life itself to such an extent that there is no question of acting against the will of God even in less serious matters for any gain or any protection whatever. On a city-wide, nation-wide or world-wide scale, this would be dynamite under our present intractable problems of peace and justice and universal access to means of decent livelihood. Perhaps the most serious obstacle is the fact that few really believe it is possible to introduce such principles into public policy. We do not really believe that Christ has conquered the principalities and powers.

If the second degree is dynamite, what is to be said of the third? The third degree exists where the followers of Jesus, to be more intimately one with him, deliberately choose his kind of poverty, his kind of rejection, his kind of folly. Perhaps we have been too quick in the recent past to equate this with a calling to the vowed religious life. It would also apply to people like Florence Nightingale and Dorothy Day; to the Quakers who won the right of conscientious objection to military conscription at the cost of execution as traitors; to the women of Greenham Common; to Steve Biko in South Africa; to Martin Luther King and many of his followers who were imprisoned and beaten and harassed for the cause of justice; and to many unsung heroines and heroes in our city slums and in refugee camps and other places of suffering around the world. In any of the genuine struggles for peace and justice there are people who have deliberately chosen to be poor and despised and considered as fools - people who have chosen that kind of humility which is powerlessness in face of violence.

It is certainly not surprising that so many of the disciples of Ignatius should be among those who do this today. It is not surprising because the teaching of the Spiritual Exercises moves so explicitly in this direction, especially in those particular meditations of the Second Week in which Ignatius makes clear what he sees as the issues of the redemption for Jesus himself.

Ignatius writes of ways of making choices, of times that are opportune and of ways to seize those opportune times. These guidelines for making choices are applicable not only to individuals in decisions affecting their personal lives, but to communal action for social justice and the alleviation of mass suffering. In those countries which have extensive networks of basic Christian communities, this appears to be happening. Ignatius writes of times when there is a clear divine attraction, and that does seem to happen sometimes in acute crisis situations for movements and groups. He also writes of times when understanding and knowledge are attained by 'discernment of spirits', and the testimony of the movements among the poor in the Third World often seems to indicate that this happens among groups who pray together and share the fruits of their prayers with simplicity and generosity. But the advice that seems most appropriate for groups acting for social justice and peace is that for making choices in 'times of tranquillity'.

If groups and networks of groups move towards decisions on goals, policy and strategy according to the rules for such choices in times of tranquillity, they will most surely become an effective force for justice and peace. To do so is to set the end of our created existence in view, shaping means to the end and not the end to the means; to cultivate detachment from all individual and group self-interest in the matter; to pray for enlightenment and empowerment together; in that spirit to consider the value and possibilities of alternative courses of action, on the best information and analysis available; and to come to a reasonable decision. This, of course, is the kind of deciding and acting that is envisioned by 'liberation theology' and by those engaged as Christians in liberation movements.

There are other suggestions of Ignatius that may be particularly appropriate in revolutionary situations. These are: to be sure before making choices or commitments that it is really the love of God which motivates them; to consider how one might advise and judge other groups in similar situations; to try to consider from the perspective of one's death-bed and from the perspective of God's final judgment what we might look back upon with peace of mind and joy of heart; and to decide accordingly. Of course, all this is projected as though all choices were open. In the situations in which most people struggle for a more just and peaceful and compassionate world, the options are severely limited because action for change involves large scale co-operation, and most of those willing to work for social justice are nevertheless not ready to accept the call of Christ in the way Ignatius delineates it. That, of course, is one reason why the Exercises do not end with the Second Week but move on to the Third and Fourth. The call of the King is not to a triumphalist sweep to victory but to a far more difficult and arduous campaign. But the focus and the tools for discernment offered in the Second Week provide a powerful dynamic towards justice and peace in the world.

CHAPTER SEVEN

The Dynamic of the Second Week

William Broderick

If anything so integrated and intricately wrought as the Spiritual Exercises of St Ignatius, with their symphonic interweaving and development of themes and images, could be said to have a centre, that centre would be the Second Week. The Second Week is carefully prepared for by all that goes before, by the Principle and Foundation, by the First Week on sin, and then by the Call of Christ the King.

Creation must reflect in its beauty and harmony, in its balance and right order, the beauty and goodness of God from whom it came, and so give rise to conscious praise and service on the part of the human creature. Thus the Principle and Foundation. The First Week showed that as a matter of historical fact this harmony has been shattered, balance and order have broken down. We live in a world characterized by sin. Salvation consists in a new order of beauty and harmony that is to appear out of the chaos, a created reflection of divine goodness. Thus the Kingdom.

The Spiritual Exercises have as their purpose to assist in refashioning the human creation. In this work of restoration human beings are to take an active and conscious part:

> . . . we call Spiritual Exercises every way of preparing and disposing the soul to rid itself of all inordinate attachments, and, after their removal, of seeking and finding the will of God in the disposition of our life for the salvation of our soul. (Exx 1)

Thus in the world of sin and disorder, something has to be rejected and something has to be embraced.

This polarity of our human existence is expressed in the Exercises in two great figures, Satan and Christ. A titanic struggle is raging between the forces of disorder and the forces of order, between the powers of darkness and the powers of light. This cosmic struggle provides the dramatic setting for the Second Week. The powers of order and light have taken visible shape as Jesus of Nazareth, the humble suffering servant of Yahweh. The decision now to put one's life into order, to find God's will, means following and conforming oneself to the historical Jesus of Nazareth. It means a total commitment to this Jesus of Nazareth and a total rejection of the 'world' along with Satan, who is 'the Prince of this world'.

Because the 'world' as representing and embodying inherited disorder is now regarded as the norm, Jesus of Nazareth in whom the harmony and order and beauty of the new creation are embodied will appear strange, bizarre, out of touch with reality. His life ending in the horror of crucifixion will appear squalid, contemptible, a pathetic failure.

Moreover, in this conforming of one's life to that of the historical Jesus there is a 'more' and a less, because of the freedom and openness of human existence. Human beings are to take an active and conscious part in the refashioning of creation, and their free response is involved. In the living of one's life one can be more conformed or less conformed to Christ. This possibility of 'more' or less gave rise to the old-fashioned distinction between the life of the commandments and the life of the evangelical counsels expressed in the vows of religious orders. This distinction Ignatius took for granted and reflects the theological perspective of his age rather than ours. However this does not affect the validity of the basic point that there is to be a search for the 'more', for a greater conformity to Christ and his way.

IN CHRIST. HOW?

How in practice is this conforming of one's life to that of Christ to be achieved? The answer is, by prayerful contemplation of Christ's life where one will experience what Ignatius calls 'consolations' and 'desolations'. It is through the experiencing of consolation and desolation that the retreatant is enabled to find God's will at this particular moment of life. As he or she holds in a single focus the life of Christ and the details of his or her own life he or she will experience 'consolation'. The retreatant will feel drawn into the life of Christ, and so into the life of God, and will also experience the dynamic of his or her own life, where it meshes with that of Christ and where it does not.

The earthly life of Jesus of Nazareth has a sacramental quality.

Christ's life is an outward and visible sign of a hidden and greater reality. This is why before each of the contemplations of the Second Week the retreatant is told to ask for 'an intimate knowledge of our Lord, who has become man for me, that I may love him more and follow him more closely' (Exx 104).

It may be objected that in the text of the Exercises, the imagery is quite different. Christ is first seen as a king, then as a baby, a child growing up, a young man leaving home, then at the Jordan epiphany discovering his deepest identity; after his desert temptations he begins calling his first disciples; 'they follow him'. And from then on the relationship between Christ and his followers is extrinsic. It starts with 'following' (*seguir*) in a literal sense of walking in his company, though of course the notion of 'following' Christ in a moral and spiritual sense is also present. This is not altogether surprising because Ignatius is basing himself heavily on the synoptic gospels and on the relationship between Jesus and his followers which is to be found there. This seems far removed from the idea of Christ's life as a sacramental reality.

The idea of Christ's life as a sacramental reality seems closer to Paul's christology, with its idea of 'mutual indwelling' as the relationship between Christ and his followers.

But even though the vocabulary used by Paul to describe this mutual indwelling, all those Pauline prepositions of 'in' and 'with' and 'through', is not to be found in the Spiritual Exercises, the reality of such a relationship is very much to be found there. This identification with Christ is present and urged on the retreatant in a multitude of different ways. The following are among the main ones:
(a) In the colloquy for the meditation on the Two Standards the retreatant is directed to ask Our Lady to obtain the gift of 'the grace to be received under Christ's standard, first in the highest spiritual poverty . . . secondly, in bearing insults and wrongs, thereby to imitate him better'.
(b) The full depth of this 'imitating' of Christ is revealed in the Third Kind of Humility,

> . . . whenever the praise and glory of the Divine Majesty would be equally served, in order to imitate and *be in reality more like Christ our Lord*, I desire and choose poverty with Christ poor, rather than riches; insults with Christ, loaded with them, rather than honours; I desire to be

accounted as worthless and a fool for Christ, rather than to be esteemed as wise and prudent in this world. So Christ was treated before me. (Exx 167)

Here the identification with Christ is total.

(c) There is the repeated use of the *Anima Christi* prayer, a prayer which indicates the kind of union with Christ the retreatant is being encouraged to seek and find. 'Blood of Christ, inebriate me . . .' '. . . . within thy wounds hide me . . .'. There is both a Pauline and a mystical quality about it.

(d) Another indication is the particular grace to be asked for in each of the contemplations, 'an intimate knowledge of the Lord'. It is not the external knowledge that can be gained by study, intellectual analysis and exegesis, but an experiential knowledge of the life of Christ, an existential oneness.

(e) This identification with Christ goes to the depths of one's affective being. When Ignatius describes spiritual consolation he must be describing the very orientation of Christ's own inner affective life.

> I call it consolation when an interior movement is aroused in the soul, by which it is inflamed with love of its Creator and Lord, and as a consequence can love no creature on the face of the earth for its own sake but only in the Creator of them all. (Exx 316)

Ignatius assumes that the retreatant will experience spiritual consolation of this kind and so share the inner affective life of Christ himself and his orientation to the Father. Ignatius and Paul are one, but Ignatius gives greater emphasis to the external historical events of Jesus's life and assumes that these external events have much to tell us. It is through them that we enter into the inner content and reality of the sacrament and mystery which is Christ.

(f) The pattern of prayer and the ordering of the day as put forward by Ignatius seem to be another indication that assimilation into Christ and the mystery of his life is what is being sought. The Ignatian day of prayer moves from activity to repose, from imaginative and discursive activity to quiet presence, from complexity to simplicity, from active assimilation of the particular mystery to total absorption in the mystery. The movement of prayer is as it were from outside to inside the mystery. The last prayer of the day, the 'Application of the Senses', before supper, is the deepest. It is total presence. The 'senses' mean a kind of knowledge which is immediate, a direct contact with the mystery, immediate presence to the mystery. The Application of the Senses is the confirmation and final stage of the movement of prayer. Direct contact has been made with the inner reality of the mystery. The Christ-life has been touched and evoked.

The contemplation of the dynamic and mystery of Christ's life enables the retreatant to get in touch with, discover, the dynamic and mystery of his or her own life. As one contemplates Christ's life one discovers one's own deepest self and truest identity. The orientation of our lives is and must be one with the orientation of Christ's own life. The Spiritual Exercises are effective because they awaken the retreatant to what is already present in the depths of his or her being, present not by nature but by grace, but still really present. The Exercises do not merely confront the retreatant with the saving truths of the gospel nor do they introduce into the retreatant's life, as it were from the outside, the truths of the gospel. They light up and evoke and make explicit what the retreatant already in some dim way knows and lives, something repressed perhaps that underlies all ordinary experiences. Every human being is now Christ-oriented in the very depths of his or her being, whether this is realized or not. What the contemplations of the Spiritual Exercises do is to make the retreatant more and more aware of this Christ-orientation in life. If this Christ-orientation were not an already present reality in the life of the person, contemplating the mysteries of Christ's life would have no power to affect, transform or bring about an identification with Christ. As it is, the retreatant begins to experience God, the world, other people, and the self in the way that Christ experienced all these.

THE TWO STANDARDS

If the retreatant is being drawn more and more into the life-experience of Christ then the great struggle of Christ's life will become a personal struggle and that struggle is the struggle against Satan whose motto is 'I will not serve', and against the externalized visible expression of Satan which is the 'world'. It is the struggle between creaturehood affirmed and creaturehood denied: the struggle between a creaturehood admitted in all its poverty and vulnerability, and creaturehood artifically concealed or built-up on what does not belong to it; between creaturehood affirmed as intrinsically relational and dependent, and creaturehood maintained as autonomous and self-sufficient, between 'I will not serve' and 'I am among you as one who serves'. This is why the meditation on the Two Standards is central to the Second Week.

Our flight from our true self is the real temptation, as is the painful sense of contingency that goes with it and acceptance of our creaturehood with all its fears in Christ's way. We can secretly betray the human creaturehood entrusted to us. The descent into hell begins in humanity's sinful flight from the self, from creaturehood with its painful limitations and uncertainties. To become human means to become 'poor', to acknowledge that one has nothing to boast of before God. To become human means coming before God and acknowledging one's total indigence. It means looking into the abyss of one's own nothingness and not hiding from this.

The Satan of the Exercises fears nothing so much as a human creature who acknowledges and remains true to his or her innate poverty ('humility'). What Satan does is to entice us to strength, to build ourselves up with what is not really our own, first through material possessions, then through the prestige that comes with these, so that ultimately we are totally in control of life and destiny; we can determine the meaning of our own existence. We are self-sufficient, we are invulnerable. Thus we are living a lie. We have become as God ('pride').

What Jesus urges is the very opposite. Acknowledge your creaturehood in all its poverty and indigence. Do not try to shield yourself from this truth. Do not let material possessions blind you, or enable you to develop a false self. Remain vulnerable. That will mean getting hurt by a hostile world ('insults and injuries'). In this way you will always live in the awareness of your own creaturehood and its poverty, and you will come to know the endless goodness of God. When you live out the truth of your creaturehood you will see the rest of creation as gift, expressions of God's providential love. Jesus says - strip away all illusions. The truth is your friend.

In the struggle going on there is something to be rejected and something to be accepted, a negative and a positive. In the meditation on the Two Standards Ignatius spells out what this negative and this positive are: 'a knowledge of the deceits of the rebel chief and help to guard myself against them; a knowledge of the true life . . . and the grace to imitate him' (Exx 139). The nature of the titanic struggle is made explicit in the meditation on the Two Standards. The whole world is caught up in the struggle but most men and women seem not to understand what is going on. Ignatius desires to throw the fullest light on the struggle. Two leaders, two strategies for happiness, two views of humanity, two value systems.

'THE ELECTION'

The contemplations of the mysteries of Our Lord's life during the Second Week are to lead to ever greater conformity with Christ, to transformation into Christ, to identification with Christ.[2] But this mystical union with Christ is not for its own sake but for service, to find and accomplish God's will for the retreatant in the particular circumstances of his or her life, either in a particular way of life if this has not already been decided, otherwise in the renewal of such a way of life. The contemplations of the life of Christ are not merely a disconnected set of devout contemplations on the gospels. There is a thrust, a dynamic, both in their ordering and their selection. They have as their purpose to present the retreatant with a choice which will transform his or her life and in which he or she will find in peace God's will. The retreatant is called upon to choose the best way, according to the grace given by God, to imitate the Lord.

The Election process had already been prepared for in the infancy contemplations and in the strange inversion of those two contemplations: 'The life of our Lord from the age of twelve to the age of thirty' and 'Jesus goes up to the temple at the age of twelve'. For Ignatius these two contemplations bear a weight of meaning that is not immediately obvious. When Jesus goes up to the temple at the age of twelve Ignatius sees this as an 'election' by Jesus 'to devote himself to the exclusive service of his heavenly Father' (Exx 135). At this point the retreatant is confronted for the first time with the possibility of imitating the eternal Lord more 'closely' and the decisive work of choosing a way of life (or renewing such a way) begins. The 'election' in the temple is repeated in Christ's departure from Nazareth to begin the real messianic task of fighting against Satan (the temptations in the desert). In between comes Jesus's baptism in the Jordan (the revelation of his true identity and the Two Standards).

Discovery of identity precedes choice. Choice is an expression of identity, of who I am. As the retreatant contemplates the mysteries of Christ's life he or she comes to know his or her truest identity, the Christ-identity, and so is enabled to make an authentic choice, a choice which expresses the authentic self. As the retreatant 'puts on' Christ, he or she becomes most truly him or herself. That is why the discernment of spirits is central to the Election. It is not the beauty or subtlety or originality of the retreatant's thoughts that matter but the experience of consolation and desolation. It is consolation and desolation that tell a person where his or her heart lies, where the deepest self is engaged. It is the retreatant's affective life which reveals who he or she really is, the real dynamic or drive of his or her being. The more the retreatant can enter into Christ's own experience of God, of life, of other people, the more perfect will be any choice or decision. It was the spiritual genius of Ignatius to see the link between discernment of spirits and the making of an Election.

However, at the time of the Election the retreatant is not just to direct attention to his or her affective state. The retreatant is to go on contemplating the mysteries of Christ's life. This safeguards the whole process. This sustained contemplation of the mysteries of our Lord's life ensures in an amazing way that justice is done to both the objective and subjective elements of an Election. The second Annotation emphasizes the objective. '. . . (the director) should narrate accurately the facts of the contemplation or meditation. Let him adhere to the points . . .' (Exx 2). The retreatant's subjectivity too is given its full part to play. What Ignatius calls the 'fruit' of contemplating a mystery is left unspecified. In each contemplation the following words or their equivalent are found: 'Then I will reflect on myself that I may reap some fruit.' So much depends on where a person is in his or her life in regard to Christ – and therefore in regard to the deepest self.

The same openness to subjectivity is to be found in the Colloquy (Exx 199).

In the colloquy, one should talk over motives and present petitions according to circumstances. Thus he may be tempted or he may enjoy consolation, may desire to have this virtue or another, may want to dispose himself in this or that way, may seek to grieve or rejoice according to the matter that he is contemplating. Finally he should ask what he more earnestly desires with regard to some particular interests . . .

Ignatius has great confidence in subjectivity because he knows that it is now a graced subjectivity, and the objective word of God is always there as a check.

Another reality check put forward in the Election process is the meditation on 'Three Classes of Men', set for the end of the day on the Two Standards. It is to help the retreatant check out his or her real oneness or lack of oneness with Christ. So many retreatants find themselves in the second class, those who are trying to manipulate God so that 'God is to come to what they desire' (Exx 154). They refuse to let God be God. They lack that total trust in, and surrender to God which is perfect creaturehood, perfect worship. To this extent they are not at one with Christ, who lived out his human creaturehood perfectly. 'I do always those things that please the Father'; 'Not my will . . .'. To the extent that they do not share in Christ's radical creaturehood and therefore are not in touch with their own radical creaturehood any choice they make will be less than perfect.

All this was admirably expressed in his *Spiritual Journal* by Jerome Nadal, the faithful interpreter of the mind of Ignatius.

> Be alert to welcome and express in action the oneness with Christ which the Spirit of the Lord bestows as a free gift and also his power, so that in the Spirit you feel yourself to be understanding things with his own understanding, to be willing things with his own power of willing, to be remembering things with his own power of remembering, and yourself to be existing, living, acting to the very depths of your being not in yourself but in Christ.[3]

CONCLUSION

The Second Week is to do with 'the King' and his Kingdom, what Paul calls the 'new creation', established in Christ, a new world centred on God, a new humanity, of which Christ is the founder and exemplar, the prototype and inspiration. There is mysticism in the Spiritual Exercises. The retreatant is called to share in the mystical experience of Jesus himself, but it is never a mysticism for its own sake. It is a mysticism for service, a mysticism which is always searching for where God is leading. It was the spiritual genius of Ignatius to point out a way of discovering this.[4]

NOTES

1. MHSJ II.2, pp. 71-3.

2. For an alternative view of election see William A. M. Peters SJ, *The Spiritual Exercises of St Ignatius* (Rome 1980, 4th edition).

3. MHSJ: *Epistolae P. Nadal* IV, p. 697.

4. Grateful acknowledgement to the following: H. Rahner SJ, *Ignatius the Theologian* (London 1968); J. C. Futrell SJ, *Making an Apostolic Community of Love* (Institute of Jesuit Sources, St Louis, 1970); Harvey Egan SJ, *The Spiritual Exercises and the Ignatian Mystical Horizon* (St Louis, 1976); J. B. Metz, *Poverty of Spirit* (Paulist Press); R. Hostie SJ, in *Christus* (April 1955).

CHAPTER EIGHT

The Two Standards

Brian Grogan

The preparation of the giver of the exercise is important. This is so of course for the Spiritual Exercises in general, but beginners especially can find difficulty in presenting the Two Standards. The deceits of the 'rebel chief' can be directed not only at the retreatant but at the giver of the exercise: the subtle temptation is to focus primarily on how to present the exercise; illuminative texts are gathered and stored in one's arsenal, commentaries are consulted, difficulties are anticipated and discussed. All of this can be good. But the primary preparation must be prayer: the more fully the giver of the exercise is won over to the way of Christ - which is the point of the Two Standards - the more helpful he or she will be to the retreatant. We communicate what we are. Paul puts it tersely if uncomfortably: 'Take me for your model, as I take Christ' (1 Cor. 11.1). If retreatants sometimes complain that this exercise seems complicated, the remedy lies with the giver becoming ever more clearly focussed on the way of Christ.

The *goal* of the exercise - the graced attraction of the retreatant to Christ and his way - must then be kept clearly in mind. Brilliant analyses of how the contemporary world, secular and ecclesiastical, is being duped by satanic illusions may simply lead the retreatant into 'head-tripping'. The mature person may only have to watch the nine o'clock television news to get a feel for the 'snares and chains' which shackle the desire for good which is in all people's hearts. The Exercises are all about desires: the desires of God to liberate us by drawing us to his Son, and the ambiguous desires in our hearts both for God and for what the world holds as important. The retreatant needs to acknowledge the deceptive attractiveness of the latter, and be encouraged to pray intensely that his or her graced desire for God be strengthened, so that the desires come more and more into harmony with God's desires.

Struggle may be anticipated and is a good sign that the heart is being engaged; if it is not, there will be little change, little conversion. To quote Lonergan: 'Without (these) feelings our knowing and deciding would be paper thin. Because of our feelings . . . we are orientated massively and dynamically in a world mediated by meaning.'[1] Conversion in us means moving out of, or being torn out of one mind-set and being placed in another; the first is that of fallen humanness, the second is divine. A retreatant put it crisply: 'I have a mind of my own; I revolt at having to put on the mind of Christ!' He knew what the struggle would involve: 'a Copernican shift' was his phrase. Day followed painful day; prayer was hard, with only occasional glimmers of light and joy. At the end of the retreat he felt he was beginning to see and surrender: the marvel was what had kept him going through the dark days. I became aware of the strength of the drawing of God, of deep calling on deep beyond this man's knowing.

There is no *earthly* reason why a retreatant should prefer poverty and insults to riches and honours. B. Kiely has written that:

> there is certainly some part of us . . . that would prefer riches to poverty, a good name to disrepute, comfort to labour, receiving to giving, doing one's own sweet will to obeying, sexual gratification to chastity . . . Such (in part at least) is the exercitant initially. He has many inordinate attachments . . . The question is whether they will prevail or whether they will be overcome by stronger attachments of a better kind.[2]

The 'stronger attachments of a better kind' are born in us, often with all the pains of childbirth, by falling in love with the person of Jesus. This process can be quite gentle and unnoticed and the quiet fruit of a good upbringing: it is in the Two Standards that the painful implications of the relationship are starkly unfolded. One may feel trapped: 'I never realized that discipleship could mean this!' One desires Christ but fears the demands of being with him; 'stronger attachments of a better kind' will come from steady prayer for the grace to imitate Christ. Yielding to the attractiveness of Christ makes it possible to yield to the non-attractiveness of his way of poverty and insults. It can help to recall Augustine's account of the attractiveness of 'the austere beauty of continence, serene and indeed joyous' who smiled on him and invited him to stop his ears against those voices which told him of delights, but not of such delights as the Lord tells (*Confessions* VIII, xi).

Indicators of readiness. The Two Standards meditation is seen by many guides as the parting of the ways. This, however, may only be clear in retrospect. Thus most retreatants are given the exercise, but with some it does not 'take' and the remainder of the retreat is worked through in a lower key. The less robust retreatant can be upset and disorientated by the content of the colloquy and even be led to a feeling of hopelessness before so high an ideal. It would be good then, to note some indicators of readiness for this exercise.

The guide looks for solid love of Christ and for basic freedom and generosity, that is, a willingness and an ability to dispose of oneself. If trust in God is still fragile and precarious, it will hardly bear the weighty demand that one place all hope of future good in the way of Christ, because the colloquy of the Two Standards requires the highest degree of trust in Christ's way as being best.

Tranquillity in the early contemplations of the Second Week is a good sign insofar as it indicates a willingness to let one's life be ruled by the Lord and that one is able to be caught out of oneself into the life of another. This is very difficult for many people; the contemplative stance is beyond them.

Tranquillity in the early contemplations is of a fundamental kind; if it were all-pervasive, one might doubt the realism of the prayer. It is to be expected that real resistances and aversions will appear, for example in the Nativity. Ignatius is writing for grown-ups in Exercises 116 – this is no child's Christmas scene where all is peace and gentleness; rather the retreatant is being prepared for a radical and demanding choice and the capacity for radical dispossession of self is being aired. Pain and death are involved; the person must be free enough to acknowledge them and so come face to face with the 'cost of discipleship'. Only then can prayer be real. Tranquillity can remain in the face of all this; it is the fruit of knowing both one's divided heart and one's need for the grace of God. John Donne's 'Batter my heart' catches the attitude one looks for, of wanting to be won over by grace and knowing that God is the only hope. A recent retreatant remarked that for days she went around saying: 'I know from my lengthy past that I'm always falling short of the ideals I should live by, so this time I won't pray the colloquy until or unless I know I can manage to live up to it!' The perceptive reader will understand what was going on in this situation.

Use of the text? This is a vexed question. But by this stage of the retreat the guide should know the reaction of the retreatant to the text and act appropriately here. If the text creates problems, it can be enough to give the content of the third prelude and of the colloquies, with suitable Scripture, but not too much thereof. The exercise is a distillation of the whole of the New Testament: key texts can help, e.g. the temptations, the opposition of the Pharisees to Jesus, the clash of spirits given in Gal. 5.13-26, the stark account of Christian discipleship given in Mark 8—10. The way of poverty, insults and humility is illustrated in Luke 16.13-14; Matt. 10.17-22; Matt. 11.29 and elsewhere.

The power of this exercise, however, is found to lie not in the text of Ignatius nor in the scriptural texts, but mostly in the dynamic interplay between the Father who steadily draws the retreatant to his Son (cf. John 6.44), and the retreatant who, in all the welter of conflicting desires, most deeply wants the true and good and beautiful. In Merton's words:

> At the centre of our being is a point of nothingness which is untouched by sin and illusion, a point of pure truth, a point or spark which belongs entirely to God, which is never at our disposal, from which God disposes of our lives, which is inaccessible to the fantasies of our own mind or the brutalities of our own will. This little point of nothingness and of absolute poverty is the pure glory of God in us. It is so to speak his name written in us, as our poverty, as our indigence, as our dependence, as our sonship. It is like a pure diamond . . .[3]

The prayer of retreatants must well up from that truth: we are made for God, made for the way of the Son, each person 'is what Christ is' as Hopkins puts it, and from being unconscious, this identification must become conscious and be ever more fully appropriated.

Learning from experience. Retreatants differ in their reactions to the Two Standards. We become better guides insofar as we reflect on our experience of giving the exercise: what went on? How did I respond? In hindsight, could I have helped more? I can think of the following cases, which may provoke the reader's own memories either of making retreats or of guiding them.

(a) The good novice in late teens. She had little difficulty and saw little problem. My efforts to provoke awareness of the dramatic but subtle conflict between good and evil were of little value, because her background was of a sheltered and untroubled home and school life. It would have been better to focus more simply on the person of Jesus and trust him to bring her over the years to a deeper understanding of the radical nature of discipleship.

(b) The university lecturer. Intelligent, articulate, she made the Exercises in daily life, full of energy and enthusiasm to do great things for God. The Two Standards dismayed and disconcerted her: she had never seriously reflected on the issue of Christ's preferred means in establishing his Father's Kingdom. Steady concentration on the pattern of the gospels revealed to her that Christian achievement relies not on human resources but on the weakness and foolishness of Christ. 1 Cor. 1.17-31 ('God chose what is foolish and weak . . .') became a major text for her.

(c) An ex-Provincial, one of nature's gentlemen, weary after a life in government and deeply aware that ambition and desire for security had shackled many a so-called exercise in discernment over the years. He needed no convincing that there *are* two standards and that the good religious is ripe for well-orchestrated temptation. His prayer was simple, wordless, deep – a humble yearning or cry of the heart to be won over to the way of Christ.

(d) A younger priest, widely read in liberation theology and defensive about it, involved in demanding enterprises in the cause of justice, and suspicious of his director who was not so involved. In several days on the Two Standards, he moved through the discouragement of realizing that in his labour for 'the rights of Christ's people' he had paid scant attention to the specific manner of Christ's approach to the liberation of humanity. 'I presumed that Christ's mind was my own!' He went on to ask humbly for light on how to work rightly for the transforming of unjust structures, how to use influence and pressure while remaining critical and free of such means. He guessed that his choice of means would have to be a matter of ongoing discernment for the rest of his life. What was given him was a 'feel' for the mystery of God's ways as shown in Christ, for bringing about the final community of humankind. His reform of life centred on getting to know the Christ of the gospels better. In the year after the retreat he found himself able to be more deeply involved in his work than before, because he was no longer dogged by frustration and fear of failure; he was helping God rather than God helping him. C. Martini's analysis of the Two Standards in terms of misunderstanding the mystery of Christ and of the incarnation was helpful reading both during and after the retreat.[4]

Witnesses. We know that Ignatius multiplied examples to help his exercitants catch on, e.g. in regard to the Principle and Foundation. Perhaps we ignore his note at the opening of the Second Week about it being 'very profitable' to read from the lives of the saints. Examples stir the imagination and the affectivity; herewith a few to end with.

(a) Ignatius of Loyola to Isabel Roser, 1532:

> . . . You speak of the enmities, the intrigues, the untruths which have been circulated about you. I am not at all surprised at this, not even if it were worse than it is. For just as soon as you determined to bend every effort to secure the praise, honour and service of God our Lord, you declared war against the world, and raised your standard in its face, and got ready to reject what is lofty by embracing what is lowly, to accept indifferently honour and dishonour, riches and poverty, affection and hatred, welcome and repulse, in a word, the glory of the world or all the wrongs it could inflict on you.
>
> . . . If we wish absolutely to live in honour and to be held in esteem by our neighbours, we can never be solidly rooted in God our Lord, and it will be impossible for us to remain unscathed when we meet with affronts.[5]

(b) Winefrid Wigmore, writing of Mary Ward, the foundress of the Institute of the Blessed Virgin Mary, *c.* 1628:

> What applause would she not have won, what friends would she have acquired and have made herself an object of admiration to the world, if she would have relented but a little on some points regarding the Institute. But she put herself aside, without regarding what was agreeable or disagreeable, her only ambition being fidelity to God, which she desired so much that it did not appear difficult whatever she suffered in so doing - to lose friends and make enemies, to despise honours and embrace contempt, to reject riches and embrace poverty.[6]

(c) Dom Helder Camara to the non-violent but involved, 1974:

> We must have no illusions. We must not be naive. If we listen to the voice of God, we make our choice, get out of ourselves and fight non-violently for a better world. We must not expect to find it easy; we shall not walk on roses, people will not throng to hear us and applaud, and we shall not always be aware of divine protection. If we are to be pilgrims for justice and peace, we must expect the desert.

101

The great and the powerful disappear, stop helping us and turn against us . . . And what is worse, those who are not powerful also avoid us . . .

There are times when we look about us and feel we are an awkward friend. People who welcome us are suspect. They want our friendship but are afraid of being compromised by our reputation.

. . . We reach the limits of endurance, desert all about us, desert within. We feel that the Father himself has abandoned us, 'Why hast thou forsaken me?'

We must not trust in our own strength, we must not give way to bitterness, we must stay humble knowing that we are in the hands of God, we must want only to share in the making of a better world. Then we shall not lose our courage or our hope. We shall feel the invisible protection of God our Father.[7]

NOTES

1. B. Lonergan, *Method in Theology* (New York 1973), pp. 30-31.

2. B. Kiely, 'Consolation, desolation and the changing of symbols' in *The Spiritual Exercises in Present-day Application* (Rome 1982), p. 134.

3. T. Merton, *Conjectures of a Guilty Bystander* (New York 1968), p. 158.

4. C. Martini, *The Ignatian Exercises in the Light of St John* (Gujarat Sahitya Prakash, Anand, India, 1981), pp. 158-66.

5. cf. *St Ignatius' Own Story*, trans. W.J. Young (Chicago 1956), p. 76.

6. M.C.E. Chambers, *The Life of Mary Ward* (London 1882), vol. 2, p. 298.

7. H. Camara, *The Desert is Fertile* (London 1974), pp. 17-19.

CHAPTER NINE

Praying the Passion

Dermot Mansfield

It is not easy to say something worthwhile on the prayer of the Third Week in the Spiritual Exercises. Looking at available literature, it can be noticed how little is written on this week. Perhaps, too, there is not a great deal to be spoken about in helping a retreatant over these days. Yet the mystery entered into here, of being with Christ in his suffering and death, is very great, so that even if statements do not come confidently it is still right to pause over the issue of praying the Passion. The few observations made here are based on my own efforts to learn in giving the Exercises and are offered for what they are worth. I should also mention that I have the closed thirty-day retreat in mind throughout.

An initial point should be made about the general meaning of this part of the Exercises. If a retreatant has been making the choice of a way of life or some other serious options, according to the paragraphs on the Election (Exx 169-189), then this time will be approached to some extent in terms of a confirmation of decisions made. Sometimes of course such concrete choosing does not arise, and would be unreal to the situation of the retreatant - although I would expect that some decisive reorientation or renewal should have been occurring towards the end of the Second Week. But in every case, I think that it should be understood that in some important way retreatants are now being invited into a deeper identification with Christ. This call to a deeper involvement, to put it in this general way, is surely a good part of the prayer of the Third Week, and needs to be kept in mind by the director.

1 ENTERING THE THIRD WEEK

What about the actual experience of entering into this week? Inevitably, I think, it is a transition which evokes many different reactions in people. The Cross and the suffering of Christ indeed, have already been present in the prayer: in the colloquy with Christ crucified in the First Week (Exx 53), in the third point of the nativity contemplation in the Second Week (Exx 116) and really in the whole sense of the third mode of humility (Exx 167), with its antecedents in the Call of the King and in the Two Standards. All of this may facilitate what is to happen now, but not necessarily. Clearly, there are some who are attracted to praying with the mysteries of the Passion, and are drawn forward peacefully, even if tired at this stage of the retreat. But others expect it to be difficult, may feel dread or have feelings of uncertainty. They may say that they have avoided this subject before, or have been uncomfortable during Holy Week. And directors too can have their own difficulties, perhaps being unsure themselves of the meaning and place of Christ's Passion, and with memories of their own seemingly unsatisfactory prayer.

However, it is good to realize that the movement of the retreat is one which will tend to carry people forward. If there are anxieties in retreatants, it can be useful to talk these over. Even if as directors we are unsure, that need not form a barrier to the way in which we are available and of help. We can go ahead, believing in the rightness of the unfolding pattern of the Exercises, wishing to entrust our retreatants to whatever the experience of praying the Passion is to be for them. The Passion of Christ relates directly to what affects us most deeply in our human experience - our own suffering, and that of others, near and far away. More than this, it opens us to the depths of the heart of God, perceived in the defencelessness of Christ broken and suffering, bearing in himself our sin and that of the world.

So we move ahead, being confronted with the reality of the Passion, and what could be called its objectivity to our Christian faith. For, no matter what way we try to understand it and whatever our feelings, the Passion is 'there'. It is 'there' in the Exercises just as in the gospels themselves, as the culmination of the life of Jesus - and so those who have been desiring and praying in the Second Week to walk with him in discipleship will wish to be with him here too, even if the prospect gives rise to pain and a sense of incomprehension. So this reality of the mystery, and the desire of retreatants to remain with Jesus, can give sufficient confidence to a director as the matter of the first contemplations is proposed.

2 IMPORTANT POINTS IN THE EXERCISES

In looking then to the prayer itself, it is well to notice some of the key elements, especially those in the text of the Exercises, which shape and give a particular quality to the contemplations.

There is above all the great immediacy of what is to be contemplated. Christ is portrayed as present and as *now* undergoing his Passion. This is seen especially in the text of the first contemplation, on the last supper (Exx 190–199), which seems to set the pattern for the contemplations of the whole week. An immediacy was there at the beginning of the Second Week, in the contemplations on the incarnation and the nativity. But the Passion seems to bring an even greater sense of it.[1]

Especially important here is the grace to be prayed for, which will be the desire present in anyone entering into the closeness of the contemplation of the Passion: 'Sorrow, compassion, and shame because the Lord is going to his suffering for my sins' (Exx 193). By the time of the second contemplation, on the agony and the arrest of Jesus, the words are stronger: 'Sorrow with Christ in sorrow, anguish with Christ in anguish, tears and deep grief because of the great affliction Christ endures for me' (Exx 203). In this phraseology there is contained the whole mystery of sin in the First Week, with the central vision even there of Christ dying on the cross, and the meaning of the incarnation and of the labours of Christ, as contemplated in the Second Week. All that has gone before is being brought forward here into earnest prayer for sorrow and for a real identification with Christ suffering.

So there is expected to be a close union in the prayer between the retreatant and Christ. This is not spoken of as passive, as is usually understood when there is reference to unitive prayer. Rather, in considering all that Christ is undergoing 'for my sins' (Exx 193, 197), 'for me' (Exx 203), the retreatant is told to make an effort and to labour (Exx 195) in the prayer, and also to think over 'what I ought to do and suffer for him' (Exx 197). It is therefore an active form of prayer, leading to practical decisions and orientations, in which the retreatant is to become more and more committed to Christ and his way, and if necessary using once again the triple colloquy from the Two Standards (Exx 199).

105

3 DIFFERENT WAYS OF PRAYER

In practice the actual prayer experience may take many different forms. A director who has guided even a small number of people in making the Exercises knows this, and will want retreatants to be guided in praying the Passion in whatever way seems most appropriate. How is this appropriateness to be assessed? That is hard to say. God alone knows best, and God it is who initiates and leads each one in prayer. There must be a real freedom here, and sensitivity to what is of God, in order truly to allow 'the Creator to deal directly with the creature, and the creature directly with his Creator and Lord' (Exx 15).[2] The best that can be done is to note briefly some of the ways which seem to occur in retreatants' prayer at this stage of the Exercises, in the hope that some of the points noted will be of value.

There is then a way which approximates to that described in the Exercises, with elements as described above. There is an evident and moving compassion with Christ suffering. There is a deep sorrow, which is once again the fruit of the grace prayed for in the First Week, being received more fully here - and perhaps it is a grace which seemed not to come before, but now is released and given in the prayer of the Passion.

There may be a certain ease in the prayer, by which the person is carried along. Perhaps it may require more obviously the effort and labour as described by Ignatius, so that even if an election has been made there are perhaps new and important questions arising now as to how to respond to all that Christ is doing. In all of this, the retreatant's involvement with Christ in his Passion is clear, with a deeply personal response to the Lord 'who loved me and gave himself for me' (Gal. 2.20).

But if this is according to what is outlined by Ignatius, it must also be said that there is another way experienced by many, where praying the Passion remains dry and difficult throughout. There is no evident consolation. There is instead what looks like desolation, in which a person may feel distant from Christ suffering, and seemingly unconcerned. 'Am I cold-hearted? . . . I can't make it real for myself . . . Perhaps the truth is that I am too afraid to face what is in it', are the kinds of questions and reflections which can spontaneously arise.

Here it might be wise to check out again the human variables of generosity, preparation, giving the time to prayer, review and general attitude (see Exx 6). Yet I may know that the retreatant is investing the right effort, and that there are still aridity and difficulty, giving rise to genuine upset that this is so and not according to expectations. Here is someone coming time and time again to prayer, desiring to be with Christ suffering, feeling helpless about it all, and still giving time faithfully despite all the conflicting emotions. That is surely a true prayer of the Passion. It is God who takes care of this prayer. There may be many human reasons why prayer is experienced as difficult, but, in the end, once we come to pray, God is there and can make fruitful what is intimately God's own concern.

It could be, of course, that a person has generally avoided suffering and conflict in life, and, noticing an instinct now to run away, comes to realize what has been happening. That can be a blessed moment, for in the helplessness of it there is an opportunity to turn to Christ and be with him in a new way.

But it can also be the case that there has been in fact much experience of suffering in life – and all of this is coming up now, leading to distress in the contemplation of the pain and sorrow of Christ. Further, anger and bewilderment at the intractability of human suffering and at the apparent remoteness of God will compound the matter, making it very difficult to contemplate a Christ said to be suffering on behalf of the world and especially for oneself. Staying with the Passion under conditions like these is a challenge for both retreatant and director. Feelings and hidden attitudes surfacing can require talking out as well as needing to be brought to prayer. It might be that even a conversion is called for, and with it the dissolution of accumulated resentment – a surprise, perhaps, because the experience of the First Week may have been considered good in some respects.

Yet only now is the truth appearing, in the painful, sustained contemplation of the beloved Son overwhelmed with suffering, bearing the unbearable burden of the enormity of the sin of the world. It appears too in the accompanying realization that one has been holding out in some situation apart from this place where eternal love is poured out endlessly, so that now there is a change and a new yielding to that love. For only here in the Passion is the

107

truth known fully, which may have been only glimpsed in the meditations of the First Week.

Now, if some conversion such as this occurs in an evident way, involving a change of outlook and consciousness, then obviously the experience will move towards that described by Ignatius. After darkness and difficulty, the grace of 'sorrow with Christ in sorrow . . . because of the great affliction Christ endures for me' (Exx 203) will most likely be given in a moving and conscious way.

But there can be that continuing and painful experience which can be hard to endure, and especially if coming after a Second Week which had much sensible consolation in it. Yet the desire to remain with Christ even if feeling completely helpless and inadequate, can surely be a sign of good prayer. After all, that is the way we are present to someone loved who is suffering or dying. For many people making the Exercises, the prayer of the Third Week is like this human experience, and that is all right. Unsure, uncertain, with conflicting emotions, they nevertheless stay with Christ suffering, and that is all that matters.

A third way of praying seems like that just described, and may incorporate elements already noted and yet I think there is some essential difference. It is what occurs when someone's prayer in everyday life has become contemplative, virtually wordless, a matter of deep and persevering faith. Coming to the retreat, then, this form in the prayer has to be respected. To impose the more active pattern of prayer given in the text of the *Exercises* would do violence to the way God is working now. The right approach is rather to allow the prayer to continue in its simple contemplative way, but with some reading and pondering of material as a preparation and with a period of reflection after each time of prayer. If this is done, one respects the person's prayer and yet follows the basic framework given by Ignatius.[3]

As I say, this may appear similar to the dry and difficult prayer of the Passion mentioned already. But the principal difference is that here the person cannot really engage in an active and meditative form of prayer, and so if this is attempted - as can happen due to pressures to 'make the Exercises properly' - there is a real lack of freedom, leading to disturbance. So let it be as God would wish. The results bear their own evidence, as a good director will see soon enough. In the prayer, but more likely out of it, various patterns may thread their way along, such as a sense of what Christ endures, his loneliness, or an experience of the distance of the sinner from what Christ alone is carrying for him or her, and also some ungraspable realization of how greatly one is being cared for, and how much too the dark and sinful world is loved.

A fourth way is one which is more evidently mystical. It might at first seem like what is expected in the text of the *Exercises* – and no doubt there is some such quality hidden in that written by a great mystic – because of the sensible and affective elements present. But what happens in mystical prayer is something given directly by God and normally part of a great and continual living in God, which has not come about in a short time. In this state, for instance, I think that 'consolation without previous cause' (Exx 330, 336) is the usual or only kind of consolation experienced. It is directly from God, and is what happens 'when an effect of the spirit overflows in the senses', as John of the Cross succinctly puts it.[4] This is quite different from what comes in some way as a result of one's own efforts to grieve and be sad (Exx 195, 206). It is something wholly from God and so the overflowing effect in the sensibility is fundamentally from above, unlike what used to come in good part from below, from one's own activity and initiative.

It could be, however, that the signs of the mystical way are hardly observable, so that what is being lived is virtually in secret. Further, it could also be that God's purposes and the needs of the Church will initiate a sharing in the Passion which may 'reach the point of an extreme powerlessness, an experience of inner darkness, abandonment and reprobation',[5] which possibly might be considered as a participation in Christ's own experience on the cross. And if this is so, then it must be a situation sustained and protected by God, and in which some other person's role is only to be alongside in faith and in prayer.

Perhaps this division into ways of praying the Passion may seem arbitrary. Still, in my experience there is some basis to the differentiation, especially between the first and the second pair, where in the latter case contemplative prayer is present in either a secret and beginning phase or else in an obvious and mystical way. And various points mentioned may overlap, as where those difficulties considered earlier may in fact signal an entry into contemplative prayer. In any case, we need to keep in mind the

109

dynamic of the prayer as given in the Exercises, while also remaining sensitive to that freedom which is the prerogative of God's leading.

4 'PASSION OF CHRIST, STRENGTHEN ME'

What generally, is happening in praying the Passion? It is hard, and possibly unwise, to look for an exact answer. But some indications have been given incidentally already, and perhaps some further notes here may point towards the meaning.

Early on it was suggested that the purpose of the week has to do generally with the call to deeper identification with Christ. If an election of some importance has been made – and which was born out of a desire to be closer to Christ – then in the contemplation of the Passion that desire is being realized and brought about in an authentic way. The identification is beginning to be lived out in the prayer itself:

> In the petition of the Third Week, we ask to be sorrowful *with* Christ sorrowful: what is at issue is a sense of identification. In fact we pray that we may be incorporated into that very *kenosis* which was the predominant feature of Jesus's life. We pray for a real participation in the radical self-forgetfulness for which he prayed and which bore fruit in his resurrection and in our redemption in him.[6]

Somehow, here, there is a renunciation of self and a poverty of spirit which is at the heart of the Two Standards and the Third Mode of Humility, as the meaning of what was asked for then becomes clearer in this time of the contemplation of Christ suffering, namely a self-forgetful love of him, shown in being with him despite the pain and the cost.

This self-forgetful love is also, as Hans Urs von Balthasar has shown, a deeper and more complete living of the First Week, where now our sin is both most conspicuous and overpowering and yet perceived only in the loneliness and anguish of Christ bearing it:

> Whether I shed tears or follow the scene dry-eyed with the gaping crowds and the soldiers affects the situation very little. Contemplation of the Passion demands self-abasement, adoration without self-regard, the simple consideration of the scenes, happenings and the inner states of the suffering Christ . . . At this particular moment, my guilt appears so evident and conspicuous that it does not need to be brought to the

light; and, on the other hand, in so far as it is mine it is insignificant, because only the burden it has placed on the Lamb of God is visible and of consequence.[7]

With this personal realization there can also be an awareness of the suffering of the world, the anguish of oppressed peoples, the pain of inequality and indignity. And yet even here, with an overwhelming consciousness of the mountains of grief and injustice, there can come about a very simple and awestruck contemplation of the one who alone bears all things. For no one there among the crowds, apart from Mary, and no one now even in the night of suffering and injustice, could claim to be innocent and just, or could avoid consciousness of personal guilt in truthfully looking on him. Even the awareness or the experience of suffering gives way to the perspective of the Lamb of God who takes away that sin of the world which is at the root of injustice, suffering and death, and who could say even in what was being done to him, 'Father, forgive them; they do not know what they are doing' (Luke 23.34).

In contemplating therefore the beloved Son, 'crushed because of our guilt' (Isa. 53.5), we are in that place where the depth of eternal love is laid open and where the world is being reconciled. We would have run away, unworthy of it, but are encompassed in its reaching out and drawn towards it and made good in it. Living there, in turn we are also called and formed to be at the disposal of such grace for the world, in a manner similar to it, by which 'God so loved the world' (John 3.16). Here we are conformed to the Son in his mission, to Christ suffering (Exx 48, 167, 203), and likewise in him can yield a rich harvest and bear abundant fruit (John 12.24; 15.5) for the Kingdom.

So it can be seen that the prayer of the Passion is not to be considered secondary to the important time of decision and mission in the Second Week, but should be viewed rather as a deepening of what has been opted for then, when the whole desire was to be close to Christ in discipleship and, insofar as one is called to it, to share intimately in his work of redemption for the world.

Of course, what is entered into in a real way in this prayer is meant to be lived out in the rest of life, beyond the actual experience of making the Exercises. To live in the great reality prayed for eventually, in the Contemplation to Attain the Love of God (Exx

230-237), will mean that in very existential and human ways one will be brought further 'to know him and the power of his resurrection, and partake of his sufferings by being moulded to the pattern of his death' (Phil. 3.10). Some people coming to the Exercises are already living these mysteries in an eminent way – and so the retreat tends to take the form of a particular deepening and appropriation of the gifts received – but more often there are those for whom the experience of the Exercises will consist in good seed sown, which is meant to germinate and come forth in all of life's future circumstances.

I would consider too, regarding the particular orientation of discipleship given in the Second Week, and especially if the choice has been difficult and with acute awareness of human inadequacy, that there is strength given in the prayer of the Passion. There would be consolation and encouragement of course in the prayer of the Resurrection, but also too there is a help in the contemplation of Christ suffering: 'Passion of Christ, strengthen me'. For just as the Lord himself was strengthened in his agony, so a person will be too, when faced with the prospect of future trials and difficulties which will arise as a result of choices made.[8] In this way, it can be said that there is confirmation given for what has been decided upon, or for a new orientation or understanding. There is strength given in looking to Christ, especially consisting in an underlying peace amid the conflicting emotions of facing the future, and which will also be there at further points along the way.

5 BEING WITH MARY

As the prayer progresses towards the end of this Week, a final point comes to mind, which I believe bears upon the issue of being strengthened and confirmed. This is the fact that Mary is near at hand at this time – 'Near the cross of Jesus stood his mother', we are told in the Gospel of John (19.25), along with the women and the disciple he loved. Ignatius wishes a retreatant to be close to her after the taking down from the cross (Exx 208, under the sixth and seventh days), in the final stages of the prayer of the Passion. It is right to be near the one person among us who stood there with an innocence wrought by her Son which we cannot claim, who walked the way of greatest faith and self-giving, and who shared terribly his pitiless humilitation. For Mary plays a great role in the Exercises, as some retreatants witness to. Whoever then is with her, and is led to consider 'her great sorrow and weariness' (Exx 208) after Jesus's death, is surely strengthened, and perhaps given to understand how we are being brought where all alienation and unlikeness are changed, and where redeemed humanity is being clothed in the likeness of the beloved Son.

The prayer may have been perceived as good in some tangible way, or it may have been dry and bitter. People undergo very different experiences of the Passion, and yet what matters is that they have remained with Christ, despite perhaps a deep sense of unworthiness. In this there is love - and there is too an opening out to the world, because that is the kind of love it is. And the rest follows now, as the fullness of the mystery unfolds in this moment. For here at the end of the Third Week Ignatius makes the prayer virtually the same as that at the beginning of the Fourth Week - it is a prayer in the presence of Mary, and it will be with her too that the Resurrection will be contemplated. She has been present throughout the Exercises. She was central to the prayer of the Incarnation, when the desire was first given in the text to appreciate Christ and to follow him more closely (Exx 104) - and with her now will also be approached the mystery of the Resurrection, when the desire will be to rejoice intensely 'because of the great joy and the glory of Christ our Lord' (Exx 221).

NOTES

1. William Peters in *The Spiritual Exercises of St Ignatius: exposition and interpretation* (New Jersey 1968), p. 136, speaks of the preferred use of the present tense now.

2. See Hans Urs von Balthasar, *Prayer* (London 1961), pp. 107-9, on freedom in the prayer of the Exercises.

3. See John Govan, 'Spiritual direction for a contemplative', *The Way Supplement* 54 (Autumn 1985), pp. 60-70; and my own essay, 'The prayer of faith, spiritual direction and the Exercises', in this volume pp. 191-202.

4. *The Living Flame of Love*, stanza 2, para. 14; in *The Collected Works of St John of the Cross*, trans. Kieran Kavanaugh and Otilio Rodriguez (New York 1964), p. 600.

5. von Balthasar, *Prayer*, p. 235, see pp. 233-46.

6. Brian McNamara, 'Jesus's prayer in Gethsemane: interpretation and identification', *The Way Supplement* 27 (Spring 1976), p. 86.

7. von Balthasar, *Prayer*, p. 241.

8. See McNamara, 'Jesus's prayer in Gethsemane', p. 87.

9. See Peters, *The Spiritual Exercises*, pp. 141-3.

CHAPTER TEN

Contemplating Christ Risen

Margot O'Donovan

To contemplate the resurrection of Christ can be a confirming experience of the choice to follow Christ, especially when done whilst making the Spiritual Exercises for thirty days. The graces of the last two Weeks of the Exercises are a multi-faceted and evolving reality, which is progressively deepened as the retreatant is drawn into the actual living of the paschal mystery. Yet often the graces of confirmation are inadequately received, or at least less richly experienced than they might be. There is much a director can do to assist retreatants. I suggest – and this is the central purpose of this article – that 'the one who gives the Exercises' will be helped in this task, in proportion to a familiarity with and a careful integration of the insights of modern biblical and theological study on the resurrection. This in no way denies the necessity for persevering prayer on the part of the retreatant to discover that freedom from all that hinders the new life offered to each one by the risen Lord.

The retreatant, who in the previous three Weeks has been progressively introduced into the riches of the mysteries of Christ, is now seeking in contemplating Christ risen the gift of a new life in the risen Saviour. How then does Ignatius propose that these contemplations be made? The Ignatian setting is surprising, in that there is no contemplation of the resurrection as such; he begins by offering a contemplation of the apparition of the risen Christ to our Lady. As Ignatius remarks, although there is no explicit reference in Scripture to such an appearance, nevertheless Scripture supposes we have understanding (Exx 299). The word is used here in the sense of the spiritual understanding that faith gives: one which grasps the appropriateness of such an appearance as being in harmony with the revealed mystery.

However, there is another reason why Ignatius chooses the apparition to our Lady as the first contemplation of this Fourth Week. It is because, to quote Cusson, 'for Christ the joy of resurrection is not the joy of breathing again, but rather the joy of bringing to the new humanity his own life now capable of being welcomed in its fullness', and only Mary is capable of taking possession of this new life immediately and fully.[1]

Yet, even though our Lady figures prominently in this first contemplation, nevertheless it is the person of the risen Lord that dominates the Week in the appearance narratives (Exx 299-311). We find no direct reference in the text to the retreatant, as was the case with the contemplations on the Passion (Exx 197). All is centred on the Risen One, who consoles his friends. The first contemplation is so structured as to assist the retreatant to enter progressively into this experience of the consoling Christ. Further indication of this can be found by carefully reading the notes for this Week (Exx 226-29). Here we find that the Additions are adapted with a view to helping the retreatant to keep a delicate attention, in a spiritual attitude best described as follows: 'And the more it (the soul), is united to him, the more it disposes itself to receive graces and gifts from his divine and sovereign goodness' (Exx 20). Ignatius is intent on promoting a harmony, interior and exterior, which disposes the person to receive the gifts of peace, love and joy.

At this stage Ignatius considers that the retreatant, if the grace asked for is received, will experience a deep joy centred on the risen Christ, which turns the whole of life towards the glorified Christ, present to the retreatant in faith. It is not a question of trying to make oneself joyful: Ignatius simply says this joy is a gift, which we are to ask for. The retreatant, having spent three weeks asking for what he or she wants, is well aware that all is gift, given in the midst of weakness and frailty. The bestowal of this gift is the proper function of the risen Christ (Exx 224), and is described in terms of spiritual consolation (Exx 316). What the retreatant is asking is the purest form of consolation: that is, the movement out of self to rejoice in the joy and glory of the risen Christ (Exx 221).

> This is the grace I ask for; to enter into the joy of the Lord, which is a joy of love, and for us, the joy of being the object of his love, his joy, of being delivered from evil, infallibly moving towards his eternal heart.[2]

Ignatius, it seems, understands the consolation given by the risen Lord as the sending of his Spirit. At this point in the Exercises, the faith-relationship with Christ has so deepened, over the long weeks of prayer, that the retreatant comes to see by experience that Christ, in comforting, is giving a share in his Spirit. So William Peters suggests that this explains why Ignatius fails to round off the Fourth Week, as many wish he had done.[3] In reality, the Fourth Week has no end.

Throughout the entire time of the Exercises, Ignatius gives instructions for the director, to help to involve every level of the retreatant's being in the prayer. Now, in contemplating the risen Christ, the aim is that the affections of the risen Lord and the retreatant's affections will be more and more closely identified. The preludes of the contemplations serve to make the retreatant present to the mystery; the points develop familiarity with every aspect of the mystery, a familiarity deepened by the repetitions, until finally the life of the senses is drawn into the contemplation. This, in brief, is the structure of all the contemplations from the Second Week onwards. But in the Third and Fourth Weeks additional points are given which give a particular tone to the prayer. It can be a very rewarding task for a director of the Exercises to try to grasp something of this particular 'tone'. It offers a director great facility in helping the retreatant to receive the gift offered in the contemplative prayer on the paschal mystery.

There is a significant shift in the nature of the petition of the Fourth Week, in comparision with previous petitions; now the request made is for knowledge of Christ in terms of what happens to him as he contemplates the Father (Exx 223). In resurrection, Jesus is for the first time in the presence of the Father. The beloved Son, now raised by the Father, knows in his humanity what it means to be glorified. What we are now seeking is an interior knowledge of what the resurrection means for Jesus, because, in the last analysis, this is what it must mean for us.

A careful study of the text of the first contemplation on the resurrection reveals the two key-points in the retreatant's prayer at this stage: what happens to Christ in the resurrection (Exx 223); and how he exercises the office of consoler (Exx 224).

In considering Christ exercising the office of consoler, Ignatius suggests that the retreatant compare the way in which Christ consoles with the 'way in which friends are wont to console each other' (Exx 224). In the accounts of the resurrection-appearances, the risen Christ is described as giving joy, confidence and peace to those who, because they remained open to him, were in a position to receive the gift of Christian faith. The appearance-scenes in the

117

gospels show how the disciples, despite their misgivings, were yet certain that the One they encountered was the same as the earthly Jesus they had known. The Lord is portrayed as consoling primarily by reassuring his friends of his identity in difference; the consolation that he gives is that he is alive and with them.

We are now in a position to give a clearer description of the kind of prayer that Ignatius hoped would be evoked in the Fourth Week. The general aim at this stage is to confirm and strengthen the retreatant in the choice of the way in which to follow Christ, so that the prayer will centre around the two pivotal points of Christ's experience of resurrection and his consoling of his brethren. It is intended to evoke what might be called an experience of resurrection, a gift God wishes to grant today. While there is a sense in which only the disciples could experience Jesus as the same Jesus they had known on earth, yet it is possible, indeed it seems almost essential to the contemplations as proposed by Ignatius, that he expects the retreatant to have an encounter with the risen Christ: one which develops faith in the risen Christ alive and present now. This encounter, it is hoped, will also be graced by the gift from the Father to the retreatant of an intense joy in the joy and glory of Christ. Ignatius, himself a man of great desires, all but assumed as certain that after the preceding weeks of purification and immersion in prayer, this gift would be given (Exx 227).

The prayer to be evoked will be such as to underline that death issues in life. There is a paschal shape to Jesus's life, and a hint of it is found in the Exercises (219), which makes a direct and firm connection between the cross and the resurrection contemplation: there is also to be a paschal shape to the life of the believer. At this point, the retreatant is, as it were, looking through two lenses, to see suffering and glory together. The process is that the suffering blossoms forth into the glory of resurrection; and the veil between the two is almost translucent. By praying to know and grasp how death issues into life, the retreatant is in fact seeking Christ's paschal shape for her or his own life.

In the light of what has been said about the kind of prayer the Fourth Week presupposes, what help can be derived from the insights of modern biblical and theological study of the resurrection? Secondly, how do these insights help us in contemplating the appearances of Christ risen?

118

THE NEW TESTAMENT WITNESS TO THE RESURRECTION

What do the New Testament writers say about the resurrection, and what did they intend to proclaim by means of the resurrection narratives? The evangelists and Paul represent varied attempts to give expression to the apostolic faith in the resurrection, and to describe the genesis of that faith. In particular, the resurrection narratives result from the combination of historical narrative and theological reflection and so diverge in details.

Paul to the Corinthians

The earliest text dealing comprehensively with the resurrection is found in First Corinthians. It is generally agreed that Paul is citing a tradition he received; but when and where he received it, how much belongs to the original formula and what is Paul's addition, whether this text is one formula or a plurality of formulae; all these questions remain open to discussion. The tradition he received was:

> That Christ died for our sins in accordance with the scriptures, that he was buried, that he was raised on the third day, in accordance with the scriptures, and that he appeared to Cephas. . . .

There follows a listing of people to whom Christ appeared (1 Cor. 15.3-8).

The phrase 'that Christ died for our sins in accordance with the scriptures' is a summary of a passion-tradition; but there is here an addition not found in the primitive passion-narrative, namely the motive, 'for our sins'. Next it is stated that 'he was buried'; this early tradition had no doubt about the reality of his death. Yet though Paul knew of the burial, it does not necessarily follow that he also knew of the 'empty tomb' tradition. The subsequent phrase, 'he was raised on the third day in accordance with the scriptures', shows that the primitive Christian community proclaimed the resurrection rather than narrated it. This was an event the inner nature of which could not be perceived but only its accompanying phenomena, the appearances and the empty tomb. The verb used here by Paul, *egegertai*, 'was raised', is the passive of *egeirein*, meaning 'to wake up', or 'to rouse from sleep', expressing how Jesus was raised from death. The verb *egegertai* is a reverential passive denoting an

119

interventive act of God.'⁴ The Father raised Jesus. The language is, for Paul, a means to describe Jesus's transition from one mode of existence to another: one which the Christians understood as resurrection, not as the resuscitation of a corpse. Jesus has been raised to a new and transformed mode of existence: one of the basic elements of the resurrection-contemplations is 'what happens to Christ in the resurrection'. Paul goes on to say that Christ's resurrection is the first break-through into a new kind of existence and the pledge that others will follow him (1 Cor. 15.20).

The debate amongst scholars as to the meaning of the phrase 'on the third day', is inconclusive. I incline to Dr Fuller's suggestion that the source for this phrase is apocalyptic. On this view, 'on the third day' is not a chronological datum but a dogmatic assertion that Christ's resurrection marked the beginning of the cosmic eschatological process of resurrection. If 'in accordance with the scriptures' is taken with the verb 'was raised', this would indicate that the resurrection, like the passion, was part of God's saving plan.

Paul uses the verb *ophthe* four times, which literally means 'was seen'. When *ophthe* carries dative it is translated 'appeared' or 'let himself be seen', the action is initiated by Christ.⁵ It is Christ who initiates these encounters with those who were open to what seems best described as a revelatory disclosure by God of the eschatological event of resurrection. This understanding of the appearances as Christ-initiated encounters can be effectively used to encourage a modern retreatant that he or she can encounter the risen Christ in faith.

According to Mark

In Mark's Gospel no appearances are mentioned (16.1-8). The account commences with the narrative of the women going to visit the tomb to anoint the body of Jesus. Mark is not wholly consistent; he has already written that the body has been prepared and buried by Joseph of Arimathea (15.46). Some say the story of burial by Joseph of Arimathea is a later, legendary account: records say Jesus was buried by his enemies (Acts 13.29). The questions of how, by whom and where Jesus was buried have no easy answer: there are various opinions as to which New Testament tradition is the earliest and closest to the actual burial. Whichever view is taken about the burial, Mark says that the purpose of the women's visit to the tomb was to anoint the body; but on arrival they find the stone rolled back, and a young man sitting inside the tomb tells them: 'He is risen, he is not here' (Mark 16.6). Leaving aside verse 7, which most scholars agree is an editorial interpolation, in verse 8 the reaction of the women is amazement and fear. There have been numerous interpretations of Mark's intention in describing the women's reaction to the news of the resurrection. I think the explanation given by Léon-Dufour is as close to the intention of Mark as it is possible to get, when he says,

> . . . the evangelist Mark did not feel it necessary to reproduce any of them (narratives of the appearances). He preferred to place his reader in the company of the women who experienced no more than the earthly presence of Jesus. They stumble upon the Easter mystery, but are not yet able to receive it. Yet it is proclaimed.[6]

Mark's Gospel, when used in giving the Exercises, illustrates well the sense of awe which is usually the accompaniment of an initial grasp of the implication of resurrection. The resurrection statement, 'he is not here, he is risen', points to transformation not resuscitation; and it is feasible to think that Mark took the women's report of an empty tomb, and used it as a means to proclaim the resurrection which the disciples already believed in on account of their own meeting with the risen Lord.

Mark's Gospel proclaims the resurrection as God's action, and uses the story of the empty tomb as a vehicle for that proclamation. It is plausible to conclude that the empty-tomb story rests on an early tradition, perhaps derived from a basic nucleus of a report given to the disciples by the women. But it must be kept clearly in mind that it was the appearances to the disciples, not the empty-tomb story, which were the origin and cause of their Easter faith.

The Matthean Gospel

Matthew follows fairly closely the Marcan text, omitting only the reference about the appearance to Peter (Mark 15.7). Matthew adds, for apologetic purposes, the story of the guards and various miraculous phenomena (28.1-4). The new element he introduces is to relate the angel's appearance with an appearance of Jesus to the women, which in turn is linked to the final appearance to the disciples. The final appearance is to the eleven disciples on a mountain in Galilee, where Jesus gives the mission-command to them (28.20). The setting for this appearance is very likely Matthew's own composition: there is an obvious Matthean touch in the phrasing of the elements of the great commission (28.20). Matthew emphasizes aspects of the Church's mission and of the teaching of the earthly Jesus as the new Law. Probably this mission-charge, in its original form, was the creation of Christian prophecy and was later attributed to Jesus. In this final scene, mission and promise are combined – a characteristic of mission scenes in the Old Testament, where God's presence is acknowledged and a mission given. Some writers consider the Matthean promise, 'Lo I am with you always', as an equivalent to the Johannine promise of the Paraclete.

Luke's Account

Luke's Gospel presents the first developed resurrection-narratives, describing meetings with the risen but not yet ascended Lord. Luke is an exceedingly artistic interpreter of tradition. His story of the women at the tomb is different from Mark's. Luke solves some of the difficulties found in the Marcan account with a characteristic smoothness of approach. Chapter 24, 6-8 is an editorial addition, recalling that Jesus's life and death were the necessary prelude to his resurrection. The mention of the apostles doubting the women's report (v. 11), followed by Peter's visit to the tomb, are so placed to show that the apostles come to their resurrection-faith first-hand, and not through other witnesses. Peter, the primary witness, must testify to the empty tomb in Jerusalem. Jerusalem is the place of the appearances, because of the city's importance in Lucan theology.

The Emmaus story is based on some nucleus of historical fact, but it has undergone a considerable process of development. Luke introduces three main theological motifs; that Jesus was a prophet, that his Passion and death were necessary preludes to his entry into glory, and one needs to know the Old Testament to understand the significance of Jesus's life and death. This story is an excellent scriptural example of how Christ acts as consoler, and can be used to advantage to explicate what Ignatius says: 'as friends are wont to console one another' (Exx 224).

Luke's almost physical account of the appearance to the eleven (24.36-52), similar to John's Gospel, is concerned to stress the identity in difference of the Risen One with Jesus of Nazareth. His concluding verses (44-49) are a summary of kerygmatic instructions. Finally, he describes Jesus's departure to heaven. The phrase 'and was carried up to heaven' (v. 51b), could be based on a primitive kerygmatic statement which Luke developed into a narrative in Acts. He differs from the rest of the New Testament tradition in putting the ascension after the resurrection. One may justifiably surmise that the deciding factor here is his theology. For Luke's theological purpose, the ascension ends the regular resurrection-appearances, so that the Spirit may be given for the mission required in view of the delayed Parousia (see Acts 1.6-8). The ascension for Luke is the climax of Jesus's pilgrimage from Galilee to suffering, death and resurrection in Jerusalem and thence to glory.

Luke's Gospel highlights the way in which Jesus's resurrection opens up the future to the witness and preaching of the gospel by the apostles, now endowed with the Spirit by the risen Christ. Accordingly, the Easter message refers also to events of Jesus's earthly life: part of God's plan 'according to the Scriptures'. The Easter event puts the Christian in touch with the living transformed Christ, to be found here and now in the word and the Eucharist.

The Gospel of John

The account of the resurrection in John is the end-product of a long process of transmission, in which two different sources have been used. The discovery of the empty tomb, first by Mary Magdalene and then by Peter and John, is described as the means to faith for the disciples, even though it has not been such for Mary Magdalene. There is a significant 'transference of the rise of Easter from the christophanies to the empty tomb which represents the most advanced development of the Easter narratives in the New Testament'.[7]

The appearance to Mary Magdalene is told in the form of a revelatory encounter (20.11-18), recognition being followed by the giving of a mission. The Johannine author adapts the story he received in terms of his own christology, in the warning of Mary Magdalene not to cling to Jesus as a figure of the past, because he is to be known now as the Ascended One. The appearances to the disciples is another recognition mission-scene. Peace and the Holy Spirit are given in view of the mission, and the recognition on the part of the believer is seen as the prelude to involvement in mission. The relationships between Jesus and the Father and Jesus and his brethren are underlined. The appearance to Thomas is peculiar to John's Gospel. In the synoptics the role of doubter is frequently assigned to Peter. Thomas's confession of faith, 'my Lord and my God' (20.28), is new, and its meaning has been much discussed. It would be congruous with John's Gospel, throughout which Jesus is revealed as the eschatological presence of God, to say that Thomas's confession means that in the risen Jesus he believes he encounters this eschatological presence. The chapter ends with stating the purpose of a gospel: to bring people to belief in Jesus as the Christ, the Son of God, so that they may have fulness of life.

John's approach to the resurrection-accounts is more personal than that of the synoptics. He highlights the new relationship established between Christ and the believer, and also the restored relationship of the disciples to the Father. The Spirit is given as assurance of the Lord's presence; and the disciples are commissioned, in their turn, to witness to this presence to others. The Johannine text, because of its personal tone, can be used in the Exercises to highlight the reaction and response of the individual to Christ, and to show how fear turns into joy and peace when the risen Christ is known to be present.

Summary

The New Testament kerygma of the resurrection is based on the witness of those to whom the risen Christ had appeared. My reading of the New Testament evidence is that the resurrection-faith of these chosen witnesses was based on the vivid undescribed appearances. In time, these appearances were developed into stories which were the effect of the resurrection-faith, not its cause. These witnesses testified to the revelation that the Son had been raised from the dead by the Father; that this eschatological event, which occurred on the borders of time, was revealed to them; and that they are assured by encounters with the risen Jesus that he was the same as the earthly Jesus they had known. The risen One, as the first fruits of resurrection, opened up the future for all believers who could now hope to share in a new resurrected life; and the life of the Spirit was the pledge of this future hope.

THE REALITY AND THE MEANING OF THE RESURRECTION

It is said that the New Testament was written in the light of the early Christians' resurrection-faith. If this opinion is accepted, then the resurrection of Christ will be seen as the central truth, shedding light on the earthly life and death of Jesus, as well as on his ascension and exaltation as Lord. The apostolic witnesses to the resurrection claimed that by reason of their personal encounters with the risen Lord, they could testify to the fact of his resurrection. The empty-tomb tradition, though an ambiguous one and not an essential part of resurrection-faith, was a strong Christian tradition and a means of proclamation of the Easter faith.

These facts were all based on human testimony; and so the question naturally arises as to the quality of this testimony. Certain pointers indicate that it is at least reasonable to credit their witness with objectivity. The apostles were not expecting the resurrection; but after the resurrection-appearances they show an enthusiasm to witness to it, even to the point of accepting death, as well as an indifference, in the sense that their message was centred not on themselves but on Christ. These marks of authenticity allow it to be said that at least the resurrection is credible. Also the historical traces of resurrection (the appearances and the empty tomb) allow that it can be said to be believable. It is these traces that were the facts interpreted by the apostles in terms of resurrection.

I would suggest that the resurrection remains a reality, whether people believe in it or not, a reality which can only be known through faith, never merely through historical investigation. For 'faith may not exist independently of historical knowledge but it cannot be reduced to it',[8] because 'ultimately an assent to the reality of Jesus's resurrection combines knowledge of past facts with an interpretation of present experience'.[9]

In the strict sense, the resurrection is not historical because it does not fulfil the conditions of historicity. Yet though the resurrection does not strictly fulfil the required conditions for historicity, there is an historical basis for belief in it.[10]

However some historical assessment of it must be allowed. 'The historian has every right to investigate the record of the happenings at Easter. . . .',[11] to decide whether or not they occurred. Indeed, the tendency to deny any historicity to the resurrection can have the effect of denying that it ever happened.[12]

The four gospels recount the discovery of the empty tomb, and John alone omits the angelic interpreter. The New Testament clearly emphasizes the appearances as witnessing to the resurrection; and I would accept that the empty tomb is ambiguous and does not compel faith. Nor need it be an original or essential part of the Easter message. Yet, although it is not an integral part of resurrection-faith, it appears to have been a significant part of the witness of the early Church.

Does the empty tomb have theological value? Can it be integrated into a resurrection-faith? Negatively, it is valuable in guarding against any Docetic interpretation of the resurrection; positively, it asserts God's intention to save the whole human person, to transform the world: the work of re-creation has begun in the transformation of the earthly Jesus. It does not seem necessary, on grounds of the incarnation (that Christ must share fully our fate) to reject the empty-tomb tradition. He underwent death; but in being raised by God to a new, transformed, eschatological existence, he was the subject of a unique and creative action of God. Jesus, although human, was not in every respect like other people; he had no personal experience of sin, he was in some respect different from the rest of humanity. Perhaps the empty tomb points up this difference, as well as indicating a whole new vision of God and his plans for humankind. Some hold the view that there is theological value in the fact that the empty tomb is an indispensable sign which confirms the appearance – the primary grounds for faith.

Paul (1 Cor. 15) is the main New Testament source in any consideration of bodily resurrection. He places the greatest emphasis on the idea of transformation (cf. 1 Cor. 15.35ff). He clearly does not conceive the risen body in a purely physical manner, even though he does seem to point to a continuity in some way of the corporeal aspect of personal existence. There is a sense of extreme tension in Paul's balancing of the themes of transformation and continuity as he tries to use various ways to express his thought. He seems to be talking about a profound total change and not the re-animation of a corpse or reconstruction of scattered remains. The descriptive expression he employs is 'spiritual body', and what that means is hard to know. The language (1 Cor. 15.35–44) swings between the idea of the 'same' and 'different' to express continuity in transformation; and perhaps this concept is better expressed in a narrative form, such as is found in the Lucan and Johannine narratives, where the seeing, touching, handling of the risen body is balanced by the other-worldly properties of coming through closed doors and appearing at will.

The central meaning of the resurrection, according to a basic credal formula used by Paul, is that Jesus is Lord (cf. Rom. 10.9). The resurrection has conferred on him a status, an authoritative function so that he is now forever Lord because the Father raised him from the dead. 'The resurrection was and remains, first of all, what God has done for Jesus . . . it was the sovereign action of God glorifying Jesus of Nazareth.'[13] This action of God confers on Jesus the status of Lord; and so he is exalted to the right hand of God where he intercedes for all. In this new risen life, Jesus lives for God (cf. 1 Cor. 6.14; Rom. 8.34; 6.10). The resurrection also makes him the source of salvation precisely as the one raised by the Father; which has its implications for the salvation and future destiny of humanity. It seems to me that these implications are understood by Ignatius in the context of the Fourth Week of the Exercises: in that the retreatant acknowledges the paschal shape of his or her life because Jesus has been accepted as Lord and Saviour.

To designate Jesus as Lord places the life of the historical Jesus in the perspective of eternity. He is now more than a prophet from Nazareth; he is the contemporary Lord. Jesus's earthly life can now be looked at with fresh insight; and the full implications of his words and deeds, as well as the meaning of his death, will be revealed. For the Christian, the earthly life of the Lord becomes the norm, the criterion of his or her own life.

In resurrection, Jesus's relationship with humanity is changed, because now he is the first born from the dead (1 Cor. 15.20). Paul does not see resurrection as an isolated privilege for Jesus. Rather belief in resurrection points to a meaningful future for humankind, or at least to the resurrection of believers. Because the Father has raised his son, new possibilities are opened up for those who come to believe.

Finally, the destiny of the world as a whole was definitively established in his resurrection. God has begun, in raising Jesus, to redeem and transform the world. The world, so closely tied to humanity, awaits redemption too (cf. Rom. 8.19-22). The risen Christ is no longer restricted in his relationship to the world. He is freed from the personal and cultural limitations of his earthly existence, and is Lord of the universe. So the God-centred world has become christocentric, and Christ speaks from within life because he is at its centre.

CONCLUSION

In the light of the discussion of the New Testament witness to the resurrection and its reality and meaning, we can now see more clearly how some of these insights can be integrated into the Fourth Week contemplations, and can form part of the background out of which the director gives the 'short or summary explanation' (Exx 2), as a brief development of the points Ignatius suggests for the contemplations.

Ignatius's ordering of the appearances in 'The Mysteries of the Life of our Lord' appears to be chronological, except that the appearance to Paul is put before the ascension (Exx 299-312). Gilles Cusson thinks that Ignatius did this because his primary concern is always to consider facts in their relationship to revealed mystery; hence he proposes the ascension for our contemplation as the sign of our return to the Father.[14] Whether or not the ordering is deliberately chronological, Ignatius has in fact followed the general progression to be found in the gospel texts.

As the director becomes increasingly familiar with the biblical texts, and the particular aspect of the kerygma underlined in each, then he or she will find increasing ease in allowing this familiarity to become integral to the manner in which the points are given to the retreatant. In a similar way there needs to be an integration of the renewed theological understanding of the resurrection. This will help to make the basic credal formula, 'Jesus is Lord', come alive for the retreatant, bearing its full weight of meaning, as it did in the early Church. Further, a careful assimilation of these insights will assist in grasping more firmly the newness of the relationship which the resurrection establishes between the risen Christ and the Father, and the significance of this for the transformation of the world and the redeeming of human history.

The retreatant knows life is redeemed, changed; and through

prayer arising from these contemplations, there will be evoked what can be termed a resurrection-experience; that is, in some sense, an encounter with the risen Christ, developing the retreatant's faith in his living presence, and giving joy and consolation as accompaniments of this presence. It is possible for the modern retreatant to benefit, in prayer on the resurrection texts, by the knowledge that it is possible to encounter the risen Lord, in a way not at all dissimilar to that in which the disciples encountered the Lord after his resurrection. Further, if it is true that a dynamic operates in the Exercises, whereby the rhythm of the retreatant is united to the rhythm of Christ, then the retreatant's instinct for Christ will develop along the lines of entering more into the glory of the risen Christ in so far as this is given to him or her by the Father.

Finally, how do these insights help the retreatant in contemplating the appearances of the risen Christ? First, it must be said that there will always be an essential difference between the experience of those first apostolic witnesses and that of any other Christian. Nonetheless the retreatant can hope to come in contact with the unexpected, as the disciples did. To find that Jesus is risen, alive. The 'seeing', the recognition is recorded in the New Testament as a gift to those open to receive it; it seems to have been accompanied by an extraordinary peace and joy. The retreatant, in so far as he or she remains open, is disposed, can hope also to 'see' and be strengthened in faith, experiencing deep peace and joy. In contemplating the apparitions the retreatant will see how Magdalene is freed from despair, Peter from his remorse and the Emmaus disciples of their spiritual pessimism; and finally Thomas of his doubts. They will see, how Christ consoles, strengthens our faith and offers us freedom, life, joy and peace. These contemplations lead the retreatant back into daily life, where the comforting of Christ continues, as he gives us a share in his Spirit throughout our time of pilgrimage.

NOTES

1. Gilles Cusson SJ, *Biblical Theology and the Spiritual Exercises*, translated from *Pédagogie de l'expérience spirituelle personelle* by Mary Angela Roduit and George E. Ganss (St Louis, Institute of Jesuit Sources, 1988), p. 306.

2. Cusson, *Biblical Theology*, p. 307.

3. William A. Peters, SJ, *The Spiritual Exercises of St Ignatius: exposition and interpretation* (Jersey City, NJ., 1967), pp. 48-9.

4. R.H. Fuller, *The Formation of the Resurrection Narratives* (London 1970), p. 17.

5. See e.g., Gerald O'Collins SJ, *The Easter Jesus* (London 1973), pp. 8-9.

6. X. Léon-Dufour, SJ, *Resurrection and the Message of Easter* (London 1974), p. 138.

7. Fuller, *The Formation of the Resurrection Narratives*, p. 136.

8. O'Collins, *The Easter Jesus*, p. 73.

9. O'Collins, *The Easter Jesus*, p. 69.

10. Walter Kasper, *Jesus the Christ* (London 1976), pp. 139-40.

11. G.W.H. Lampe and D.M. MacKinnon, *The Resurrection* (London 1966), p. 33.

12. See the comment by Raymond E. Brown, *The Virginal Conception and the Bodily Resurrection of Jesus* (New York 1973), p. 125.

13. Brown, *The Virginal Conception*, p. 128.

14. Cusson, *Biblical Theology*, pp. 307-11.

CHAPTER ELEVEN
The Exercises in Daily Life
Martha Skinnider

Ignatius suggests in the nineteenth Annotation (Exx 19) that:

> One who is educated or talented, but engaged in public affairs or necessary business should take an hour and a half daily for the Spiritual Exercises. (Exx 19)

He considers that the full Exercises can be followed in the stream of life by one who because of public or business affairs cannot withdraw for the full thirty days. Yet he would limit the ability to do this to those of some intellectual standing with or without formal education.

He sees the Exercises in a modified form as valuable to a wider range of people. In Annotation 18 he makes this clear:

> The Spiritual Exercises must be adapted to the condition of the one who is to engage in them, that is, to his age, education and talent. Thus exercises that he could not bear, or from which he would derive no profit, should not be given to one with little natural ability or of little physical strength. (Exx 18)

He considers that nothing beyond the exercises of the First Week should be given 'to those of little natural ability or who are illiterate' (Exx 18).

This appears to have been the early practice in Ignatius's own lifetime. Francisco de Strada writes to Ignatius and Favre in 1539 from Siena:

> With respect to the Exercises, may I tell you that I gave them to four Sienese who came here to Montepulciano. I did not lose much time with them, since they were all very ordinary fellows, and in this I followed the rule of our own father. They all made a general confession and agreed that they had drawn great fruit from the Spiritual Exercises.[1]

Further on de Strada writes:

> I would like to tell you what the Exercises have been christened. They are

now called 'Purgation' or 'General Confession' and since this is more descriptive, they do not shrink from it as they do from 'Exercises'.[2]

This appears to be the limit expected of ordinary people. In the same year we hear of Favre in Parma preparing many people through the meditations of the First Week to make a general confession.[3]

As I live and work in a peripheral housing scheme in Glasgow – the equivalent of the inner-city – I did not expect to give the full 'Exercises in daily life'. Areas of multi-deprivation do not house the educated or talented 'engaged in public affairs or business'. Our housing scheme was built in the early 1950s for the families of unskilled and semi-skilled workers living in the over-crowded slum conditions of post-war Glasgow. Not much real planning was put into it. Over the years when better housing became available many moved out. As the particular area where we live was least popular, nobody wanted to live in it. We became an area where families with specific problems, or families who cannot cope, were housed because they had no choice.

Yet the community is still made up of a rich variety of people. There are those in their late fifties and sixties who came to the scheme when it was first built. Their early childhood and young adulthood had been spent in the grim poverty of the Glasgow of the depression and war years. They built up a real community here which in recent years they have had to watch break up. Those in their late thirties and forties have also contributed to the growth of the community and have witnessed its decline. They have known regular employment but now experience redundancy for themselves and unemployment for their teenage children as they leave school. Younger married couples, many of whom were brought up in the area, see living here as a temporary measure until better housing is available. They are bringing up young families on unemployment benefit or low wages with the threat of unemployment ever present.

Secondary education in these groups has been confined to two years post-primary or three years in a junior secondary school at a time of teacher shortage, or more recently four years in a comprehensive school. Among Catholics, except for the younger adults, the Bible is not known, and religious education stopped when they left school. Vatican II theology has had little impact on the majority.

132

As I live in the area I meet my neighbours as a neighbour in the streets, on the buses, at the shops, at residents' and parish group meetings. As we meet informally, I can be approached informally about the problems and anxieties of family life: a mother feels strangely empty and useless as her family begins to leave home; an active person finds difficulty in adjusting to a quieter life after a heart attack; a wife suffers from hyper-tension in her anxiety for a husband who cannot cope with redundancy; the young wife of a broken marriage struggles with the loneliness of her task of bringing up her family by herself – the ordinary anxieties of many people today.

Most often, all that is wanted is a listener, someone to take an interest. However, as I listened to people talking out their anxieties and problems, I suggested to a few of them that we take some time to learn to pray, to find God more in our lives. The suggestion was welcomed, particularly because I was not merely suggesting that we pray to God to remove the problem. What gave most hope was the suggestion that God could be found in the problem.

Those who accepted the offer committed themselves to coming to see me individually once a week for about an hour. It was necessary for each one to come to me, for there is little opportunity for a parent to have uninterrupted privacy in the family home. However, our house is in no quieter position than any other house in the area, and both the retreatant and I had early to learn to cope with conducting the interview amid the external noises of dogs, children and neighbours' televisions.

With each one I began by talking of her present life experience, not merely the present problem, and then we looked at some significant event where she had found God. Without formally working at a full faith history this normally sparked off a looking back at the most important life events, and a realization of God's presence in them. At the first meeting this was planted as a seed which grew and developed in the weeks following.

Prayer was introduced to the interview in one of the stillness exercises of *Sadhana*.[4] Both the retreatant and I relaxed and became still as we concentrated on our breathing, and shared with each other our experience of stillness. I introduced some *mantra* into the exercise – one that seemed natural to the retreatant. This was the total prayer content of the first interview.

I encouraged the repetition of this, where possible, each day for a short time during the following week. Being still for even five or ten minutes a day proved to be a gentle but powerful well-spring of awareness of God's presence in everyday life, and of a deeper appreciation of God's love and care. By the second interview I found that even such a small beginning was bearing fruit.

The early interviews had a simple pattern - listening to the ups and downs of daily life, more obviously now shot through with the awareness of God, to be followed by some stillness exercise.

When it seemed most appropriate for the retreatant at the second or later interview, I moved on to the contemplation of her 'joyful mysteries'.[5] Here she re-lived some peak experience of her life - actually feeling again the joy or the love first felt years ago. Once again I did the exercise with each one and shared my experience. This exercise quite naturally flowed into a prayer of thanksgiving.

I suggested that this be repeated each day at home. Sometimes the same joyful experience would be returned to and deepened; at other times different ones would be contemplated each day. In this way the seed of faith in God's presence in life increased its growth.

After one or two weeks spent in this contemplation I found it time to introduce a Scripture passage. It was not difficult to find one flowing from the retreatants' own prayer experience of the past few weeks. Obvious ones are Psalms 131 and 139 and Isaiah 43.1-7. I first of all lent a Bible until the retreatant could afford to buy one. At this point the passage is the important thing, so we found it, marked it by page number and verse, read it over to make sure there were no insuperable difficulties, but learned nothing about the Bible as a whole.

For the first two interviews after the introduction of Scripture both the retreatant and I prayed the passage during the interview and shared what we had experienced. This I find is the most helpful way of giving an introduction to *lectio divina*. The retreatant could then take a further passage to pray on during the week and report on this prayer at the next interview.

When a certain ease in this Scripture prayer had been established we moved on to Ignatian contemplation. As I have worked with mothers and grandmothers I find that the simplest and most natural introduction to Ignatian contemplation is through Mary's joyful mysteries. Each one has had the experience of contemplating her own joyful mysteries, which invariably are connected with childbirth and the early life of her own children. They can feel with Mary the joy and wonder of carrying the child; the joy of motherhood with its accompanying anxiety for the responsibility it brings. The first of these contemplations I shared with the retreatant, but after that each one was able to take one incident for prayer each week, reporting on it in the following interview.

We followed Mary in the early years of her motherhood, using passages from Luke's Gospel from the annunciation to the finding in the temple. By this time I would have introduced the retreatants to the beginning of the prayer period – the placing of oneself in the presence of God, the prayer for the grace sought, and the colloquy (without using that word). Almost without knowing it, over the weeks, the retreatant had begun to learn what repetition is, and was making a simple review of prayer.

During this introductory period we worked out what commitment could be given daily to prayer; where prayer could be made, and what was the most suitable time in the sense of what was possible and helpful.

When retreatants had covered all this and were at ease with it I moved on to a simple First Week theme of God's goodness to me, my poor response and God's loving mercy. As this involved moving round the Bible, we took some time to learn the difference between the Old and New Testaments, and the names of the writers of the four Gospels. It was helpful to know such a simple thing as the fact that the Gospels are at the back of the book and the Old Testament is at the front. I found that sufficient for general information. I could give any essential information on a passage at the interview.

I considered that this would be my goal – an 'Eighteenth Annotation' retreat. But as I came to this point with my first set of retreatants I realized that I was working with a group of people who were showing a great desire to be open to God. God was responding to that openness in their prayer and life and they in return were responding to God. Their desire was so strong that they could keep to a commitment to spend time daily in prayer in noisy surroundings and liable to family interruptions. Their only possible place for prayer is a bedroom. No one here can afford to heat bedrooms. Several prayed daily in their unheated bedrooms through the winter when the temperature dropped to fourteen degrees fahrenheit.

Considering this, and considering also that the retreatants showed ease in both *lectio divina* and Ignatian contemplation, that they had grown used to the simple Ignatian pattern of prayer, that they were able to organize their prayer during the week, and could report on it simply and clearly, I could see no reason why we should not undertake the full Exercises.

As my work sprang informally from people's life experience, my first group of retreatants were all at different stages, having begun at different times. When I judged the time appropriate for each one, I asked if they would like to follow a longer, planned series of prayer which would especially help them to find God in all things in their life. I gave them the title of the planned series: 'The Spiritual Exercises of St Ignatius'. The mention of St Ignatius drew no response. To my retreatants he was completely unknown as was also his order. As far as they were concerned they were following a planned way of prayer guaranteed by me. It was with this assurance that my first group launched into the full Exercises.

The commitment was a period of prayer each day. The aim was half an hour, but in the stream of family life the full time could not be guaranteed. Over and above this was the commitment to the weekly interview. During the nine months we took to complete the Exercises some interviews had to be missed, usually because the director had to be away. Even when I had to miss two interviews, the retreatants were able to cope with prayer on their own and keep a record of two weeks' prayer.

The interview followed the pattern established in our introductory weeks, except that now we set aside at least an hour and a half. I had more instruction to give - simple background to Scripture texts and explanation of the text of the Exercises themselves. Retreatants had shown that they could cope with meditation and contemplation of Scripture, but working with the text of the Exercises was new.

This I found, however, offered no difficulty - whether the Puhl translation was used or the Fleming.[6] Retreatants borrowed the book of the Exercises when any specific text was being used in prayer, with the proviso that they read only the appropriate section.

The only Ignatian texts I have hesitated to use are those of the First Week, as they come so early in a new undertaking. I paraphrased them and supplemented them with Scripture readings. We began the Exercises with some introductory prayer highlighting the main points of the Principle and Foundation; then in the light of each retreatant's prayer we looked at the text of the Principle and Foundation. From the Kingdom meditation onwards to the Contemplation to Attain Divine Love all texts were used from the book of the Exercises with no Scripture to supplement them. The retreatants prayed on the text alone. Time was taken during the interview to read them over and explain any difficulties without in any way interpreting the text for the retreatant.

The Ignatian text is basically simple; its images, although of an early age, are clear, and rather than posing a difficulty to retreatants proved helpful. There was a difference in the retreatants' infancy contemplations made after reading Ignatius's text on the incarnation, compared to their early infancy prayer of the introductory weeks. The imagery of the Two Standards, instead of reinforcing older attitudes to sin, revealed to the retreatants how evil was tempting them through good.

I have found it most important to keep everything simple. I gave no background reading, as this can be muddling to those not used to much reading and not familiar with the Bible. One text per week, either a Scripture passage or a text from the Exercises, was found to be most helpful. We did not seem to lose anything of the depth of prayer in this way, rather we gained. I found that it was important to have a narrow focus in prayer; a broader one could dissipate effort and become overwhelming. As retreatants grew at ease in the Exercises I saw the week's prayer move gently to its still point by the end of the week. With any more than one text we would not have reached this.

If there is not great ease in using books among the retreatants, there is less ease in making notes. At first, therefore, while reporting could be done from recall, I did not ask for any writing. I waited until there was some difficulty in remembering and suggested making notes after the review. This made the writing an aid to memory and not an end in itself.

It may be asked if, with these limitations, I can be sure we were really following the full Exercises. Of this I am certain, because of the unerring way in which the prayer of each retreatant moved - different for each individual within the same general movement.

When I undertook to direct others in the Exercises in daily life, I had the simple belief that my work would be merely 'to permit the

Creator to deal directly with the creature, and the creature directly with his Creator and Lord' (Exx 16). Otherwise I would not have had the courage to undertake the task. I discovered this to be true. It was as if I was working a computer. I gave my message to the retreatant whose powers to receive it were very simple. Then it was for me to watch as the programme unfolded, quite out of proportion to my little input and her power to receive. Women who knew nothing of the intellectual concepts of spirituality, nothing of Ignatian spirituality and little even of the Bible found wonder in the Principle and Foundation, in the realization that all of life is gift, and that God loves each of them uniquely. They desired to respond to that love.

During the prayer of the First Week the revelation of what sin really is and of their own sinfulness overwhelmed them, as they have normally considered sin in individual actions, and on the whole considered themselves 'all right' - not really sinners. However, the revelation that, at the same time, God loves each of them in spite of that sinfulness helped them to realize just how gratuitous this love is and yet how steadfast. This gave them in varying degrees a trust in that love which enabled them to offer to follow Jesus in the Kingdom meditation and to carry out that following in the prayer of the Second Week.

During the prayer of the Second Week each one learned gradually more of what was involved in that following. In the prayer of the Two Standards, the Three Classes of Men, and the Three Kinds of Humility each one discovered what choice God wanted her to make in her life. As none could change her state in life, and none had been living a really evil life, the choices they were asked to make were subtle but important changes of attitude: the realization that they judged others from a Pharisaical standpoint; the letting go of the desire that they do work for God - their work, but rather allowing God to work through them - God's work.

In the Third Week their prayer automatically became a being with Jesus in his suffering and a seeing of his suffering continuing in the world today.

In the Fourth Week they did experience the Risen Christ and with this came a fuller realization of his presence in the world today, particularly his presence in others. The Contemplation to Attain Divine Love, which closes the Exercises, gathered together all that had come to them in their prayer and life experience of finding God in all things - a looking back, and a looking forward in deep trust and love to a life changed by the experience of the Exercises.

We studied this movement as the Exercises progressed, taking time at the end of each stage to look back over this prayer to see what had been happening in it, why we were ready to move on, and in what direction we were moving. In this way the retreatants were aware of the movement not only in their prayer but in their life. For as throughout the Exercises their prayer affected their lives so also did their life experience affect their prayer. When the Exercises were completed, we spent at least three interviews looking back at what had happened in the whole experience.

It follows naturally that from the experience of the Exercises the retreatants learned a new theology - a new way of looking at God and creation, or rather God in creation. The most valuable thing about this theology is that it has not been learned intellectually but experienced personally. It is not something to be known but to be lived.

In finding a God present in the whole of creation, loving individuals just as they are, they discovered a freeing truth that they cannot earn their own salvation: everything is gift. The important thing is not what they can do for God, but what God can do in and through them. They discovered the true humanity of Jesus - that he had to discern his Father's will. They realized that he did suffer and that he gave himself up in faith and trust to his Father. Because of this they can find him in the suffering, the helpless and hopeless - in all the agony of this world. Because they have experienced his resurrection as the outcome of his suffering they now have a quiet but deep hope.

To one retreatant in particular who had never heard of the doctrine of the Mystical Body, the knowledge of the union of each of us in the Risen Christ has become a real force in her life. She experiences this oneness not just in Catholics, not even just in Christians, but in all whom she meets.

From this has come a deep change in attitudes. The inner security, which has grown from the acceptance of oneself as loved and valued as one is, has fostered an acceptance of those who hold different ideas or who have different standards; a greater understanding of teenagers in a family; a fuller appreciation and deepening love for a husband. A growing stillness within has given a better ability to cope with family crises. With this change of attitude there has grown a desire to help others, not by giving things to those who cannot cope, but rather by supporting them in their own efforts. Those who have been mere passengers in the parish have become active in its life. Of course the Exercises have not produced ready-made saints. These changes are merely growing from deep roots, and the daily examen of consciousness helps to encourage the growth.

After-care can be continued in the stream of life. Most of it can be informal. Retreatants and director still live near each other, still meet in daily life. If we really believe that we find God in all things, what would normally be called spiritual direction can take place as we meet in the supermarket, at the shopping centre or in the street.

Throughout this article for convenience I have used the terms 'director' and 'retreatants'. This is not the real relationship; we are friends and neighbours. I prefer to see myself as a companion - a companion on the way. Moreover, as I receive so much from those that I accompany, I consider they are valued companions with me on my way.

Already I have a working companion. The greatest desire of one retreatant - Anne - is to share the gift she has been given by helping others through the Exercises. Already she has begun simple Eighteenth Annotation work with one person. The retreatant is a fellow worker who noted the change wrought in Anne as she worked through the Exercises. Anne has no anxiety about undertaking this, because if God worked through me to reach her, God can use her to reach her friend. I accompany Anne as she accompanies her retreatant.

Who are the Exercises in daily life for? It is obviously for those who cannot afford the time or money to withdraw to a retreat house for thirty full days. But I cannot say that it is only for those who are talented or educated. I have not found that to follow the Exercises in daily life demands an academic education, an ease in handling books, any knowledge of the Bible or of theology. I have found that they can be given to 'very ordinary' people (Exx 18). But with these ordinary abilities there must be the desire to open oneself to God and God's will in one's life. It is the strength of that desire that enables anyone to undertake the six or nine months' commitment and to be steadfast in that commitment.

Our area may not be rich in academic education or intellectual ability, but it is rich in the life experience of its people. None have lived sheltered lives or particularly easy ones. Our main support has been in each other, and even now as 'an area of multiple deprivation' mutual care and concern still thrive in a deteriorating situation. For such people, Catholic or non-Catholic, the Spiritual Exercises are a simple instrument to enable them to be aware of God in their lives, and to enable them to express that awareness.

The answer to our question then is simple. The Nineteenth Annotation is for 'very ordinary' people (Exx 18) who cannot afford time or money to withdraw for thirty days, but who have a deep desire to open themselves to God in their lives, and to do God's will.

NOTES

1. George Schurhammer, *Francis Xavier, his life and times* (Rome 1973), vol. 1, p. 514.

2. ibid.

3. ibid., p. 527.

4. Anthony de Mello, *Sadhana, a way to God* (Gujarat Sahitya Prakash and St Louis, Institute of Jesuit Sources), pp. 22, 23.

5. de Mello, *Sadhana*, p. 65.

6. cf. *The Spiritual Exercises of St Ignatius*, trans. by Louis J. Puhl (Chicago 1951), and David L. Fleming, *The Spiritual Exercises of St Ignatius: a literal translation and a contemporary reading* (St Louis 1978).

PART THREE

Prayer and Discernment

CHAPTER TWELVE

Ignatian Contemplation Today

John F. Wickham

The renewal of contemplative prayer is spreading to more and more people, and thus proving its relevance. Perhaps, in view of the desires for social justice re-awakening in the Church, as well as a new sense of the public (political, economic, social) dimensions of faith, it is time to reflect on the direction which this prayer-movement ought to take in the future. My exploration of this fairly complex question is limited to 'Ignatian' contemplation as described in the *Spiritual Exercises*: a traditional form of imaginative presence to the mysteries of the gospel as popularized by St Ignatius.

By 'mystery' here is meant any story-unit of Scripture in which God is acting in human history. Examples are the 'mysteries' of the rosary or those presented in the medieval mystery plays and religious paintings. A lengthy list of them is given in nos 261-312 of the *Spiritual Exercises*. Ignatius best describes the method of entering into these mysteries in his detailed discussion of the Nativity (Exx 110-17). In addition to 'seeing the persons', 'hearing what they are saying' and 'considering what they are doing', he suggests: 'I will make myself a poor little unworthy slave, and as though present, look upon them, contemplate them, and serve them in their needs with all possible homage and reverence' (Exx 114-16).

The mystery thus becomes an action of God which is going on now; and in this method of prayer I make myself present through my imagination (however it suits me to do that), but in such a way that I may actually take part in what occurs. 'Reverence' - a specifically Ignatian word - describes the right attitude of one who is in the presence of a divine mystery. It avoids the extreme of utter prostration which would inhibit personal involvement, and the other extreme of carelessness which would mean that one misses the transcendent power of God's presence. The particular mystery becomes real for the person praying - it is actualized for him or her at that moment in its eternal significance. It follows that the individual should become personally present by imaginatively taking part - through some contribution - in what is going on. Experience proves that this might also be realized by 'identifying' with one or other of the persons involved in the mystery.

It should be emphasized that the mysteries in question are not to be merely reconstructed by an imaginary return to the past, and entered into by a sort of movie-making effort. This is not, in fact, how people who contemplate them actually experience the mysteries. Because Christ is risen, all his mysteries somehow partake in his eternal now, and become really present to the person at prayer. However difficult it may be to explain this fact logically, the fact itself has long been recognized in the feasts of the liturgy. Christmas is more than the remembering of an ancient birth: it is that birth itself made real among us now; and at Easter we say not merely that Jesus arose from the dead long ago, but that he is risen today in our midst. In the same way, all the other mysteries of Scripture are realized in the now of prayer, and retreatants may experience the sacred events as actually happening to them.

What has been said so far, of course, merely describes the method of disposing oneself for prayer, and not the prayer proper. The divine Lord may communicate in some quiet or some unexpected manner (or may withhold a tangible sense of presence for a time). The prayer itself is experienced as what is received by the one who is entering into prayer. All the person can do is try to be well disposed: that is, to be receptive to whatever the Lord may give.

I have been describing the elements of Ignatian contemplation in order to lead into the more crucial matter of social and public involvement. The usual discussion confines itself to two main movements: (a), the person praying enters into the mystery by becoming imaginatively receptive; (b), the divine Lord enters actively into the depths of the one praying (God communicates God's own life to him or her).

I wish now to introduce two factors which, in effect, extend and complete their significance. These are: (c) that the one praying should carry an awareness of the whole life-world into the mystery; (d) so that God in the power of the mystery may pour divine life into the life-world of the one praying. My argument is that, if (c) and (d) are not allowed for in Ignatian contemplation today, the original aim and function of this sort of prayer will probably not be realized.

The reason is simply that in our day (a) and (b) can too easily become confined within a merely private and subjective realm. The object of stressing (c) and (d) is to attempt to break out of the withdrawn spirituality of our time, and to make more explicit the public meanings that otherwise remain latent and implicit in personal prayer. And this should begin at the very core relationship of Christians with God.

St Ignatius was, of course, very careful to insist upon the entirely concrete realization of such contemplations, but he did so in a manner and terminology proper to his age, when our modern difficulties of privatization and existentialist subjectivity were not pressing. At the conclusion of each 'point' in his directions for contemplating the incarnation and the nativity, Ignatius goes out of his way to emphasize what I have proposed to call the retreatant's 'life-world':

> I will reflect upon this to draw profit from what I see (Exx 106). Finally, I will reflect upon all I hear to draw profit from their words (107). Then I shall reflect upon all this to draw some fruit from each of these details (108).
> Then I will reflect on myself that I may reap some fruit (114) . . . and then to reflect on myself and draw some fruit from it (115).
> . . . and all this for me.
> Then I will reflect and draw some spiritual fruit from what I have seen (116).

Until fairly recently, these expressions, 'reflect', 'draw profit', 'reap fruit', were taken to refer to supplementary activities of a meditative sort: that is, they were interpreted as efforts of reason and of will in applying the lessons of the prayer-subject to one's individual life. I believe that this interpretation is a serious distortion.

Ignatius has not forgotten that he is dealing with a method of contemplative prayer in which personal insertion in the mysteries by means of the imagination is the appropriate way of disposing oneself. Certainly, the remarks quoted above make clear how eager he is that the retreatant should feel the full effects of the mystery upon his or her personal life-world. The same would be said, for example, about the application of the senses: at the end of each 'point', Ignatius again insists on the need to reflect and to draw fruit (Exx 122-5); and yet this is surely not the place for acts of reasoning and of willing, but rather for immersing one's whole self in the consolations already received. It should be added that Ignatius uses similar expressions in the points for contemplations on the passion (Exx 194), and in the Contemplation to Attain the Love of God (Exx 234-7).

Perhaps our difficulty with these expressions used by Ignatius comes from the deep divisions in our own cultural world: divisions between private and public realms, between the individual and social aspects of life, between subjective and objective experiences. While these disjunctions were not unknown in the time of Ignatius, they were very far from being institutionalized in his culture in the way in which they tend to be in our own. What I mean is simply that Ignatius could take it for granted that what a person felt inwardly would at once reverberate through social relations. In his day, personal and social were concretely known as one.

This difference between the cultural worlds of St Ignatius and of our own time can perhaps be most vividly seen in late medieval and Renaissance paintings of gospel mysteries. The persons in each mystery are often dressed like fifteenth-century men and women. Sometimes the patron of the picture, or even the painter himself, is humbly and reverently present in the mystery. In background scenery, sometimes medieval ploughmen are seen at work in the fields, or Renaissance ladies and gentlemen travelling down the roads.

In short, anachronism was no problem in those times, because the main intention of the artist was to realize each mystery in his or her own life-world. The power of each divine mystery did not make itself felt merely by transforming the secret inner soul of the individual person at prayer and remaining hidden in those depths, but rather by flooding into the social, public world where alone each individual could be realized as a person. Ignatius did not need to mention these facts: no one would expect anything else in his day. When he urges me, therefore, to reflect on myself and to draw profit from each detail of the mystery, he of course assumes the public impact of divine action in the world, and wants to make sure that I personally do not evade its influence.

Consider the following conversation, from Shakespeare's *Macbeth*, in which two minor characters talk about the impact of the secret murder of King Duncan:

OLD MAN: Threescore and ten I can remember well;
Within the volume of which time I have seen
Hours dreadful, and things strange, but this sore night
Hath trifled former knowledge.

ROSSE: Ha, good Father,
Thou seest the heavens, as troubled with man's act,
Threaten his bloody stage: by the clock 'tis day,
And yet dark night strangles the travelling lamp.
Is't night's predominance, or the days' shame,
That darkness does the face of earth entomb,
When living light should kiss it?

OLD MAN: 'Tis unnatural,
Even like the deed that's done. On Tuesday last,
A falcon, towering in her pride of place,
Was by a mousing owl hawked at, and killed.

ROSSE: And Duncan's horses (a thing most strange and certain)
Beauteous and swift, the minions of their race,
Turned wild in nature, broke their stalls, flung out,
Contending 'gainst obedience, as they would make
War with mankind.

This was written more than a generation after the death of Ignatius; and yet it still clearly assumes that any important event, even if secretly done, will at once have noticeable effects at every level of public life. The normal direction of interior motions, in fact, is outward into the external world. A dagger in the heart will put blood on the moon.

It was much later that Galileo and Descartes began to urge the separation of 'objective' and measurable dimensions from interior feelings and 'subjective' sensations. Furthermore, it was only in the eighteenth century that the habit of extracting general or universal truths from the mysteries became popular. From that century, 'reflection' has tended to mean a standing back and an exercise of conscious reasoning to formulate abstract propositions that would belong equally to everyone, and of a conscious willing to apply universal truths to one's particular case.

All this is quite foreign, I believe, to the intentions of St Ignatius in the Spiritual Exercises. For him, reflection was understood in the more elementary sense of letting the light of truth shine upon the life of the one contemplating. When he said, 'Reflect and draw fruit',

149

he could assume a natural and direct impact of the divine mystery in the public life-world of each person: that was not his concern. His problem was the prior one: how to make sure of a personal involvement in the divine mystery. Once that individual response was obtained, once the mystery was allowed to have a bearing on the person's life, the public consequences were certain to follow.

In our cultural situation, on the other hand, the opposite results may be expected in those who have already been deeply affected by the popular forms of existentialism and analogous cultural movements. They will very easily take the mystery 'personally': that is, individually and privately. It is the social and public outflow that is usually blocked off.

For us, whatever is most meaningful in subjective terms seems, for that very reason, to be alien to the institutional forms of public life. A strongly reinforced dividing wall has been erected between subjective experiences, however powerfully felt, and the social implementation of their seemingly obvious consequences. So long as the meaning of 'social' is restricted to inter-personal and inter-subjective realms, the effects will easily flow. But as soon as 'social' is extended to public structures, the cultural gap or division tends to prevent any further influence.

Very often this has reached the proportions of fatalism. The political and economic world appears to be controlled by such powerful alien forces that no relationship between 'in here' and 'out there' seems possible. Ignatius, were he to return today to help us adapt his Exercises to current needs, would likely spend a good deal of time marvelling at the peculiarity of our ways. After he had grown used to us, he would probably warn us energetically against misinterpretations of his meaning.

He would urge us in particular, I believe, to put the emphasis today on bringing with us, into our contemplation of the divine mysteries, our whole life-world, the concrete reality of our social and political existence. The purpose of this imaginative effort to dispose ourselves aright in prayer is that the power of the Lord's divine initiatives, as received in our prayer experiences, may not be intercepted and turned merely inward, but rather pour itself into the public sphere and make itself felt in the social realities of our time.

What will this amount to in practice? To discover this, it will help to note the difference between the level of direct experiences in prayer and the level of interpretation of those experiences. When it comes to interpretation, a whole range of new difficulties arise from the conservative, liberal, radical or reactionary bent of retreatants, their ideological approach to the issues lurking in their life-situation. While I am convinced that ideologies are inescapable for Christians in their public life today, I cannot begin to deal with that important question here. The level of interpreting prayer experiences belongs to the review of prayer, to interview with a director, and in fact both to longer-range preparations for retreat and to a later pondering on the whole series of repeated prayer-periods. I wish to limit my discussion here to the prior, more elementary level of direct experiences themselves, and to seek a basic openness which will enable the retreatant to move freely about in the public realm rather than become confined to the inter-subjective and private realm from the start.

With these limitations to our discussion, we can say that at the level of directly experiencing the divine initiatives in prayer, where there is genuine openness to the public realm of the praying person – whatever ideological commitments may in fact be influential with that individual – then the power of the incarnate mysteries ought in concrete fashion to shape or motivate or illuminate the person's life-world.

What, then, might this 'concrete fashion' be like? Let me take the example of an Ignatian contemplation: the episode of the calming of the storm in Mark 4 (35-41).

Let us assume that I am a business executive currently embroiled in a dispute over new income distribution policies to be adopted by my firm. This conflict has been upsetting me both at the office and at home. Because my own level of income is directly involved, not only has my standard of living in a highly inflationary situation become uncertain, but my future role in the company will be affected by whatever decision is taken.

If my prayer experiences are restricted to the private realm, perhaps I will sense the storm in the boat, as I take my place alongside the sleeping Lord's disciples, to be nothing more than the upset feelings that I tend to take out on my spouse after work. Perhaps I will recognize the storm as fears disturbing my inner peace, or exaggerated anger directed at my children's petty

151

behaviour at home. I might well experience a consoling peace, when Christ awakes to rebuke the wind and waves and to remind the followers how firmly they ought to trust him. I could easily respond with real confidence in the Lord's dominion over my inner anxieties. Jesus is here the master in the sense of one who enables a disturbed person to find 'peace of soul'.

But all this prayer, in itself very good, has clearly been channelled into the realm of subjectivity alone. The interior confidence gained would indirectly influence my way of relating to my spouse and children and even my private dealings with business partners. It would not, however, bear directly on the public issues of my family's attitudes towards their material standard of living, and of my company's decisions on income distribution policy. Such areas of contention are usually excluded from prayer; and I am suggesting here that they ought not to be excluded. Our whole life-world is relevant to the mysteries of Christ, and the divine power incarnate in our midst ought to flow freely into the full concreteness of that public existence.

I should insist again that the ideological questions raised for interpretation of these prayer experiences cannot truly disappear even if we dislike them. When ignored, they become even more enslaving, they bind our hands behind our backs. Whether we wish it or not, the Lord is nudging us today into the public realm. The gospel of Jesus must make itself felt in our actual world; otherwise through our intransigence, it will be relegated to the back rooms of power, and silently listed with what is easily controlled by others.

Should the contemplation be entered into with an entire openness to the public realm, then (in the example given) the storm is felt not merely internally in private or subjective areas, but as blowing strongly in the social, political and economic fields of life. And Jesus who sleeps awhile can be awakened by our own concern. He is Lord of that public storm and not merely of our inner states. He commands the winds of consumer exploitation and the waves of political oppression. His word of rebuke to the storm reveals to us personally, not of course any removal of the issues from our lives, but the ways in which blocks to public commitment, doubts about the value of the struggle, depression over reverses, resentments against differing views, and every other stay to involvement in the public realm, can be overcome by the power of the gospel.

One objection should perhaps be mentioned. It could be said that a retreat by definition, and even contemplative prayer in the everyday situation, implies a withdrawal from the cares and concerns of ordinary life. The proposal to open them more firmly to the public realm, because it appears to reverse this direction, would therefore seem to make prayer more difficult. To this it should be answered that the 'apartness' of prayer must always be maintained: not the actual circumstances of daily cares and concerns, but a consciousness of their deeper reality and meaning should be brought to prayer apart. What is desired today is that the person in full awareness of the concrete life-world may be brought into the presence of divine mystery. What is opposed to this is the tendency to turn 'apartness' into 'withdrawal' from consciousness of the real situation of our public lives.

Naturally, the questions mentioned so briefly here are large ones, and new emphases in prayer alone will not make them go away. But amid a wide range of efforts to tackle the larger problems of our day, this matter of our special orientation during the quiet moments of contemplation cannot be neglected. After all, it is often 'in prayer apart' that God enters our lives, converts our hearts and begins to renew our real existences. The question here is to remove blocks in our earliest dispositions, blocks that might from the very start prevent God's operations from having their proper effect.

CHAPTER THIRTEEN

The Ignatian Examen

Donald St Louis

The sixteenth-century world of Ignatius Loyola was one of profound change and upheaval, in which the Church, long the centre and stabilizing force of a united Christendom, was experiencing tensions and challenges from both within and without. In this context, Ignatius's vision was of a new style of religious life that would be free to be more actively responsive to the multiple and diverse needs of the Church, and so the apostolic body he founded differed from the religious institutes which had preceded the Society of Jesus. Ignatius sought to form a group of prayerful, highly-disciplined and well-trained men poised in availability for mission. Mobility was to be a key: 'It is according to our vocation to travel to any part of the world where there is hope of God's greater service and the help of souls.'[1]

From beginning to end, Ignatius's ideal was love and service, a love which makes itself known in deeds.[2] God's glory in apostolic service was ever the measure and the norm, that towards which all else was focused and in terms of which decisions and choices were made. Thus Ignatius and his men would leave the seclusion of traditional religious communities for a life of active engagement in the world. Contemplation and action were not enemies for Ignatius: he was a mystic, but his was a mysticism of service and action.[3] And if active ministry was to be the arena in which to seek and find God, then reflection on one's experiences of ministry would be critically important for Ignatius. In both his personal spirituality and in his direction and guidance, whether of religious or others, it is clear how important for Ignatius was the practice of prayerfully reflecting on one's experience of service. To this end, 'he seemed to count primarily on the examens of conscience from which he never dispensed',[4] and 'on which [he] laid more stress and considered of greater importance than meditation'.[5]

There can be little doubt but that Ignatius saw the Examen as a central element of the spirituality of his new body of active religious, and succeeding generations of religious and others have inherited the Examen as a practice of piety. But, Ignatius's clear and prominent valuing of this method of prayer notwithstanding, the experience of most people is that it is the first thing to be abandoned as an irrelevant interruption in a life of committed, active ministry. This very fact would seem to betray a fundamental misunderstanding of what Ignatius intended this prayer to be.

My thesis is that rather than the moralistic exercise in self-scrutiny that it has become for many people, Ignatius saw the Examen fundamentally as a prayer of discernment, a vitally illuminating and dynamic experience of prayerful reflection that both celebrates and enhances one's awareness of and response to the Lord who is ever-present in our human experience. In the language of contemporary pastoral theological literature, it is what is commonly called a method of theological reflection on ministry.[6]

Ignatius was no literary stylist, a fact which may well contribute to a misunderstanding of the Examen. Avery Dulles and Harvey Egan have both argued that for a seminal thinker such as Ignatius, whose theology was essentially pastorally based, it is important to examine his writings in the light of the total 'horizon' within which he represents his approach.[7] Such is certainly the case with the Examen, whose five points, tersely and laconically stated, reflect a wealth of pastoral experience and profound spiritual insight that becomes apparent only when one sees them in the context of the larger sweep of Ignatius's spiritual theology.

Accordingly, what follows is an effort to explicate the rich and profound vision of this prayer of reflection by viewing the Examen in the context of the Exercises, relating the five 'points' to aspects of Ignatius's doctrine and practice as developed in the various weeks of the Spiritual Exercises as a whole.

THE FIRST POINT

The first point is to give thanks to God our Lord for the favours received. (Exx 43)

This first point establishes the Ignatian Examen as an existential, experientially-focussed experience. Having learned during his months

155

at Manresa to attend carefully to his own inner experiences as the graced context for encounter with the divine, Ignatius thus begins this prayer with where one is, which includes a reflective awareness of the events, circumstances, relationships and experiences that have shaped one's history and led to this present moment of self-awareness before God. What is important here is not an exhaustive list of 'the favours received', but rather a deepening sense of one's life as richly blessed by God, as suffused with the gracious presence and action of God (cf. Exx 230-7).

If Ignatian spirituality is one of 'finding God in all things', this presupposes, of course, that God is present and involved in all of reality. Clearly, Ignatius is no deist. His God is vitally, dynamically active, an emphasis in Ignatian thought that is clearly evidenced in the Exercises, and which becomes an underlying presupposition for the entirety of his spiritual doctrine. As seen in the Exercises, the God of Ignatius freely, deliberately and compassionately chooses to enter into the fullness of the human condition in all its poverty, weakness and sin (Exx 103, 116), and in all its historical particularity (Exx 103), inviting the retreatant to labour with God in companionship for the liberation and salvation of this world, in order to share with God in the joy and freedom of God's victory (Exx 95).

This active presence of God is also highlighted in the Contemplation to Attain the Love of God which both caps the Exercises and also recapitulates all that has gone before.[8] Here, Ignatius would have us consider 'how God dwells in creatures . . .' (Exx 235) and 'how God labours for me in all creatures upon the face of the earth . . .' (Exx 236). For Ignatius, this God who is so present and active labours precisely in order to lavish on us divine gifts in a reciprocity of love, for 'love consists in a mutual sharing of goods . . .' (Exx 231).

Ignatius has the retreatant consider these gifts not only in a global way, but in all their concreteness (Exx 233, 234, 237), again emphasizing that God is present and active in all reality at every moment. As the individual becomes progressively aware of this active, generous divine presence, the stance becomes one of humble thanksgiving. And gratitude in turn yields to still deeper levels of awareness, to new depths of openness to encounter the gracious presence and action of God in one's present and future.[9]

Our giftedness by God is the heart of the Principle and

Foundation (Exx 23), Ignatius's presupposed world-view for a committed Christian,[10] and it is also the reason for its eventual inclusion in the Exercises. In this sense, the first point of the Examen may be seen as a summary of the Principle and Foundation, a reminder of who one is before the living God in all the graced concreteness and uniqueness of one's personal history, and with such an awareness leading to a deepening gratitude and desire to respond in ways that are increasingly 'more conducive to the end for which we are created' (Exx 23).

THE SECOND POINT

> The second point is to ask for grace to know my sins and to rid myself of them. (Exx 43)

Having become more consciously and reflectively aware of one's self as gifted by God through the first point of the Examen, one now seeks light. For Ignatius, this is a profound opening of one's life and spirit to the illumination of God's own spirit. Hence, Ignatius is not interested merely in gathering data, nor in an introspective preoccupation with the self; the focus *is* the self, but the self as experienced in the presence of God, moving toward greater authenticity as responsive to the divine initiative. Ignatius seeks that illumination which leads beyond mere information to freedom: 'to know my sins *and* to rid myself of them'.

This dual grace petitioned here – 'to know . . . and to rid myself' – echoes the purpose of the Exercises as a whole (cf. Exx 21) and also exemplifies an often-repeated pattern of petitioning in the Exercises. Knowledge, as an object of Ignatian petition, is never an end in itself, but is always a means of moving to deepening freedom. One asks to know and understand precisely in order to choose more freely. Note, for example, the petitions of the contemplation on the incarnation:

> This is to ask for what I desire. Here it will be to ask for an intimate knowledge of our Lord, who has just become man for me, that I may love him more closely. (Exx 104)

Similarly, the petition of the meditation on Two Standards:

> Here it will be to ask for a knowledge of the deceits of the rebel chief and

help to guard myself against them; and also to ask for a knowledge of the true life exemplified in the sovereign and true Commander, and the grace to imitate him. (Exx 139)

These petitions become the recurring prayer patterns throughout the Second Week of the Exercises, as knowledge of Christ becomes the source of deepening illumination and the touchstone of deepening personal authenticity and freedom, for the mystery of oneself is illuminated in the mystery of Christ as one contemplates the events of his life, seeking to 'put on the mind and heart of Christ' (Phil. 2.5).

Finally, this same petition pattern is seen in the Contemplation to Attain the Love of God:

> Here it will be to ask for an intimate knowledge of the many blessings received that, filled with gratitude for all, I may in all things love and serve the Divine Majesty. (Exx 233)

For Ignatius, then, the petition for light is a prayer for the grace of a discerning heart, for a deepening connaturality with the Spirit and heart of Christ. Ignatius's Rules for the Discernment of Spirits help to provide some specific criteria and hermeneutical principles for identifying and interpreting the action of God and the enemy (i.e., the Two Standards as existentially experienced in one's own life), to detect the subtle interplay of grace and selfishness that weave into the fabric of one's response to the grace-gift of God.

THE THIRD POINT

> The third point is to demand an account of my soul from the time of rising up to the present examination. I should go over one hour after another, one period after another. The thoughts should be examined first, then the words, and finally the deeds. (Exx 43)

The two-fold grace prayed for in the second point of the Examen – 'to know . . . and to rid myself' – and its rootedness in the purpose of the Exercises and the petition patterns should make it clear that the review called for in the third point is not simply an informative listing of what one has done well or poorly since the last Examen. Rather, it is a search for that understanding which leads to purification of choice. 'The operative questions are: what has been happening in us, how has the Lord been working in us, what has he been asking of us. And only secondarily are our own actions to be considered.'[11]

Thus, rather than a preoccupation with self, this review is primarily a focus on the 'epiphanies'[12] of God, those often subtle yet persistent ways in which the divine seeks to reveal itself in and through one's experiences. The uniqueness of one's own life provides the setting for this review and translates the images of the Exercises into here and now reality: e.g., one seeks to understand how the Lord has been calling in the 'synagogues, villages and towns' of one's own world of experience, and whether one has been 'deaf to his call' or 'prompt and diligent to accomplish his most holy will' (Exx 91). How has one's life progressed in that characteristically Ignatian movement from knowledge to love to service (Exx 104)? How has the drama of the Two Standards been played out in one's life, and how have choices and actions surfaced attitudes and subtleties of response as in the Three Classes of Men and the Three Degrees of Humility (Exx 149-57; 165-8)? The very pattern of reflection suggested by Ignatius (thoughts, words, deeds) is not so much meant to suggest a formally structured approach as the pattern of consideration in the contemplation of the Second Week. Rather it points to the human experience (cf. Exx 106, 107, 108). What does the totality of one's life-experience say in response to God?

The recognition of patterns in one's experience as a means to achieving greater freedom is reflected quite clearly as a central concern of the Rules for Discernment of Spirits, especially those of the Second Week. Ignatius exhorts the retreatant to 'observe carefully the whole course of our thoughts . . . beginning, middle and end . . .' (Exx 333), to trace their progression, to note the connections, to become more familiar with the subtleties of one's characteristic snares and delusions (cf. Exx 344). Ignatius takes care that nothing be lost, that one learn from experience, even the experience of temptation, sin and infidelity. All is potentially a rich source of that knowledge and understanding which leads to deepening freedom and growing capacity for commitment to the Lord who calls. Hence, the importance of this type of reflection for Ignatius. One makes progress as one becomes more nuanced in interpreting the language of one's inner movements: the patterns, the recurring themes, issues and images – those characteristic ways one is moved by God, self, the enemy.

Accordingly, though the focus is the self, it is not an irretrievably interior focus: it is on self as becoming more authentic under the impulse of God's gracious activity, the self as responsive to the divine initiative towards companionship in service. The Principle and Foundation[13] provides Ignatius's implicit definition of the authentic human person as one who is free precisely in order to respond in a mutuality of love. And so the heart of this review is an effort to answer the questions: how has one responded to that divine love which seeks to share itself in mutuality (Exx 231)? And how have the concrete details of one's life authenticated one's love by drawing it beyond words to more fruitful action (Exx 230)?

THE FOURTH POINT

> The fourth point will be to ask pardon of God our Lord for my faults. (Exx 43)

The movement through the first three points of the Examen – from memory of God's gracious gifts, to prayer for deeper and more sensitive awareness, to seeing in one's most recent history the action of the Lord – inevitably leads to a deepening experience and awareness of the inadequacy of one's response to the initiative of the Lord. Hence, the fourth point: to seek forgiveness.

The Ignatian attitude towards the recognition of one's sin and responsibility in the sin of the world is perhaps best and classically reflected in the famous colloquy of the First Exercise of the First Week (Exx 53). Note here, as seen above in the third point of the Examen, that the focus is *first* on the Lord ('Imagine Christ our Lord . . .') *secondly* on the self as responsive ('I shall also reflect upon myself . . .'). The grace Ignatius would have the retreatant seek in the First Week of the Exercises – in which one reflects on the mystery of sin in the world and in one's personal life – is the experience of oneself as a 'loved sinner'. Thus, the retreatant sees the involvement in sin, and yet the love of God ever remains as the all-pervasive context calling us beyond our own sinful inadequacy into a companionship of service (Exx 95). Hence, for Ignatius, reflection on one's sins is never meant to trap one in a morbid guilt that focusses simply on the inadequacies of self, but rather is intended to point all the more insistently in awe and wonder (Exx 60) and thanksgiving for the merciful love of the Lord (Exx 61, 71). Always, the focus is on the Lord's love which draws one beyond who and where one is in one's sinfulness. And for Ignatius it is precisely the contrasting polarities of sin and grace that truly reveal the depths of this love: we know the Lord's love as the utterly free gift that it is to the extent that we also understand our sin, our personal place in the history of sin, and all this against the backdrop of the unwavering fidelity of God's love.

Thus, in contemplating the Passion, the costliness of our forgiveness, Ignatius continues to focus on the Divine Lover, poured out to the fullest degree, seeking ever to draw us into union and companionship. The Third Week of the Exercises emphasizes the totality of the incarnation, the radical depth of Christ's identification through love with the human condition. His additional directives, which he suggests be persuasive themes throughout the contemplations on the passion, reflect this same awareness and emphasis: 'Consider what Christ our Lord suffers in his human nature, or . . . what he desires to suffer' (Exx 195) and 'consider how the divinity hides itself . . .' (Exx 196). Again, Ignatius underscores the radical totality of this love which seeks to share itself in identification with the loved one (cf. Exx 231).

Ignatius is concerned, then, that the retreatant come to a deeply personalized, experiential awareness of being saved here and now by the active love of Christ. And, as absolutely everything for Ignatius is oriented towards service, 'this experience of salvation leads most naturally to the desire to share with others the "good news", to do something for this Christ who has done so much for me; it leads . . . to a desire to be a disciple, to follow Jesus'.[14]

THE FIFTH POINT

> The fifth point will be to resolve to amend with the grace of God. (Exx 43)

For Ignatius, gratitude is the stepping-stone to love, and love seeks to express itself in deeds (Exx 230). Hence, this concluding step of the Examen is focused towards the future and its choices, decisions, postures and attitudes. How does one look to the future now, in light of this process of reflection? As in the second point it was noted that the prayer for light was not simply for knowledge of its own sake, but 'to rid oneself' of faults one now looks to the future with specific decisions and choices to be made, with resolutions that embody new attitudes and purified choices.

This commitment to the future must be specific and concrete if it is to be real. How will one's life continue to live out ever more authentically the vision of the Principle and Foundation (Exx 23), the Call of the King (Exx 91), the drama of the Two Standards (Exx 139)? How, concretely, will the Three Degrees of Humility (Exx 165-8) and the Three Classes of Men (Exx 149-57) continue to reflect and illumine one's stance before the Lord? That is, this step of the Examen seeks to de-romanticize and to concretize choices, promises, decisions. At times there will of course be obvious and specific choices that need to be faced; at other times, perhaps, the decision may be for a subtle change in attitude or a renewed commitment of effort to be more aware, more grateful.

Now one prepares to enter again that real world of experience and action, but with a newly heightened sense of the divine action, and a greater depth of human freedom for authentic response. So, in a progression of Examen reflections, the future towards which one looks in this Examen becomes the graced past of one's next Examen, as one strives to continue to 'find God in all things'.

CONCLUSION

The whole point of the Examen is to heighten and deepen one's experience of this God one has found. Though presented by Ignatius as a form of personal prayer, the Examen is not a 'private' exercise in the sense of promoting an individualistic, 'me and Jesus' kind of piety. In the Ignatian view, attention to one's interiority is not an end in itself, but is for a more authentic self-giving in service. One moves *ad intra* in order to move more freely *ad extra*: everything, for Ignatius Loyola, is oriented toward apostolic action: towards a continuing purification of choices for greater service in a response of love to the divine initiative. It was in the changing circumstances of his age, and in the constant flow of active ministry, that Ignatius sought to find God - not in a monastic withdrawal from activity.

This prayerful reflection sought precisely to create those sensitivities which enabled a person to be more genuinely, freely active in God's service, to 'find God in all things', and to be a 'contemplative even in action'.

NOTES

1. Rule 3, Summary of the Constitutions, 1599, excerpted from *The Constitutions of the Society of Jesus* (no. 304), *Rules of the Society of Jesus* (Woodstock, MD, 1956).

2. Ignatius Loyola, *Spiritual Exercises* (no. 230). Hereafter, all references to the *Exercises* will be included in the text, citing the numbered paragraphs of the edition of Louis Puhl SJ, (Westminster, MD, 1954).

3. Robert L. Schmitt, 'Ignatian mysticism: a mysticism of action', *Journal of Dharma* 4 (1979), pp. 126-42.

4. Alexandre Brou, *La Spiritualité de Saint Ignace* (Paris 1928), p. 23, cited in Mary Hugh Campbell, 'The particular Examen - touchstone of a genuinely apostolic spirituality', *Review for Religious* 30 (1971), p. 775.

5. Josef Stierli, 'Ignatian prayer: seeking God in all things', in *Ignatius of Loyola: his personality and spiritual heritage, 1556-1956*, ed. by Friedrich Wulf (St Louis 1977), p. 162.

6. cf. for example: Raymond F. Collins, *Models of Theological Reflection* (Lanham, MD, 1984); James E. Hug, (ed.), *Tracing the Spirit: communities, social action, and theological reflection* (New York 1983); James Whitehead and Evelyn Eaton, *Method in Ministry* (New York 1980).

7. cf. Avery Dulles, 'St Ignatius and the Jesuit theological tradition', *Studies in the Spirituality of Jesuits* 14 (March 1982), p. 2. Also, cf. Harvey D. Egan, *The Spiritual Exercises and the Ignatian Mystical Horizon* (St Louis 1976).

8. cf. Michael J. Buckley, 'The contemplation to attain love', *The Way Supplement* 24 (1975), pp. 92-104.

9. cf. Exx 234, Ignatius's famous *'suscipe'* prayer, the fruition of such an awareness deepened through the experience of the four weeks of the Exercises.

10. Hugo Rahner, *Notes on the Spiritual Exercises* (Woodstock, MD, 1956), p. 294.

11. George A. Aschenbrenner, 'Consciousness Examen', *Review for Religious* 31 (1972), p. 18.

12. cf. Daniel Araoz, 'Positive Examination of Conscience', *Review for Religious* 23 (1964), p. 622.

13. cf. Exx 21. What is articulated here is Ignatius's goal for the Exercises, a vision which informs not only the Principle and Foundation, but each succeeding exercise of the Exercises.

14. William A. Barry, 'The experience of the First and Second Week of the Spiritual Exercises', *Review for Religious* 32 (1973), p. 107.

CHAPTER FOURTEEN

'The Serpent's Tail': Rules for Discernment

David Lonsdale

The brightness of a bright idea is no indication of its divine origin. That was a comment of one of my former teachers in response to our less practical proposals for changing 'the system'. The same is true of the strength of feelings. Strong movements of feeling and bright ideas are what impel us interiorly to decisions and to action. Two of the fundamental convictions underlying both sets of Ignatius's Rules for the Discernment of Spirits are firstly, that God communicates with people through feelings and ideas, and particularly through feelings, and secondly that we are open to deception through our feelings and ideas.[1] The Second Week Rules for Discernment (Exx 328-36) explain how this comes about and how such deceptions can be recognized and appropriate action taken. In this essay I shall outline some of the dispositions that Ignatius expects to find in a person to whom the Second Week Rules would be helpful and then discuss some typical instances of the practical application of these Rules.

Before that, however, some brief comments about Ignatius's main presuppositions. The Second Week Rules need the First Week Rules as a building needs a foundation. Reading the Second set of Rules in isolation from the First can give the impression that Ignatius was a pessimist about grace and over-preoccupied with deception. In fact he has full confidence in the willingness and ability of God to lead a Christian to full maturity (Exx 15). He wrote in a letter:

There are very few persons who realize what God would make of them if they abandoned themselves entirely into his hands and let themselves be formed by his grace. A thick and shapeless tree trunk would never believe that it could become a statue, admired as a miracle of sculpture, and would never submit itself to the chisel of the sculptor who . . . sees by his genius what he can make of it.[2]

165

Nonetheless, it is a fact that people are led astray through apparent good, and a spiritual director needs to be able to recognize 'the serpent's tail' (Exx 334). The main elements from the First Week Rules which are needed for appropriate application of the Second Week Rules are: the necessity for the director to know whether he or she is dealing with a fundamentally 'maturing' or 'regressing' Christian (cf. Exx 314, 315, 335);[3] the ability to recognize and know how to deal with 'spiritual consolation' and 'desolation' (Exx 316-24); the knowledge that it is in the very nature of our resistance to the Spirit of God to be tricky and deceptive (Exx 139, 142, 325-7). The Second Week Rules have to do with the more subtle deceptions, and the focus of these Rules, as the previous ones, is on the individual's experience of thoughts and especially feelings which are signs of the presence and action of the Spirit of God and of one's harmony with or resistance to that Spirit (Exx 315-7, 322, 229, 335).

DISPOSITIONS FOR APPLICATION OF SECOND WEEK RULES

When Hamlet says that 'the devil hath power to assume a pleasing shape' (act 2, scene 2), he is quoting a fundamental principle of both sets of Ignatius's Rules for Discernment (Exx 332). There are, however, important differences between the two sets of Rules, and one of these lies in what constitutes a 'pleasing shape' for people at different stages on the Christian journey. If my basic orientation is towards a comfortable, peaceful existence, I will be discouraged by thoughts or images of a way of living or acting that involve strenuous activity and considerable cost. If I am the sort of person who feels genuine enthusiasm for higher Christian ideals, I will be fallaciously attracted to the lower or the less good, if it is disguised in the 'pleasing shape' of a higher. It is largely to this second category of people, maturing Christians, whom Ignatius calls 'souls that are progressing to greater perfection' (Exx 335), and to their spiritual guides that the Rules for the Second Week are addressed.

Ignatius did not think that any and every person was suited to making the whole Exercises (Exx 18). Similarly, not everyone who makes the First Week is necessarily ready to go further.[4] Among those who do go on to make the Second and subsequent Weeks' exercises, some though not necessarily all would be helped by the

Second Week Rules for Discernment, since some would be 'assailed and tempted under the appearance of good' (Exx 10).

We have some idea of the dispositions that Ignatius sees as compatible with the exercises of the Second and subsequent Weeks and the forms that a person's resistance to the action of God might be likely to take. In the context of the Exercises, the necessary basic disposition seems to be that a person is inwardly so free from being bound to a significant course of action that he or she is effectively able to follow God's leading in practice. An early Directory instructs that the First Week should be prolonged for 'all those who are not as yet resigned into the hands of God our Lord, etc., so that he can act on them and incline them toward that which is better for them, but they enter with certain plans and intentions . . .'.[5] The exercises of the Second Week, especially the election, seem to ask for more: both that a person be open and able to follow God's leading in life, and that he or she desires to live at all times in a way that is *better* suited to giving praise and glory to God. That is to say 'not only to will and not will as God inspires' (Exx 155), but also to be at a point on their journey where 'the desire to be better able to serve God our Lord will be the cause of their accepting anything or relinquishing it' (Exx 155, cf. Exx 151, 179, 180, 338, 339). This orientation towards and effective desire for what is *better* able to serve God is one of the distinguishing marks of a person who can profitably continue with the Exercises after the First Week.

This desire will include, in Ignatius's view, some kind of apostolic orientation, a movement of life towards others in charity and imitation of Jesus (Exx 95). It will also involve a close following of the path that Jesus took. Provision is made for people who want to be 'prompt and diligent' (Exx 91) to follow Christ and even to 'distinguish themselves' and 'give greater proof of love' (Exx 97, 104). This means not only a willingness to accept the cross for the sake of Christ but even an 'earnest desire and deliberate choice' of 'poverty with Jesus poor rather than riches; insults with Christ loaded with them, rather than honours; . . . to be accounted as worthless and a fool for Christ rather than to be esteemed as wise and prudent in this world. So Christ was treated before me' (Exx 167; cf. Exx 146, 147, 157). If the way of weakness and poverty was the true way for Jesus, it will be so too for his disciples. Even those who are already engaged in a particular Christian way of life and not faced with a life choice in the course of the Exercises should show one of two dispositions:

> First, if it be to the equal glory of God and without offence to him . . . to *wish* to suffer injuries and opprobium and to be humiliated with Christ . . . or second to be *ready* to suffer patiently, out of love for Christ our Lord, whatever of like nature may happen to him.[7]

This desire to be associated with Christ, and even to suffer with him, forms a crucial part of the setting in which the Second Week Rules may be applied even outside the Exercises. The insidiousness of the deceptions described in these Rules lies in their apparently being wholly in conformity with this uncommon and abundantly graced orientation of a person's life (cf. Exx 139).

It is also important to note, however, that the two sets of Rules for Discernment overlap in their application. Few people outgrow the First Week Rules completely. Sometimes the Second Week Rules are helpful to a person in the Exercises of the First Week.[8]

PRACTICAL DISCERNMENT ACCORDING TO SECOND WEEK RULES

I would now like to reflect upon some concrete instances in which the Second Week Rules for Discernment seem helpful. The examples are taken from recent experience of spiritual direction.

Ignatius's writing on discernment implies that in practice it is a matter of some subtlety requiring careful observation, perception, reflection and judgment. Even towards the end of his life, when his union with God was profoundly mystical, he was careful to observe, sift and reflect on his experience, aware of the possibilities of deception.[9] Not all great spiritual directors, however, would agree that discernment of spirits requires such painstaking care and method. The Russian *staretz* Seraphim of Sarov said:

> I Seraphim am a sinful servant of God, and what the Lord orders me to say, inasmuch as I am his servant, that I say to the one who seeks profitable counsel. The first thought arising in my mind I consider to be a sign from God, and I express it without knowing what there is in my visitor's soul; all I do is believe that God will inspire me thus for that man's benefit.[10]

The differences in approach indicated here have present-day

relevance. One meets people, and especially perhaps some who have come under the influence of the charismatic movement, who claim to know quickly and without very much reflection what 'the Lord' or the Holy Spirit 'is saying to us' in a given set of circumstances. The value of Ignatius's Second Week Rules, so it seems to me, is that they are at least a reminder of the human heart's capacity for deception in good faith, of its ability to deify its own predilections and desires, to justify this by rationalization and to interpret the disguised urgings of egoism as the call of the Spirit of God.

Recent interest in apophatic forms of Christian prayer, in 'centring prayer' and in eastern non-Christian forms of meditation and contemplation, have rightly reasserted the values of stillness, interior peace and quiet in prayer. One difficulty that can arise here is that a pleasant, more or less self-induced state of interior peace and stillness can be mistaken for what Ignatius and others mean by the 'peace' of spiritual consolation. People with little experience in a life of prayer or who have taken most of their information about prayer from books, as well as those facing very difficult circumstances in life, seem to be susceptible to this kind of misunderstanding. It is true, of course, that genuine spiritual consolation often includes an experience of real stillness and peace (Exx 316). Not all experiences of peace are to be seen as deceptive or misleading. In some instances however, prayer can become, though not deliberately or consciously, a kind of peaceful cocoon into which a person moves and which is being used as a cushion against harsh realities and a resistance against the pain of further growth.

The signs that this 'peace' is deceptive seem to vary from one person to another but might include some or all of the following. A person's prayer, in the first place, might show little connection with his or her life; might not touch or be touched by the circumstances, especially the harsher circumstances of life. In this case, if a director suggests a change in the style of prayer (to a more 'active' way, for instance) the suggestions could meet with obstinate resistance, perhaps largely dominated by fear. Another sign might be that the director discovers that a person has a timid and markedly unadventurous approach to life, a shrinking from challenging circumstances, which are dictating the style of prayer. If one explores such a person's images of God, as a spiritual director naturally would at some stage, they might turn out to depict a God who is one-sidedly comforting and comfortable, and who is found in prayer but rarely in life. If the director sees that this kind of 'consolation' may well be deceptive and hindering growth, he or she can begin to help. The person in question is staying with the lesser good and not moving towards the greater, although the lesser may be clothed in the form of the greater.[11] This highlights two facts about Ignatius's Rules and their application. The first is that it is not helpful to emphasize one element of a description of consolation (namely 'peace') in isolation from others (Exx 316). Secondly, Ignatius's Rules are a reminder that the full discernment of the leading of the Spirit of God in prayer and life calls for external, objective criteria, as well as the interior, subjective touchstones that Ignatius gives.

A similar possibility of misleading 'consolation' can also occur within other styles of prayer, including those in which the imagination plays an active part. For some people, times of prayer (as well as other times) can become a pleasant, stimulating and even exhilarating exercise involving imaginative flights with which are associated feelings of 'love' towards God and other people and generous desires to suffer with Christ and to live as the saints lived. A person who shows a propensity to this might seem to have an outstanding capacity for prolonged imaginative contemplation of gospel scenes.

There is clearly no doubt that some people do have such a genuine gift and that this can lead to real growth in Christian love. But this can also indicate a penchant for fantasy as a defence against life. As always, a director will look at the effects over a period of time that prayer has upon life and growth. Genuine prayer leads to changes in attitudes and practice and towards an integration of prayer and life. These are some of the touchstones by which the genuineness of any kind of prayer can be known. If there is little sign of growth in the gifts of the Spirit, it could be that the 'consolation' of such prayer is deceptive. A director can also ask about the 'afterglow' of such prayer: if the 'residue' tends to be dissatisfaction or anxiety, this can be a sign of resistance to a greater good, as Ignatius discovered in his own experience.[12]

Apart from these and similar instances in the area of prayer, we can also consider examples of misleading consolation from wider areas of experience. The alleged experience of feeling 'wholly at peace' about a decision or course of action past or future is one form of consolation often cited in Ignatian discernment. Such peace, when it is genuine, confirms the decision of a course of action undertaken. One meets instances, however, in which this experience of peace appears deceptive, at least to an external observer. Sometimes people, believing that they are guided by the Spirit of God, adopt courses of action which are divisive in a community, offensive or hurtful to its members, apparently self-willed and headstrong, and which show few of the features of Christian love enumerated by Paul (1 Cor. 13.1-7). The perpetrators of these courses of action sometimes justify themselves by appealing to the experience of feeling 'wholly at peace' about what they have set in motion. Here again a director, if consulted, can explore more exactly what is meant by 'peace' in such a case, and can foster further growth by showing that to focus on a single aspect of consolation – 'feeling at peace' – can be misleading. The criteria of affective movements, moreover, have to be supplemented in discernment by external signs of genuine Christian love and of the presence of other gifts of the Spirit.

We can look at another example. It is often being said at the present time that an essential (or at least an important) ingredient of being a Christian is the call to be a 'prophet'. We are said to be called to form a 'prophetic' Church. While this is obviously a too long neglected dimension of Christianity, the experience of such a call is one in which people can in good faith be deceived in the ways described by Ignatius in the Rules for Discernment of the Second Week. The 'consolation' itself, that is the alleged experience of a call to be a prophet, can be deceptive (Exx 331) in the sense that enthusiasm for a cause in a person who naturally responds to challenges can be mistaken, perhaps in the atmosphere of a retreat or a prayer-meeting, for true, spiritual consolation. Alternatively, the deception, the leading to a lesser good, can arise as Ignatius describes (Exx 332-3) in thoughts and decisions consequent upon a true experience of consolation.[13] So as always, the vital procedure in such a case, when this call seems to be leading to courses of action about which discernment is needed, is to trace, 'the whole course of our thoughts' (Exx 333).

Ignatius gives two signs by which the 'serpent's tail' can be detected here. One is cognitive, that is to say, if the thoughts that

171

come to mind are 'less good' or 'distracting' or 'terminate in something evil or less good than the soul had formerly promised to do' (Exx 333). This is a sign of deceptive good. The other sign is in our affective experience. If the course of thoughts ends in 'what weakens the soul, or disquiets it; or by destroying the peace, tranquillity and quiet which it had before, it may cause disturbance to the soul', this too, is a sign of subtle resistance to God. If one or more of these signs is present, it will be helpful, partly too as a guide to future occasions, to trace back the course of reasoning to discover the point at which the fallacy or distraction towards the lesser good began (Exx 334).

We can look at a more precise example. A married man, father of a family, may experience a true call to make his life more 'prophetic'. Afterwards, in the 'afterglow' of this consolation, reflecting on and reasoning from this experience, he may be led to take up a lifestyle or form of work which seems to be more 'prophetic' but which perhaps causes harm to his marriage and family and in fact diverts him from a fuller way of living out his Christian vocation and from a more profound way of being 'prophetic'. Here then it would be helpful to go over the course of thoughts which led to decisions and choices, to see where the distraction to a lesser good occurred. Contemplation of the gospel accounts of Jesus's temptations to a lesser good can be useful (Matt. 4.1-11; Luke 4.1-13).

The underlying assumption of Ignatius's Rules of Discernment is the conviction that God communicates through our feelings. Affective states can be a guide to the activity of God within us. These same states are influenced by psychological forces or factors which are largely unconscious or on the boundary between the conscious self and the unconscious. Discernment of spirits in Ignatius's terms is not a matter of looking into the person to try to discover natural or supernatural influences (in any case, an impossible task). Discernment is not introspection. It is rather a matter of noting significant affective 'movements' in a person's experience and the perceptions, decisions and courses of action associated with these, and through that observation to try to perceive the leading of the spirit of God and the resistances to that leading that might be operating.

So although discernment is neither introspection nor psychological analysis, it is helpful if a spiritual director is aware of at least *prima facie* possible similarities between genuine spiritual consolation or desolation on the one hand, and on the other hand affective states which are due to unconscious psychological factors. Let me illustrate this by another example. The spiritual director has to be guided by his or her client's report of what has occurred in the client's experience: thoughts and feelings which seem significant in this context of discernment. In good Christian people the effects of, for example, a mild psychological compulsion can be very similar to the alternations of spiritual consolation and desolation.[14] This fact can be specially important when it is a question of trying to discover one's 'vocation'. The effect of a psychological compulsion is disquietude, anxiety or feelings of guilt when the compulsion is not acted out in a person's behaviour. When a person is able to act out this compulsion, this disquietude is removed at least for a time. 'Good' feelings (e.g., peace, tranquillity, a desire to be generous) can be associated with my being able to live out my 'vocation' as I conceive it. 'Bad' feelings (e.g., anxiety, guilt, disturbance) appear when I am not living that out or when I conceive of a future for myself, which does not include my being able to live out my (alleged) 'vocation'.

The signs which would indicate mildly but not pathologically compulsive behaviour with regard to a 'vocation' or a particular course of action would vary slightly from one person to another, but might include one or more of the following features. In addition to anxiety and feelings of guilt attached to what goes contrary to the supposed 'vocation' or preferred course of action, discussion of the images of God with which a person operates might reveal a God who inspires chiefly fear and who is unwilling to allow people to be free or to act freely. This may mean that earlier images of God in a person's life, which suggest that God does allow freedom, have been suppressed, but it may also mean that they have never been present. A person suffering from a compulsion will often associate similar features with the figure of Jesus and stress the strictures in the gospel teachings of Jesus. From these and other signs the director can see that a man or woman whose behaviour in this area is largely compulsive may be more helped at this stage by psychological counselling. At first sight, this might appear to be an instance in which the Second Week Rules for Discernment would apply, in the sense that the 'vocation' to which a person feels called might seem a spurious or deceptive good. This may in fact turn out to be the case, but the more urgent need is to focus on the compulsions. Here spiritual direction and counselling, insofar as they are distinct, can work together, especially if the compulsion is powered by the images of God. In fact, in Ignatian terms, the person in this case is not yet ready for the First Week of the Exercises since he or she lacks the necessary freedom and sense of the love of God presupposed in the First Principle and Foundation. A spiritual director might be able to help by suggesting contemplations of some images of God from Scripture which might help towards a more balanced image of God and Jesus. But this sometimes only serves to reinforce already powerful distorted images. If the main problem is a psychological one, it should be treated psychologically.

In this article I have moved from some of the presuppositions of Ignatius's Second Week Rules for Discernment, through a consideration of the dispositions that Ignatius associates with a person for whom these Rules would be helpful, to a discussion of some practical applications of the Rules taken from recent experience. The examples, of course, could be multiplied. Enough has been said, I imagine, to illustrate both the Rules and their limitations. They were intended not as complete guidelines for discerning the will of God in particular cases but rather as a way of helping a person to perceive, reflect on and overcome interior resistances to the leading of the Spirit of God, however subtly and deceptively 'in pleasing shape' these resistances might be clothed.

NOTES

1. cf. Michael Buckley, 'The structure of the Rules for Discernment' *Way Supplement* 20 (1973), pp. 19-37, and Chapter 18 of this book.

2. I do not have an exact reference for this extract from a letter of Ignatius.

3. Jules J. Toner, *A Commentary on St Ignatius' Rules for the Discernment of Spirits* (St Louis 1982), pp. 48ff. His commentary on the Second Week Rules is found on pp. 213-56.

4. cf. *Autograph Directories of St Ignatius Loyola* (Program to Adapt the Spiritual Exercises, New Jersey), pp. 14, 17 and 19.

5. ibid., p. 26.

6. cf. ibid., p. 9.

7. ibid., pp. 10-11. My italics.

8. cf. W.H. Longridge, *The Spiritual Exercises of St Ignatius Loyola with a Commentary* (London 1919), p. 14. Longridge's notes (pp. 13-14, 184-93, and 262-7) are still among the clearest concise guides in English to Ignatius's Second Week Rules.

9. This is clear from Ignatius's own decisions recorded in his spiritual journal.

10. G.P Fedotov, (ed.), *A Treasury of Russian Spirituality* (London 1950), pp. 261-2.

11. This was the case with the 'consolations' that Ignatius himself experienced in Barcelona and Paris, which tended to distract him from studying. cf. Ignatius's Autobiography, sections 54-5 and 82.

12. ibid., sections 6-8.

13. To go into a discussion of *consolación sin causa precedente* here would take us too far afield. There is a full exposition of the latest thinking on this topic in Toner, *Commentary*, pp. 291-303.

14. Useful working definitions of compulsion and compulsiveness can be found, for example, in P.L. Harriman, *Dictionary of Psychology* (London 1972); H.B. and A.C. English, *A Comprehensive Dictionary of Psychological and Psychoanalytical Terms* (London 1958).

PART FOUR

The Spiritual Direction Relationship

CHAPTER FIFTEEN

The One who Gives the Exercises

Brian Grogan

I would like to begin by speaking of the fear which I face in giving a retreat, and thus may find some common ground with other would-be directors. First, I want to admit that for me each retreat is a new beginning, a risk, a moving into the unknown; I experience inability and a sense of dread; I go through periods when I wish the whole retreat would be cancelled, or that some worthwhile excuse might free me from the engagement without too much loss of face. I have found that many potential retreat-givers are put off from ever beginning by just this sort of fear. This apostolic paralysis is a tragedy when such a person is judged to have the basic qualities for the work of retreat-giving. One meets, for example, people who are excellent spiritual directors, who have sensitivity and good judgment; and yet when confronted with the apostolate of the Exercises, they experience a sense of uselessness, or ineptitude or a fear of failure; and these prove decisive. Such a fear is not from God and must be resisted. Perhaps it may help if I explain how I confront it myself.

WHO IS THE DIRECTOR?

In trying to come to terms with my fears over the years, the light has slowly dawned that in the retreat situation there is indeed a director, who is, however, not human but divine. God is the director; I am a helper, the *giver* of the retreat. To view the apostolic task in this light does effect a radical change in one's approach; or perhaps I should say that at least it has changed everything for me. My beginning fear usually is: I cannot make a success of this retreat, so it will be a failure. When grace enters my heart, I come to see that while I cannot make a success of the retreat, God can and will. My fear then becomes something more like 'holy fear'; a fear that I may get in God's way, that I may be a bad and useless instrument. I sense that I am not sufficiently familiar with God and with God's ways to understand what is to happen in the encounter between the

179

retreatant and God. My 'doubtful dread' becomes a holy fear when it leads away from paralysis and escaping from the task of the retreat, but to prayer, to repentance, to penance if need be; in short, when it leads me to conversion and to deeper union with God.[1]

Ignatius, whether by good instinct or by careful reflection, does not speak of the 'director of the retreat'. Instead he uses the term 'the one who gives the Exercises' (*el que da los exercicios*).[2] Involved here is something far more important than words; for me it is the basic truth that the director is God, and with God lies the main responsibility for the success of the enterprise of the retreat. It is God who has invited the retreatant to 'come apart' (Mark 6.31), and it is God too who gives the grace whereby the retreatant responds generously to that invitation. It is God too who has been preparing the way for many a year, and who knows the needs of the retreatant 'infinitely better' than I.[3] So the burden of 'success' must rest with God who alone can bear it. In my ungraced moments – and they are many – I fear that nothing will happen, because I cannot make it happen. In my graced moments that fear fades: I plant and water, and God truly makes things grow, as every retreat experience proves abundantly.

Not only do the retreatants grow, but through each retreat I too have grown in my appreciation of the marvellous ways in which divine providence leads each of us uniquely. When I see others generously struggling to accept the radical values of the gospels, I find a like desire in myself, and an urge to become more familiar with God, so that I may be a more faithful interpreter of God's call to the individual retreatant. Something of Christian humour has grown in me too: humour is some measure of our appreciation of divine providence, as Hugo Rahner indicates in his book *Man at Play*. The dread which both retreatant and giver often experience at the opening of the retreat can be suitably lightened by that humour, which expresses a trust that all will be well, that something worthwhile will happen, since God knows what is really going on.

SERVING MY BETTERS

When I accept the truth that God is the director and I the helper and instrument, I am free enough to undertake the work of retreat-giving, no matter how aware I am of vast gaps in my inner life and my spiritual experience. I may very well be shown up as one who is indeed very poor in spirit; but does this matter, since the standards, the pace and the goal of the retreat are set, not by me, but by God? I once asked a man to guide me in an eight-day retreat: he refused. 'I'd have nothing to say to you' he said; 'you're on the inner track with all this spirituality stuff!' He was in fact a holy man; but like most of us, he had reflected all to little on his long experience of God. He was rich but did not know it, nor did he know who had made him rich. And so he declined my request because he felt that he had nothing to give. I have felt the same temptation myself: at least half of my retreatants are further along the path to God than I! But however poorly I am responding to God's calls in my own life, I can at least present Christ and the Scriptures to retreatants, accompany them on their journey, support them and help them reflect on what is happening in their encounter with God, and hold them at those critical junctures where they see clearly what God wants, but experience the temptation to evade the issue and move to something else. And so, though I may be far from the goal myself, I know the way, and so can help others find it.

The retreat-giver, then, does not present himself or herself as a *guru*. By this I mean one who has become a 'master' of the interior life, and who communicates knowledge of the path to God to chosen disciples who are capable and anxious to receive it. The disciples' role is to ask questions, to listen and to learn the wisdom which the 'master' offers. Perhaps in preached retreats of the older style, relationships were of this guru-disciple type; but such is not the relationship between the giver and the retreatant in the mind of St Ignatius. Rather, it should be characterized by a growth in maturity and freedom; it should be a voyage in which one learns to sail the ship for oneself, by responding appropriately to the different winds that blow. It should be a voyage of personal discovery, rather than a guided tour conducted by a non-stop commentator.

THE PRAYER OF INTERCESSION

The retreat-giver who has a right sense of order, that is, a sense of the primacy of God in the whole enterprise of the retreat, will spend much time interceding with the Lord for the retreatant. This is something which any Christian can do for another; it requires no

181

special skill, only concern. For when I am sufficiently concerned, I give the time, and over the years I have found that the amount of time I have given to the prayer of intercession has grown a good deal (I blush to think of my earliest retreatants reading this!). The late Anthony de Mello proposed that unless one believes effectively in the prayer of intercession, it would be better not to undertake to give the Exercises. Ignatius's advice to the giver does not include the obligation of praying for the retreatant, which is perhaps remarkable; Polanco, however, may be quoting his master when he says somewhere that it is the task of the giver of the Exercises to love and pray for the retreatant. This tradition of praying for and loving the person entrusted to one's spiritual care goes back to the early Fathers, to Polycarp, in fact, the disciple of St John.[4] St Monica's prayer for Augustine might serve as a paradigm.[5] The prayer of petition is centrally emphasized in the New Testament, more than any other form of prayer; the Letter to the Hebrews reminds me that I do not intercede alone, but that Christ joins my prayer to his own and presents *our* prayer for the retreatant to the Father (Heb. 7.25).

It often helps to tell the retreatant that you are praying for him or her. I usually express it as part of my side of the contract in the retreat, and I find that retreatants are usually both surprised and very grateful. The effectiveness of this form of prayer is truly extraordinary: one sister confessed to me: 'Knowing that you were praying for me just changed everything. It kept me going when my prayer was a mess, and made me believe that God does care for me after all. We sisters are not used to the idea that a priest could be concerned enough about us to give up his time to pray for us.'

It is through praying in this way that I come to love the retreatant properly: sustained intercession is the antidote to the development of unhealthy relationships, whether of antipathy, of possessiveness, or whatever. One comes to regard the retreatant as God does, with a love which is reverential and hopeful. Before me is the image and likeness of God, a masterpiece, God's work of art. I pray that in the daily meeting with the retreatant I may remember this truth. I find that when I do, the retreatant begins to grow in the realization that he or she is high in the Lord's favour, and when this happens, the retreat 'takes off'.

DON'T PUSH THE RIVER!

I have been told that I suffer from 'N-ach', which is the psychologist's shorthand for 'Need for achievement'; certainly in my earlier days of retreat-giving I tended to have a too-ambitious programme for the retreatants. I found, however, that once one gets a reputation for forcing the pace, the volume of requests for one's services tends to diminish. I learned slowly that one needs the patience of God; God takes a lifetime (and longer, if purgatory is somehow in time!) to bring about our full conversion. So I have had to learn to walk at God's pace, and that pace is that of the honest retreatant. The graces of the Exercises are lofty ones; it is a critical yet a liberating moment when a retreatant says: 'I know what I should be praying for, but I'd be dishonest if I pretended to you that I'm praying for it.' It is preferable to stand still and admit that one is doing so, than to dance sluggishly and unwillingly to another's music. The admission allows both retreatant and giver to grasp where the real problem lies. God does not give immediate response to all our requests. It is not failure on the giver's part if the retreat ends without a resolution of the problem. The real failure would be if the retreatant felt that she or he had to be dishonest. Hurried along by the giver's desire that all the graces prayed for should be won, the retreatant can be blocked from revealing the true state of affairs. I find that I now often ask: 'What were you praying for?' When the answer is, 'Quite honestly, nothing', both of us can look at the situation and try to puzzle out together what to do next.

RAISE THE ANTE!

This section appears to contradict what has just been said. It is intended, however, to illustrate the need for flexibility in the retreat-giver, so that the approach can be adapted to differing situations. It is true that the giver should walk at the retreatant's pace, and not be anxious to 'push the river' or hurry the retreatant along. This quality of patience comes appropriately into play when there is genuine movement. However, in my experience, many retreatants come to the retreat in a state of quiet resignation to a life of 'safe, uninteresting mediocrity' – the phrase is Newman's. They are innocent but often dull; their horizons are narrow: they lack any sense that they have a unique role to play in God's redemptive plans; and so they can read and pray their way through the radical passages of the New Testament without a shiver, because they do not grasp the fact that the Lord is challenging *them*. Where this sense of challenge is absent or only dimly present, there is little genuine movement, and the giver of the exercises must intervene. Let us listen to the advice of that master retreat-giver, Peter Favre. He speaks of those

> . . . who believe themselves always to be impelled by one and the same spirit, though - as they will acknowledge - with greater or less intensity at different times. . . . They neither entertain thoughts such as would deviate from truth and goodness, nor have they any clearly wayward inclinations. . . .
> Now a highly effective way by which a man can learn to distinguish the spirits is to propose first that he should choose a state of life, and then choose from among the varying degrees of perfection within it. Try proposing to him higher standards regarding his ways of acting, his beliefs, his hopes, his charity: put the challenge in such a way that he can apply himself to it both in heart and deed, and you will usually discover that this method makes it much easier for him to experience the difference between the good and evil spirit.[6]

Should the giver of the Exercises be ready to challenge the retreatant in the manner Favre describes, when he speaks of leading people to examine themselves concerning a higher degree of perfection in their lives? I believe so, and I do not think that this contradicts what I said above about moving at the pace of the retreatant. I give the Exercises without any predetermined agenda or time-schedule: yet I must constantly ask: Where is God leading? What is the next feasible step? There must be a relationship of honesty such that the retreatant can admit: 'Nothing's happening', and I can respond with tentative suggestions, which may range from proposing that the retreatant might pray more, for example, at midnight, or that some suitable form of penance be tried, to questions which would involve a definite broadening of horizons, such as: 'Have you ever thought of living among the poor?'; 'Have you considered putting your talents at the service of some voluntary organisation?'. Ignatius's directive about the need to ply the retreatant with questions when he or she is not moved by the differing spirits is in question here (Exx 6). Perhaps in doing so one runs the risk of provoking anger or loss of the retreatant's friendship; but more often I have found that the retreatant is somewhat flattered that I have such an exalted view of the plans which God may have in store for him or her. Looking back, I regret those retreats which I have made or given in which there was no element of challenge: they were largely, I fear, wasted time.

REFLECTION ON EXPERIENCE

The best preparation for giving the Exercises is to make them in a personally-guided manner, such that one comes to experience the various graces, and begins to practise the art of discernment. As to the graces, perhaps that of the First Week is the most subtle: I can well remember the day it dawned on me that I was truly a sinner, yet loved with infinite compassion; it was a hot, sticky day in upstate New York, and I had been labouring long, with the help of a happily insistent tertian master. We were due to end the First Week in a few hours' time, and I was aware that I had not yet appropriated what Ignatius was talking about. Suddenly the light dawned, and I remember saying to myself: 'God forgive me for trying to tell others what the grace of the First Week was, before experiencing it myself!' The grace may have dimmed since then, but I can still recognize it or its absence either in myself or in others. The art of discernment! Since the central role of the giver is to help the retreatant to discern the spirits, we must be in touch with our own feelings, tugs, aversions, inclinations. By nature and by training I see myself as over-cerebral; for long I was unaware of the world of feelings and affectivity. 'Feelings don't count!', my Master of Novices used to say, and I learnt the lesson well. Over the past few years I have tried to learn - without too much help from my brethren, I must confess - to get in touch with my feelings, to acknowledge and articulate and recognize how they influence my decisions. For me, this is a new language, and I speak it poorly; but unless I try to speak it, I cannot teach it or understand it when it is spoken by the retreatant.

This follows the need for spiritual direction; I need to be developing in self-knowledge and in knowledge of God. I have presuppositions, prejudices and blind spots; I easily warp the good; I set limits to the demands of God on me because my openness is limited. Good spiritual direction helps me to uncover those limiting attitudes in myself which are certainly not from God; through it I become a little more aware of what is going on in my heart, and so I can have some idea of what is going on in the heart of another. Why was Peter Favre so highly regarded by Ignatius as a giver of the Exercises? Surely it was because he was so spontaneously in touch with his feelings, as the *Memoriale* reveals on every page. At an early age he fell under the influence of Ignatius. He was immature; but with Ignatius to reflect with, he travelled a long road. We see him, on page after page, adverting to and responding appropriately to his rich inner experience.[7]

The importance of the supervision of the giver during the retreat itself is accepted much more these days at least in theory. The occasions on which it is feasible will be limited, since the giver is often working alone. Nevertheless, it is an excellent idea: which of us is so transparent as not to cast any shadows? How free am I in regard to what God is doing in the retreatant? Am I presuming that God must act in certain ways? Do I advert to my likes and dislikes of various retreatants? Am I aware of the retreatants' reactions to me – such reactions may extend all the way from falling in love to antipathy – and how am I to deal with them? These and a host of other questions should arise; and a good supervisor with whom one can 'check out' during the retreat would be invaluable. Another help would be a feedback process, whereby retreatants' comments would be passed on, where helpful, to the giver.

Some capacity for teamwork is important, especially where a number of retreat-givers are working in the same building. If one of the group has no desire nor capacity to co-operate with the others when the situation arises, I doubt his or her capacity to listen or to learn; and if either quality is lacking, the person is hardly suited to retreat-giving.

A GOOD LISTENER

Are you a good listener? Ask your friends. To be able to listen well is an essential quality of the retreat-giver. To listen sensitively, without intruding oneself, is the best way to help the client to articulate, clarify and distinguish what is going on in prayer. The retreat situation may be a unique experience for the client; perhaps never before and never again will someone be there simply to listen. The rapport essential for a relationship between giver and client is established by listening; for listening shows acceptance. Clients yearn to be taken 'where they're at'; they dread being forced onto some Procrustean bed of the retreat-giver's making. Through listening, one helps the client to become aware of those unconscious attitudes which set the course of life for good or ill. To illustrate: at the end of a retreat a retreatant told me that two words I had said in the course of an interview had changed everything for her. I enquired what these two sapiential gems might have been. I had simply said, 'And then . . . ?', at a point where she had paused, unwilling to recount a very painful experience. My question had enabled her to go on to share something of which she had never spoken before. Thus she looked at it openly for the first time, and became free of it.

KNOWLEDGE

I have spoken of the need for personal experience of the Exercises and of their graces; I have indicated that one needs to be practising discernment at some level (whether through spiritual direction, supervision during the retreat, or through the examen of consciousness, or all three), and that one must be trying to stay close to God in prayer, especially that of intercession for the retreatant and for oneself. One needs to have a living awareness that the primary role in the retreat is God's, and so one needs to be able to listen both to God as well as to the client. Lastly, I would add that there are some intellectual requirements: among these I include a basic competence in theology. Good theology has always been delicately poised between extremes: one needs to know what are correct and incorrect positions on sin, christology, grace, providence, salvation, and so on. Not that interviews are to degenerate into theological debates, but rather that both giver and client operate out of certain theological frameworks. The more correct these are, the more easily the Spirit can operate. Familiarity with Scripture and with contemporary exegesis is also important. There are many collections of helpful texts available now, and most clients are reasonably familiar with the New Testament at least; and so the retreat-giver need never feel at a loss for texts. What one needs is to be able to illuminate the passage briefly and point the retreatant towards the riches contained in it.

Some basic counselling skills are needed to give the Exercises; if one does not have them by nature, one must try to acquire them. Good programmes for training are available: the trainee learns to pick out the skills of good counsellors, and to rate himself or herself and the fellow-trainees in play-back sessions. In supervised interviews and group sessions the trainee can explore his or her own inner world and learn to spot the reactions of indifference, hostility, fear, and so on. Authenticity or genuineness in the trainee becomes crucial; when present it facilitates the emergence of a trusting relationship, so that the client becomes free to reveal the true self in its strengths and weaknesses. Empathy can be learnt. It is a sensitivity to the other's feelings and a verbal facility in communicating what one has understood. The client can then say, 'The director's with me, understands me and seems to like me, no matter what I say!' A client has the right to expect this of any retreat-giver. A client should not expect psycho-therapeutic skills, but that the giver should be able to spot psychological problems when they arise: that he or she should be aware of the difference between counselling and spiritual direction, and know the limits of his or her own ability.

PROMOTION OF JUSTICE

Giving the Exercises is an ecclesial event: the work must relate to the contemporary situation of the Church and the issues which she authoritatively calls us to embrace. Thus in more recent years, I have had to relate to the Exercises the Church's new emphasis on the promotion of justice in our world. How this is to be done well is a matter of continuing debate; but it is a debate which no one giving the Exercises can afford to ignore.

Various ways of linking the Exercises with the justice issue are proposed: experience of and reflection on unjust situations might precede the Exercises, so that the retreatant brings to prayer a wider dimension, a greater compassion. Likewise, similar reflections after completing the Exercises can bring about a creative response in a person who is generous, capable, captivated by Christ and the demands of the gospel, and anxious to do only what God wants. Few retreat-givers of experience would wish to use the Exercises themselves to educate the retreatant to justice. This would be to pre-empt God's freedom to set the agenda. God's concern with the retreatant may lie elsewhere during the time of the Exercises. God may, for instance, be calling a person to the contemplative life. What is important is that the retreat-giver should be sensitive to the dimension of justice. Awareness of it will be heightened if the retreat-giver has lived among the poor and deprived, and he or she will be better able to guide others if sensitive to his or her own reaction, whether of attraction or rejection, to the issue.

CONCLUSIONS

God is the director: positively this expresses itself in intercessory prayer for the retreatant; negatively it means that one leaves God and the creature free to encounter one another directly. Responsibility for growth and development lie with them, since they are the partners in the relationship. The retreat-giver is present, not to teach, but to guide and facilitate. He or she needs enough imagination to grasp that God leads everyone in a unique way. There can be no pre-determined agenda, no package deal; rather, the approach must be tentative, pragmatic, experimental. Capacity to listen accurately, an attitude of loving respect for the retreatant, and an ability to be genuine and honest: these are the qualities which help the formation of a trusting relationship with the retreatant. One's personal experience of God, which comes through prayer, through making the Spiritual Exercises and, in general, through living out the Christian life, can be enriched and made available to others, if reflected on with the aid of good spiritual reading and spiritual direction. Such qualifications are sufficient, I believe, for one beginning the ministry of retreat-giving.

NOTES

1. The fourteenth-century English spiritual writer, Julian of Norwich, is perhaps outstanding in her treatment of the distinction between this paralysing fear, which she calls 'doubtful dread', and the 'holy fear' to which the author of this article refers. She calls it a lovely or reverent fear. cf. E. Colledge and J. Walsh, *Julian of Norwich: Showings* (New York 1978/London 1979), pp. 324ff.

2. Louis J. Puhl, whose edition of The *Spiritual Exercises* (Westminster, MD, 1951) is the most widely known of the English versions, is regrettably careless in his translation of the Spanish *el que da los exercicios*; in the Annotations - Exx 1-20 - he translates correctly in the majority of instances; but in Exx 7 and 18, he renders the phrase 'the Director of the Exercises'.

3. cf. Exx 89.

4. cf. Irenée Hausherr, *Direction spirituelle en Orient autrefois* (Rome 1955), pp. 130-41.

5. cf. *Confessions* IX, 11.

6. Bl. Peter Favre, *Memoriale*, in MHSJ *Fabri Monumenta* (1914), nn. 300-02, pp. 638-9.

7. cf. Brian O'Leary, *The Discernment of Spirits in the Memoriale of Blessed Peter Favre: The Way Supplement*, 35 (Spring 1979), *passim*.

CHAPTER SIXTEEN

The Exercises and Contemplative Prayer

Dermot Mansfield

In the life of prayer, an important time comes when there is a change from a relatively active, sensible phase, to one where the emphasis will be more on faith, on receptivity, and on God's part. Such a time will also be an important and critical one in the work of spiritual direction.

In retreats, and in the giving of the Spiritual Exercises, a real challenge is posed when such an issue as this arises. Directors can find that a considerable number of retreatants pray in a very simplified manner: perhaps with quite an affective element still present, or else in an almost continuously dry way, in pure faith. What kind of adaptations can be made in giving the Exercises – especially in the case of much dryness in prayer, which can seem the opposite of what Ignatius expects, especially regarding the graces to be sought?

My purpose here is not to attempt answers to the practical questions which arise, but rather to say that a proper understanding of prayer is the more basic requirement, and to offer some points especially on what has been called the prayer of faith. I believe that this issue is quite important at the present time, when so many people are accepted for the thirty-day retreat or make shorter directed retreats based in some way on the Ignatian Exercises, among whom are those unable to make much use of the material suggested because of what is happening in the prayer.

1 THE PRAYER OF FAITH

The phrase, 'the prayer of faith,' occurs in the classic book, On Prayer, by Jean Pierre de Caussade SJ, and indeed could be considered his principal theme.[1] More recently, it was used in a helpful way by Dom Eugene Boylan for the impossibility to meditate in Difficulties

191

in Mental Prayer.[2] And it then became the title of the book by Leonard Boase sj, meant to be a treatment of the topic especially for laypeople.[3]

The description conveys the positive meaning of the experience of many people who pray, who find themselves unable to concentrate in the prayer, who try to accept as best they can their helplessness and offer the time to God in faith. Once it may not have been so for them, but was good and satisfying. Then gradually it changed, and the earlier sense of satisfaction began to evaporate. Usually now it is a matter of giving time, making space, being faithful. For periods, perhaps, this can be relatively easy, but it can also be very difficult and dreaded in anticipation.

How can this virtual nothing be described, especially to a director in retreat? It can remain like a secret, hardly admitted to and unrecognized, due maybe to a general expectation that the active use of Scripture should be the method of prayer, and that the notions of 'consciousness' and 'movement' must be the significant factors of its evaluation. But such an expectation will leave little room for what is happening now, and what is needed is a better understanding of how we grow in the life of God.

Of course, prayer is a very individual matter, and God deals personally and uniquely with each of us. Yet certain clear outlines have been sketched in the Christian spiritual tradition, which need to be kept in mind. It will then be seen that what has happened in the prayer is inevitable.

At first, there is normally a more or less prolonged and attractive period in the spiritual life - an active phase which has something of the method of *lectio divina* within the prayer itself, with a movement from reading, imagining and pondering to the simplicity and depth of praise, sorrow, longing, love. It is often designated as meditation or discursive prayer,[4] but contains many contemplative elements - in it, we work first, so to speak, but then God takes over, giving us the taste of communion. The simple and affective part of it may come to predominate, and can seem to be the best kind of prayer, eliciting so much of our human sensibility and the depths of human response. Yet, most likely it precedes the prayer we are discussing here: it will have given way gradually to this dry helplessness, devoid of feeling and seemingly engaging none of our personal responses, where the call is to remain in faith without tangible reassurance or any immediate criterion by which to assess the prayer.

2 THE MEANING OF THE PRAYER

In much of the tradition of recent centuries, and following the important distinctions in the writings of Teresa of Avila and John of the Cross, this prayer is called the beginning of the state of contemplation.[5] It is where the deepest self is set on God, looking to God alone, due to the more immediate presence and activity of God within the soul. It is a 'dark and secret contemplation', according to John of the Cross: 'nothing else than a secret and peaceful and loving inflow of God, which, if not hampered, fires the soul in the spirit of love'.[6]

At the more ordinary level of experience, contemplation seems like nothing at all in comparison to the earlier, satisfying time. But with regard to the working of God, it is, if one remains perseveringly and with longing, allowing God to come more immediately – God who is mystery, who could never be encompassed by our knowing or reached by our effort to love, but who will now deeply communicate God's own understanding and love in the more intimate divine self-giving. In the active, more outward orientation of one's life, it is where all that is done will be more directly under the influence of grace, being ordered more purely and consistently to God.

The signs of the onset of contemplation include the inability to think or imagine in prayer, the lack of sensible consolation, and the helplessness of recurrent distractions. A person in this state wonders what to do, where to turn. It may seem as if one has gone wrong somewhere or is losing faith – and yet nothing else in life satisfies, and beneath all the surface feelings and thoughts it will be realized that the sole desire is to be for God and to serve God in everything. There is in such a person's life what could be called a preoccupation with God, and when it comes to prayer itself all one wants is to be lovingly attentive.[7]

The time of prayer then is a matter of just being there in weakness, but coming to it with belief and hope in the faithfulness of God, the divine purposes and mysterious approach in love. Outside of prayer, indeed, the conscious mind will continue to be nourished by pondering the mystery, but in the prayer it cannot, because being brought within the mystery. 'Because God is showing *himself*, however dimly,' Ruth Burrows says, 'the deep self loses its taste for what the mind can bring to it by way of ideas and concepts.'[8] If we are now under the influence of the more direct action of God 'our inmost heart will tell us that, for us, this sort of activity at prayer is a distraction and an infidelity'.[9]

If prayer has changed in this way, there is a further important point regarding the place of Christ. For it should not be concluded that we have become incapable, in Teresa's words, of 'enjoying the sublime blessings that lie enclosed in the mysteries of our good, Jesus Christ'.[10] Teresa, wary of some theories of prayer and very conscious of what she had learned in her own experience, tells us that Christ is always both our companion along the right road and also the one we contemplate and in whom we see the Father.[11] The difference is between the former need to meditate discursively *about* him in prayer and a deeper but quiet drawing to be contemplatively present to him and with him. Such an orientation, she says, can be helped by calling to mind one of the gospel events, but after which it is right to want to be with Christ in this more immediate and loving way, without initiating active thought, because now 'the soul understands these mysteries in a more perfect manner'.[12]

Such is the beginning of contemplation, dark and secret at this stage, but which is, to repeat the words of John of the Cross, already the inflow of God which, if we will allow it, 'fires the soul in the spirit of love'.[13] It is a new journey in the way of faith, signalling a great change in the life of grace and which has often been described as the process of a second conversion.[14]

It is not, however, something completed, but rather opens onto the whole landscape of the mystery of God, hardly glimpsed before, and over which we are to travel with even purer faith, being led onward to a greater communion in the divine life. There will be deeper suffering, due to increasingly painful self-awareness, to the wound of the longing for God, and to the extreme aridity arising from the sense of God's seeming remoteness as even our depths are thoroughly purified.

God, unceasingly faithful, enables us, as God alone can do, to abide more and more in the divine life. God instructs the soul now 'in the perfection of love without its doing anything nor understanding how this happens'.[15] Everything is given by God, but in a way which is dark and difficult, because so utterly beyond what can be comprehended or endured, until our knowing and loving is taken up more fully into that of God. All of the concrete circumstances of life are involved in this transformation, so dark to us, but being accomplished divinely as we are brought to let go of our own direction in life and can therefore be led securely. 'God takes you by the hand and guides you . . . You would never have succeeded in reaching this place no matter how good your eyes and your feet.'[16]

In this way prayer grows, the life of God increases. There can be different emphases both in the way it is described and in the form it takes in a person's life. Certain writers will stress the darkness and others not so much – John of the Cross clearly does so, in comparison to Teresa, due to his doctrine of the transfiguration of the senses and the extreme purification of the spirit, by which we rise to the 'divine sense, which is a stranger and alien to all human ways,'[17] and are 'reborn in the life of the spirit by means of this divine inflow'.[18]

These changes occur under different forms, depending on whether people are given more to the purely contemplative way or to an active or apostolic life. 'They do not always appear under so definitely contemplative a form as that described by St John of the Cross', Garrigou-Lagrange says.[19] The prayer in itself may have fewer signs of change, and what is happening will be discerned more readily in the changing quality of all the activities of life. In terms of Jesuit spirituality, for instance, since the apostolic life is itself 'a pathway to God,' to be travelled with eyes kept first on God,[20] there will be a deepening realization of what it is to 'always aim at serving and pleasing the Divine Majesty for its own sake',[21] in the growing self-forgetfulness of journeying and labouring, 'ever intent on seeking the greater glory of God our Lord and the greater aid of souls'.[22] Again, it may be according to the similar grace desired by Mary Ward for the members of her Institute, when she received her vision of the Just Soul, of a person brought to 'a singular freedom from all that could make one adhere to earthly things, with an entire application and apt disposition to all good works', and being enabled in that freedom 'to refer all to God'.[23]

As Mary Ward further saw, this could only be so in the case of 'a soul wholly God's'.[24] The way to that state of being in God accords with what I have said about growth in grace, although the more marked signs will include the lack of sensible consolation in the apostolate itself and times of extreme darkness where even the most valued of commitments are concerned. Once again, this is so because of what we are, who God is, and how God works in our being changed more and more into the divine likeness, who 'is light' and in whom 'is no darkness at all' (1 John 1.5).

In time there can come about what has been prayed for and longed for, when God will take over completely, mysteriously, and divine love becomes everything. This is the abiding state of union in God, of wholly belonging to God, so that all understanding and willing is God's, and what is done is within the great activity of God. Yet in the night and way of faith there is already something of this essential reality, in the silent and interior loving of God, and in our contemplation of God in the vision of faith.[25] What is happening and how it happens must be left to God. The kingdom grows, we do not know how, in secret (Mark 4.26-9). Our part is to be detached and faithful, in simplicity of heart, content to let God work, affirming the divine presence in faith, and doing what we are able with willingness.

3 SPIRITUAL DIRECTION

When it comes to helping another in this prayer, it is important to know the meaning of growth in prayer and grace. This is the most important requirement without which many mistakes will be made.

Without an adequate appreciation of how God works, a director will fail to grasp the real significance of the difficulty and darkness described above, and may respond in a harmful way even with the best of intentions. There can be, for instance, a suspicion that something has gone wrong, and so the person's prayer and life are analysed on this presumption, based on an initial misreading of the situation. This is not to deny the reality of human difficulties, or how valuable it is to help when these are uppermost in a person's consciousness, or when they may need special attention. But it is to say that the principal focus must be the mystery of God. Again, there can be expectations of readily-discernible movement in a person's relationship with God, when in fact the deepening mystery of grace is quite beyond normal comprehension.

The best approach is to affirm the prayer, and to do this especially by referring to the faithfulness and love of God. To someone in this contemplative way, not sure what to express or wondering how the words spoken will be taken up, this affirmation and understanding brings support. Some personal explanation or reading matter on the nature of the prayer can be part of that help.

It is also good to encourage the pondering of Scripture and other material outside of the prayer. But there may be a disinclination to read much and a feeling of saturation after very little, because of what is happening in the prayer, and since the mind will have received much already in earlier meditation and reading. In any case, it is always worthwhile mentioning how much is acquired in the liturgy, which may form a preparation for the prayer or be taken up as a conscious articulation of the longing, praise or intercession in the heart of the prayer, which itself is deeply rooted in the prayer of the Trinity and in the action of Christ.

Obviously the many issues of life may need to be talked about, as they enter into the mystery of God's leading, and particularly now because of the growing concern to refer all to God.

In many instances, people have been led without the help of a director, and it is well to remember this, and to be reminded that everything is God's work. Where direction is available it is a situation where the director's own orientation towards God is very important, for one can only be of help to another in God and under the influence of divine grace.[26]

4 THE SPIRITUAL EXERCISES

In the matter of the Spiritual Exercises, and how best to deal with a retreatant whose prayer is contemplative, it will be seen that some important alterations must be made - but not out of line, I believe, with what Ignatius offers.

First of all, I take it that the method of prayer outlined by Ignatius is generally 'meditative' - and this includes even what Ignatius terms 'contemplation' from the Second Week onwards though there is a process of simplification in the prayer and over each day. It follows that if the prayer of faith has become the habitual way of a retreatant he or she cannot use the method outlined in the Exercises, and should not be expected to do so.

It seems advisable that alterations should be along the following lines. Since Scripture or other material cannot be used, or only very sparingly, it is good to suggest some meditation on key elements of the Exercises outside prayer, with a short period of reflection after each time. In this way there is an appropriate framework to the retreat, and at the times of meditation or reflection there can be helpful insight, a sense of God's leading, of how love is being given, and freedom in the service of Christ. It is a more active side to the retreat – although how much of it will happen, and whether it can be perceived to any extent, will vary from one person to another – and is a situation where the director may have a role in discussion and elucidation.

Let the prayer itself be truly contemplative, without the constraint to use material in a discursive, active way. Help may be needed because of inevitable pressures to become more active again in prayer – which, if yielded to, will do violence to what God wishes to do and will cause disturbance. The director must beware especially of mistaken expectations which force the retreatant to pray and report on the prayer in the more accepted manner. The right approach is to leave the prayer to God, and to affirm and to encourage the retreatant in this. For what formerly needed to be worked through in some detail in order to be open to a particular grace, according to the method of Ignatius, has now given way to a simplified awareness or to a prayer of being there in faith.

It may be that during the prayer at this time there will be a more conscious awareness and response than usual, occasioned for instance by particular aspects of the mysteries of Christ. If this is so, I do not think that it contradicts what has been said about the prayer of faith, but can be good, once the underlying emphasis remains that of receptivity and dependence on God. Again, some people may be at the stage where they still tend occasionally to come back to meditation in prayer, without doing violence to it. In such cases, I think it better to encourage the simplicity of the prayer of loving attentiveness, a contemplation of the mysteries of Christ 'with a simple gaze', as Teresa puts it,[27] rather than to incline towards a more literal following of the prayer of the Exercises. In all of this it may take time, with trial and error, to find what is best for each person.[28]

In conclusion, it is good to mention why I consider that such an approach is in keeping with the intentions of Ignatius. For it could be felt that an insistence on the prayer of faith, based especially on the teaching of John of the Cross, seems to deny the richness of more active and imaginative prayer and is out of place in Ignatian apostolic spirituality. I do not believe that this is the case. Rather, it is a question of noticing what is being opened up in the Exercises about prayer, and of appreciating the subsequent ways of God's leading, that occur even in people whose lives are very active.

The Spiritual Exercises were meant primarily for those who seek the will of God and who wish everything to be ordered to the love and service of God (Exx 5, 20, 21), so that they are open to choose that state of Christian life which God most desires for them (Exx 135). Such people are usually not far from the beginnings of their formal spiritual life, when they started to give regular time to personal prayer, and so require that more active method as outlined by Ignatius. But the prayer of contemplation is given to people further along that path who have most likely made their definitive choice of a way of life – and who have not stood still or gone backwards, but made good progress. There is a link, a sequence. And it is surely the case that a generous person who has made the Exercises in the more usual manner is being prepared for the whole range and depth of grace, as all of it is meant to be received and to unfold over a life given to God's praise and service.

What is happening, then, in someone making the Exercises yet being drawn beyond the more active engagement with the mysteries of Christ in prayer, and beyond the expected, tangible effects of consolation? I would say that what is being aimed at by Ignatius – in the Second Week for instance, regarding the understanding and love and following of Christ – is now being lived interiorly and ever more fully, by the direct action of grace. Certainly, a measure of this occurs in the more literal making of the Exercises – and indeed the Word, in its external and objective forms, will never cease to be nourishment and living revelation for us.[29] But in the darker way of contemplation, Christ comes to be formed and to abide in us more completely, the mysteries of faith are lived increasingly from within, through a greater conformity with what they really are, because realized by the more intimate and secret working of the Spirit of God.[30]

In this way, the Exercises are fulfilled in their deepest meaning, and there is no need to fear that some other path is being followed, not intended by Ignatius, who desired that those called to an active life would be truly contemplative.

At the end of the Exercises, in the Contemplation to Attain the Love of God, Ignatius leaves us to make the extraordinary offering of the prayer, 'Take, Lord, receive' (Exx 234). In subsequent living, perhaps full of active concerns, it is not surprising if the love prayed for here, nothing less than the divine and trinitarian life abiding within (John 14.23), becomes more and more the fullness of our existence and, to adapt Mary Ward's phrase, make us belong wholly to God. It is what Christ has promised, and alone enables us to bear much fruit for the kingdom in the world (John 15.7-9). Ignatius opens us out to all of that, although we need to go beyond the Exercises to understand the process of it. And so it is that in coming to appreciate the meaning of contemplation, or the night of faith, we can see how what was necessarily incomplete and fitful in its beginnings is now being changed into the mystery of a life of uninterrupted prayer, a life lived supernaturally in and for God.

NOTES

1. J.P. de Caussade, *On Prayer* (London 1931, revised 1949), introduction by Dom John Chapman and originally published in 1741; the phrase 'the prayer of faith' appears on pp. 110, 209, 266, and is from Bossuet, whose teaching in turn relied on John of the Cross, Francis de Sales and Balthasar Alvarez.

2. Eugene Boylan, *Difficulties in Mental Prayer* (Dublin 1943).

3. Leonard Boase, *The Prayer of Faith* (London 1950). More recently, the theme is taken up in Thomas H. Green, *When the Well Runs Dry* (Indiana 1979).

4. See Thomas Merton, *Spiritual Direction and Meditation & What is Contemplation?* (Wheathampstead 1975), pp. 43-86.

5. See the writings of Reginald Garrigou-Lagrange, especially *Christian Perfection and Contemplation* (St Louis and London 1937), based on Thomas Aquinas and John of the Cross, but made more accessible and readable in *The Three Ways of the Spiritual Life* (London 1938). See also Louis Bouyer, *Introduction to Spirituality* (New York 1961), pp. 261-85; Merton, op. cit., pp. 89-112; Antonio Moreno, 'Contemplation according to Teresa and John of the Cross', in *Review for Religious* vol. 37, no. 2

(March 1978), pp. 256-67; Francis Kelly Nemeck and Marie Theresa Coombs, *Contemplation* (Wilmington and Dublin 1982); Ladislas M. Orsy, 'From meditation to contemplation', in *Review for Religious* vol. 22, no. 2 (1963), pp. 172-9.

6. *The Dark Night*, Bk 1, ch. 10, n. 6; in Kieran Kavanaugh and Otilio Rodriguez, *The Collected Works of St John of the Cross* (New York 1964), p. 318.

7. See John of the Cross, *Ascent of Mount Carmel*, Bk 2, ch. 13, nn. 1-7, and *The Dark Night*, Bk 1, ch. 9, nn. 1-9, for the signs of the onset of contemplation (Kavanaugh and Rodriguez, pp. 140-1, 313-6); and Nemeck and Coombs, op. cit. pp. 53-71.

8. Ruth Burrows, *Guidelines for Mystical Prayer* (London 1976), p. 33.

9. ibid., p. 35.

10. *The Interior Castle*, 6th Dwelling Places, ch. 7, nn. 6, 9; in Kavanaugh and Rodriguez, *The Collected Works of St Teresa of Avila* (Washington 1980), pp. 399-401.

11. ibid., n. 12: and see also nn. 5, 7.

12. ibid., n. 11; and Teresa has an earlier treatment in her *Life*, chs 22 and 24. See Antonio Moreno, 'St Teresa, contemplation and the humanity of Christ', in *Review for Religious* vol. 38, no. 6 (1979), pp. 912-23, and *Mount Carmel* vol. 28, no. 3, pp. 149-65.

13. *The Dark Night* Bk 1, ch. 10, n. 6 (Kavanaugh and Rodriguez, p. 318).

14. See for instance Garrigou-Lagrange, *The Three Ways of the Spiritual Life*, p. 32, where he quotes from Lallement on the second conversion.

15. John of the Cross, *The Dark Night*, Bk 2, ch. 5, n. 1 (Kavanaugh and Rodriguez, p. 335).

16. John of the Cross, op. cit., Bk 2, ch. 16, n. 7 (Kavanaugh and Rodriguez, p. 365).

17. op. cit., Bk 2, ch. 9, n. 5; but here I quote from E. Allison Peers, *The Complete Works of Saint John of the Cross*, (London 1953), vol. 1, p. 399. See Jean Mouroux, *The Christian Experience* (London and New York 1955), 'A note on the affectivity of the senses in St John of the Cross', pp. 305-20. On the purification of the spirit see Garrigou-Lagrange, *The Three Ways*, in what he calls the third crisis or conversion, especially pp. 91-93; as well as in this book, see his treatment of the three conversions in *The Three Ages of the Interior Life*, 2 vols (St Louis and London 1947, 1948).

18. John of the Cross, *The Dark Night*, Bk 2, ch. 9, n. 6 (Kavanaugh and Rodriguez, p. 348).

19. *The Three Ways of the Spiritual Life*, p. 109; and see pp. 63, 73, 74, 79, 91.

20. Ignatius of Loyola, *Constitutions*, n. 3; as in George E. Ganss, *The Constitutions of the Society of Jesus* (St Louis 1970).

21. ibid., n. 288.

22. ibid., n. 605.

23. See Mary Catherine Elizabeth Chambers, *The Life of Mary Ward* (London 1882), vol. I, p. 346; M. Emmanuel Orchard, *Till God Will: Mary Ward Through her Writings* (London 1985), p. 40; and Immolata Wetter, *Mary Ward's Prayer* (talks given in 1974 and circulated among members of the IBVM), p. 15.

24. Chambers, vol. 1, p. 474.

25. See Hans Urs von Balthasar, *The Glory of the Lord: a theological aesthetics*, vol. 1: *Seeing the Form* (Edinburgh 1982), 'The light of faith' pp. 131-218.

26. To help understanding of the right approach to spiritual direction here, one can hardly do better than read Dom John Chapman, *Spiritual Letters* (London 1935), noting especially 'Contemplative prayer, a few simple rules' pp. 287-94; and see Ladislas M. Orsy, 'Contemplation: some practical considerations', in *Review for Religious* vol. 24, no. 2, (March 1965), pp. 248-64.

27. *The Interior Castle*, 6th Dwelling Places, ch. 7, n. 11 (Kavanaugh and Rodriguez, p. 402). But again with Teresa, contemplative presence to Christ and looking to him within the prayer goes beyond imaginative representation; see the study of this question in Thomas Alvarez, *Living with God: St. Teresa's concept of prayer* (Dublin 1980), pp. 12-18, based on her *Life*.

28. I have been helped by the points given in Robert O. Brennan, 'The retreat director and the contemplative', in *Review for Religious* vol. 40, no. 2 (March 1981), pp. 168-181.

29. Hans Urs von Balthasar's *Prayer* (London 1973), is an exposition of the place of the Word in contemplation, by which we are drawn into the 'objective' reality of God's love for the world and in the Church.

30. See Joseph Patron, 'Christ in the teaching and life of St John of the Cross', in *Mount Carmel* vol. 30, no. 2 (Summer 1982), pp. 94-110, and especially pp. 101-2; see also Louis Bouyer, op. cit., p. 305.

CHAPTER SEVENTEEN

Spiritual Direction and Social Consciousness

Elinor Shea

The current popularity of doing theology through story-telling provides an exceptionally apt vehicle for presenting one concrete answer to the frequently posed questions: 'What is the connection between spiritual direction and social consciousness? Is there a connection at all, and if so, how can it be identified and developed?' One concrete experience recounted here may encourage and assist others who are exploring those questions.

The story is that of the Center for Spirituality and Justice, a centre established primarily for the training of spiritual directors.[1] The Center was founded in the Bronx, New York, in 1980 through the initiative of Sister Miriam Cleary OSU an experienced spiritual director who had just returned from four years in the Caribbean and South America. The horizon of the Third World and its needs was therefore a significant influence in her decision to create a training programme for directors in the United States.

From its inception, the Center was based on a strong faith that the two foci – spirituality and justice – were essentially interconnected, and on an equally strong commitment to discovering where the essential connections lay and how to foster their dynamic interaction. The fact that each person who joined in the work as staff had some experience either in foreign or domestic missionary work ensured that the horizon of the Third World and the poor would not be overlooked. While believing in the interconnectedness of spirituality and justice, it soon became clear to staff that the task of shaping a training programme on its foundation would not be easy nor would the methodology be obvious.

The directed retreat movement and the growing phenomenon of ongoing spiritual direction, familiar as part of the current life of the Church in the United States, had early on encountered the question: how does the practice of spiritual direction and the marked increase

203

in interest in interior prayer, prayer forms and all that was embraced by the term 'spirituality' relate to the equally strong and equally engaging world of social action? The equation was sometimes framed rather facilely: 'Do you picket or do you pray?' but the concern was much more serious and searching.

The Synod of Bishops in 1971 had declared unequivocally that 'action on behalf of justice and participation in the transformation of the world fully appear as a constitutive dimension of preaching the gospel'. The implication of this for Christian spirituality was challenging, but a methodology for implementing it had yet to be created. Directors trained in the Ignatian tradition had been taught to focus primarily, if not exclusively, on the prayer of the directee as the locus for God's action: the movements, affections, attractions, repugnances, enlightenments which were noticed by the directee. The director was to be contemplative before the person directed, and was not to function as teacher, preacher, pastoral counsellor or advocate of a particular form of Christian presence or action in the world. However, after a number of years in the work, directors began to ask themselves why, in the lives of so many good and praying persons whom they were directing, concern for the crying needs of the world did not appear in any significant way except perhaps in expressions of guilt, or 'shoulds' and 'oughts'. Conversely, why, in the lives of dedicated and deeply committed social activists, did contemplative prayer and, for that matter, spiritual direction, appear to be somewhat irrelevant to their passionate concern for the creation of a more just society? As the staff of the Center for Spirituality and Justice began their work, they were conscious of these questions both within their own lives and in the lives of the persons who were attracted to the programme, precisely because of their own search for the vital links between justice and spirituality. The challenge was to shape a programme which would be faithful to the principles of spiritual direction as understood and experienced, and, at the same time, faithful to the belief that whatever was constitutive of the Christian life would be operative and manifest in the lives of praying Christians.

The study of the Spiritual Exercises of St Ignatius provided the basic structure for the programme. Of themselves, however, the Exercises do not address this tension directly. The staff eventually needed to find an anthropology which would adequately undergird the search for the links between spiritual direction and social consciousness, and which would be in harmony with the dynamic of the Spiritual Exercises.

As early as 1974, the Center for Concern in Washington, DC., had published the work of a task force set up precisely to explore the relationship between 'social consciousness and Ignatian spirituality'. The term 'social consciousness' rather than 'social action' gave a new clarity to the question, and the paper, *Soundings*,[2] proved to be an invaluable resource for the Center staff. Particularly enlightening was an article by Peter Henriot sj, 'The public dimension of the spiritual life: the problem of "simultaneity" '. This article, coupled with one by Thomas Clarke sj, 'Societal grace: for a new pastoral strategy', offered the basis needed for the next steps of the process.

Henriot's thesis is that

> it is only possible to speak of the reality of the human person today by taking into full account the three dimensions of human existence: the individual, the interpersonal and the public. These are not three separate and distinct dimensions so much as three moments in our perception of a single reality, or three interrelated interpenetrated aspects. Thus the identity of the human person is inadequately situated outside of a consideration of all three dimensions simultaneously.[3]

These three aspects of the human person are described by Clarke as 'intra-personal, inter-personal and public or societal'.[4] Every human person experiences her/himself simultaneously in all three dimensions existentially, but the nature of human consciousness is to be attentive to only one of them at any given moment. Without a theoretical understanding of the triadic nature of human experience, however, it is likely that only one or possibly two dimensions will be noticed, reflected upon and appropriated, with the consequence that human experience is only partially known and acted within. In working with this insight, the Center staff began to intuit that perhaps directors were suffering from some kind of blindness or bias which inclined them to focus too narrowly on the intra-personal and inter-personal dimensions of their directees' experience and not to notice how God was drawing and engaging them in the societal dimension of their faith.

Using the triadic model for human experience provides a more suitable lens for expanding the range of the director's attention to include the societal dimension. Then it is not a matter of imposing the societal dimension or of manipulating the directee's experience, and in so doing, moving out of the contemplative stance appropriate to the director. Rather, the screen is widened and the directee is consistently perceived as a person simultaneously engaged in intense intra-personal activity and consciousness, on-going inter-personal relationships, and living within a set of established and defining structures and institutions in the societal arena. A different and more freeing challenge was offered the director. Rather than trying to make the connections between justice and spirituality, she/he was to become alert to recognize how God was initiating this activity in the lives of believers.

As the staff worked with this model, the fruitfulness of the approach became more apparent. However, since spiritual direction is primarily concerned with the *religious* experience of the person in its totality, not only in prayer experiences, a theological vision and language was needed which would be an adequate complement to this anthropology and would be useful in spiritual direction training and practice. Two articles of Karl Rahner's answered this need in wonderfully congruent ways.

The articles, 'The experience of God today',[5] and 'The experience of God and the experience of self',[6] at first glance appeared to the trainees as too dense, unnecessarily complex and not obviously useful. However, serious work with Rahner's thought paid a rich harvest. The essential fruit gathered was a working understanding of Rahner's thesis that the experience of God today is *also* an experience of simultaneity, that is to say that any experience of God is simultaneously an experience of self and an experience of the neighbour. Moreover, the experience, wherever it begins, develops and moves from a non-thematic stage to a reflective and finally an interpretive level. As the staff gradually familiarized itself with these concepts and juxtaposed them with the insights of Henriot and Clarke, a grid began to emerge which became a frame of reference and teaching tool in the training programme. The grid began to look something like this:

The experience of the directee

	intra-personal	inter-personal	societal
non-thematic			
reflective			
interpretive			

Of what use is this grid to the spiritual director? An example may illustrate, drawn from an actual session of spiritual direction in which the director's consciousness had been shaped by this grid and was the receptive screen receiving the communication from the directee. The directee recounted a series of experiences, some in the mode of almost casual conversation or information, some with more explicit religious focus, some of significance but not consciously part of the formal religious experience. The directee is a person who has consistently experienced herself as having received a strong and deep gift of faith and has experienced God's fidelity in her life. She has also been drawn to involvement in peace and justice issues in her life.

The session opened with an observation that her little nephew was feeling sad because of the birth of a new baby in the family. He had lost his place of importance and was suffering from it; this was reported with feeling and compassion. The conversation then moved to two experiences of the directee during liturgies, one in her own parish and the other on vacation. In each instance the setting was familiar – a church filled with Sunday worshippers – and in each instance an unfamiliar interior word expressed itself as, 'What in hell am I doing here?' accompanied by feelings of surprise, confusion, alienation and anger. Later in the conversation, a sense of loss was expressed over the departure of an intimate friend from her community, intensified by the acknowledgment that the friend was entering into a lesbian relationship. Loss was present, as well as a desire to be faithful to the person as far as possible. There was also a rather disheartened reference to the reversal of many programmes of social welfare due to the direction being taken by the Reagan administration. Finally, the directee, who was just beginning the programme at the Center for Spirituality and Justice, recounted an experience of formal prayer. The participants had been asked to spend some time allowing their prayer to offer them an answer to the question: 'What do you desire from your participation in this programme?' The answer came, clearly, surprisingly, somewhat disconcertingly: 'To be faithful to God even if God is not there'.

For the purposes of this essay, what is important is the fact that the director, attuned to the grid described above, noticed connections related to loss, alienation, death, sadness, fear, experienced in each of the three arenas. The director noticed, too, that some of the experiences were on the non-thematic level (at the liturgies), some had moved to the reflective, (the relationship with the friend), some more interpretive (the consequences of the Reagan policies). The director could also note the underlying thread of desire: to be faithful to a faithful God, to friendship, to peace and justice commitments, *no matter what*. A single focus, rather than the triadic one here, might have meant that the unity and simultaneity of this directee's experience of herself, and her neighbour (inter-personally and societally) and her God would not have been perceived and reflected on.

The actual movement in the session is more dynamic than the grid and its static, geometric shape suggests. While not every session touches upon all three areas quite so clearly as in the one described, experience suggests that with heightened consciousness and trained attentiveness, the director will, over time, perceive this pattern of experience. In being able to reflect this perception back to the directee, the director can facilitate in a fuller way the directee's recognition of the movement of God's grace. The meaning of the experience may not be immediately available, indeed, cannot be when the experience is at the non-thematic level. But meaning is not the initial concern. Rather, in the session, the directee is assisted in re-experiencing the non-thematic, in describing it as best she/he can. Through the director's reflecting, questioning, noticing, the experience may begin to unfold, and be appropriated more fully by the directee. In the process the experience will eventually move from the non-thematic to the reflective and ultimately the interpretive level, the latter being the level of meaning, of theological interpretation. All the while the conversation and experience may be moving around within and among the three arenas of the experience, the intra-personal, the inter-personal and the societal.

While the director gives primary attention to the arena in which the directee initiates the interview, he/she is also listening attentively to where and how the essence of the experience may be appearing in the other two areas. Since the grace of God affects us through the principle of attraction, this will exercise the same attraction in each of the dimensions of the person's life, although the connection may not be immediately apparent. The synchronicity of the inner and outer worlds appears again and again. The attentive director, from the vantage point of the above grid, is in a position to be affected by the attraction operative in the directee and will be able to tease out the possible connections. The grid, then, places in the director's hand a kind of Ariadne's threat, the golden thread of desire, attraction, specific and unique in each directee, and enables the director to detect and follow the movement of God's grace in the religious experience of the directee, and help the directee to respond to this movement in all its richness and mystery. 'The mystery we call God' touches, challenges, and is free to capture our attention at any place, at any time, and in any way. As the programme at the Center developed, it became clearer to the staff that the director not only witnesses the activity of God and the response of the directee, but also works in the triadic maze as a translator and de-coder, attuned to the language of 'the experience of God today', and not limited to only the traditional language which often obscures as much as it illuminates.

Having come to this point in the evolution of the Center, their initial faith now supported and elucidated by an operative anthropology and theology - a process which took about three years - the staff was nevertheless aware that in the case presentations and verbatims of the trainees, even though this theoretical apparatus was in place, operationally the majority of the supervised direction sessions remained chiefly in the intra- and inter-personal areas and rarely included in any integrated way, the area of social concern, the public, structural area of the lives of the directees. At this point the staff sought a methodology for the training which would finally bridge the gap.

Up to this point, the format for the training was not unlike a number of other programmes. Among the resources and tools that had consistently been used were the *Spiritual Exercises* of St Ignatius, and various published materials on the dynamic of spiritual direction and on the psychological principles operative in any helping relationship. Each trainee was providing spiritual direction on a regular basis for at least two people and meeting weekly to present a verbatim to a supervisor. These individual sessions were complemented by case conference presentations. In looking for an additional tool which would bring to light the societal dimension of experience and affect the social consciousness of the staff and trainees, two members of the staff recalled the model of the praxis cycle, developed by Peter Henriot and Joseph Holland,[7] and used in a workshop conducted by Thomas Clarke which staff members had attended. While this was developed for use with groups which were trying to come to some effective social analysis and pastoral action within a commonly shared structure, it occurred to the staff that it could be adapted for individuals, and that the conscious and systematic reflection on a structure in this mode could provide an avenue to a transformed consciousness in the director who would then be more able to facilitate this process in her/his directees without violating the principles of spiritual direction.

The praxis cycle, also called the pastoral cycle, soon began to be referred to in the programme as the experience cycle which connected it more directly with the basis of all spiritual direction, the experience of the directee. Some of the staff, shaped in their earlier days by membership in Young Christian Students, readily recognized the experience cycle as based on that natural impulse to 'observe, judge and act'. However, as Freire had demonstrated, particularly in *Pedagogy of the Oppressed*, what is *seen* and its underlying meaning, in terms of structural analysis and naming, are quite different realities. The de-coding process which Freire developed in his literacy programme not only enabled people to read but also to name their reality as subjects, and, in the process, take the first step toward transformation of their lives through transforming the structures which shaped their consciousness.

The staff decided to adapt the focus and structure of the pastoral cycle and create out of it a form for a verbatim. Whereas the traditional verbatim recorded not only the spoken dialogue between the director and directee, but also the non-verbal, and especially the affective responses of the director, this second verbatim form would provide a format for reporting on a dialogue between the director (in this case, trainee) and a structure in her/his life which impinged on or seemed to control her/him precisely in the public, societal dimension of life. The staff experimented with the process to test its validity. Their experience confirmed their intuition about the possibility of a break-through in finding the elusive links between spiritual direction and social consciousness.

What does the process involve? At the beginning of the year, the trainees were introduced to the four phases of the experience cycle: insertion, social analysis, theological reflection and pastoral planning. They were then instructed to dialogue with their own lives and, with the help of their supervisors, to choose a structure in their lives that they wished to investigate. Initially time had to be taken to narrow down the scope so that the structure selected was as specific as possible. A working definition of structure emerged: an independently operative set of relationships in which one is involved but which has a life of its own and would continue to operate whether one was involved in it or not. Some of the structures selected will illustrate the concept: membership in an on-going covenant community, membership on a parish pastoral team, membership within a religious community (local, provincial, international), membership on a retreat house team, membership on a college faculty, a seminary faculty. In each instance, the person influences and is influenced by the structure, while the structure has an independent existence.

The structure having been selected, a series of questions was offered as a help to enter into the phases of the cycle. The most recent form these questions took, plus a diagram of the cycle, follow. In each phase, the questions helped to get at the underlying reality, assumptions, inter-relationships involved in the structure in a manner not unlike the dialogue that would ordinarily be recorded in a spiritual direction session verbatim.

INSERTION PHASE (surfacing actual experience and affective response)

What is happening to you and to others, relative to the structure? What are your feelings about your experience? How do you find yourself responding, in behaviour, in feeling, in prayer? Where and with whom do you locate yourself or identify as you consider this

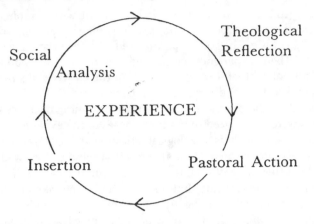

structure? When you consider this structure or discuss it do you find that you tend to leave out certain people or groups? Relative to the structure, who are the poor, the oppressed? What role do they play in your considerations? Pray for the light to discern the presence of the Spirit in the midst of the experience you are considering.

SOCIAL ANALYSIS PHASE (becoming objective; getting at the facts and interconnections)

What is the history? How did the structure come about, develop, change? What analytical tradition(s) have been operative in this history? What one(s) are you using as you analyse the structure? (For example, if the structure is economic, is the tradition socialist, capitalist; if political, is it participative, authoritative; if ecclesial, is it hierarchical, communitarian?) What are the operative assumptions flowing from the tradition(s) being used? What are the social relationships involved (class, race, sex, etc.)? How is power being exercised? Who has it? Who makes decisions? Who benefits? Who bears the cost?

Are any trends emerging? What will happen if the situation continues as it is now? Pray to discern the 'signs of the times' and the sources of creativity and hope.

THEOLOGICAL REFLECTION PHASE (becoming contemplative; allowing the gospel values involved to surface)

What reinforces, or undercuts gospel values, or social teachings of the Church in the situation under consideration? What theological stances are involved (e.g., God as loving or condemning; creature as good or evil; the Church as pyramid or people of God)? What Scripture passages apply to the situation? What is graced, open to God? What is sinful, turning from God in the situation? Have there been any transformative aspects to the experience as you have moved through the phases so far? Any spontaneous insights, understandings? Pray to be aware of the movements of light/darkness, peace/disquiet, encouragement/discouragement which have occurred.

PASTORAL ACTION PHASE (becoming concrete as to action to be taken)

How much freedom do you experience as you move toward this phase? What concrete responses arose in you to the movements you noticed in the theological reflection? What concrete actions are possible to bring about what you see as needed relative to the situation under consideration? Which of these do you consider most effective? Who would be involved in carrying out the action(s)? Are the poor and oppressed involved? Is service *for* or *with* others involved? What are the implications of the actions? (e.g., hostility/acceptance; enthusiasm/apathy, etc.) What means will be used to evaluate the effectiveness of the actions? Pray for the strength to move into the decisions and actions which have emerged.

These questions have undergone several revisions in the process of working with the cycle and applying it to the structure of the training programme.

In the training programme of thirty weeks, the verbatim on a spiritual direction session with a directee was alternated each week with a 'verbatim' on the trainee's dialogue with the selected structure. As each phase of the cycle was completed, the trainee was invited to move to the next phase. An interesting dynamic appeared. In the first two phases, analytic and cognitive skills were called upon primarily. The transition into the theological phase showed that this

213

phase remained elusive and somewhat sterile until a more contemplative and receptive stance was assumed by the person using the cycle. Then the theological connection, which had the character, usually, of the non-thematic level of experience, was noticed. At times it came through the awareness of a familiar and significant Scripture passage, or an image, or a word. The revision of the questions for this phase reflects this insight rather clearly.

The movement into pastoral action was strongly influenced by the quality of the theological reflection. The actions which proved to be most appropriate to the process frequently were less dramatic than the term 'social action' often connotes; however, within the structures selected, they often had a transforming effect on the trainee and on the structure, partly because of the action and partly because of the consciousness which emerged out of the various phases.

A cardinal principle of spiritual direction is that the initiative is always God's; the responsibility of the directee, and of the director, is to pay attention to where God is acting, initiating. Just as in prayer traditionally understood, so too in the realm of social consciousness, the initiative is God's. If 'action on behalf of justice and participation in the transformation of the world fully appear as a constitutive dimension of preaching the gospel' then faith informs us that God will act in harmony with that belief. The story of the Center for Spirituality and Justice offers one concrete example of how directors were enabled to be attentive and responsive to that action.

NOTES

1. The author is indebted to the staff and participants in the Center for Spirituality and Justice for their assistance and encouragement in writing this essay, and for allowing the author to use their experience.

2. *Soundings* (Center of Concern, Washington, DC., 1974).

3. ibid., p. 13.

4. ibid., p. 15

5. Karl Rahner, 'The experience of God today', *Theological Investigations* XI (London 1974), pp. 149-65.

6. Karl Rahner, 'The experience of God and the experience of self', *Theological Investigations* VI (London 1969), pp. 231-49.

7. Joe Holland and Peter Henriot SJ, *Social Analysis: linking faith and justice* (Orbis Books in collaboration with the Center of Concern, New York, 1983). See Ch. 1, p. 7ff.

PART FIVE

Interpretation and History

CHAPTER EIGHTEEN

The Structure of the Rules for Discernment

Michael J. Buckley

While the contents of the Rules for the Discernment of Spirits have been analysed and applied over the past four centuries, the structure or internal unity in which they are presented has almost escaped attention.[1] Enormous weight has been given to their individual instructions, but almost no significance has been attributed to their collective form and anatomy. They are treated as individual units or groupings brought to bear as occasion warrants or as temptations indicate their use, both within the Weeks of the Exercises and within the discriminations made every day of conscious Christian living. In such employ, they have offered an enormous clarity and prudence to prayer, choice, action, and direction, except when their understanding degenerated into simpliste maxims and painfully obvious platitudes.[2] It is the contention of this brief essay, however, that the renewed interest in discernment should engage an inquiry into their formulation precisely as a tight-knit collectivity, that they should be submitted to a structural analysis analogical to that which the entire Exercises are undergoing, and that from this examination an understanding should emerge, both about the meaning of the individual directive and about the location of these within the general organization of the Exercises. The basic claim here is identical with that of any structural analysis: that the argument by which the elements are conjoined specifies their meaning and illumines the function which they may serve.

There is a particular urgency about this task now. Western religious culture is submitted to a variety of religious experiences and a heterogeneity of religious traditions as multiple as anything it has confronted in over a thousand years. Variety and hetereogeneity have become characteristics of our times, whether one refers to them in terms of future shock or as the collapse of the modern world. They offer the Church a unique *kairos*, standing amid the confluence and even chaos of so many religious traditions, both within and without the Christian community. Some old stabilities and enclosed cultural forms have perished, and the Church must choose among the myriad and complex voices that surround it. Even more fundamentally, the Church must decide whether its posture in this contemporary encounter with newness will be synthetic or polemic, whether the Church is to assimilate even while transmuting that which is assumed, or whether it is to battle even while admitting that there is much to commend in its adversary. This essay contends that the Ignatian structure of discernment reveals and offers to the Catholic spirit the means by which various strands of religious traditions can be assessed in a reverent attempt to discern the progression of the divine Spirit through the world, that the integration which this structure achieves allows for an openness to all authentic religious experience without reducing it to magic and superstition, rationalism and enlightenment, or sentimentality and enthusiasm. The structure of the Rules for Discernment of Spirits should provide for a synthesis which is more than an undifferentiated syncretism, whether that synthesis illumine a grace given for individual choice or a providence by which the Body of Christ may be present to more civilizations and cultures.[3]

A fundamental conviction founds and supports the history of religious consciousness and commitment: God will direct a person's life. Within this religious context, God emerges more personally than the ultimate source of meaning, being, and value, more engaged even than that which stands primary in any process and that towards which things ineluctably move, more immediate than an explanation for the existence of contingencies or a presupposition for the imperatives of the ethical enterprise or an horizon within which beauty and spirit are gathered and made available to human beings. All of this the religious person may sense or intuit or accept, but none of these constitute the primary focus or motive. Such a person longs for God, not as people think about marriage, but as they search for a spouse. God is known not so much in the inference that the cosmos is rooted in a source, but in the contemplative experience of personal longing. Within the religious context, God is not so classically 'He' or 'She', as 'Thou'; just as in religion, a person stands not as another fact within the universe, but as someone who is called by name out of nothingness and to whom a word is spoken.

Religion differs from the academic as its engagements are particular, its modalities are interpersonal, and its aim is transforming union.[4] The religious person is vitally persuaded not only that God has offered union as such a possibility and fulfilment, but that God will guide human life towards this realization; God offers not only finality, but consistent direction.

The pressing question is about concrete means; how does God direct human life? What are the means of contacting or of being guided by God? Where does one locate this directing power of God? Three variant and complex answers historically have been given.

Some have sought their guidance from God through the mediation of the preternatural, personalities or realities which – while not divine – so transcend and influence the human that they alter thoughts or control destinies or marshal forces or tempt resolution or effect liberation or deceive intention. Joan of Arc had her voices, Socrates his *daimon*, Antony his devils, and even Rilke fell back upon the angels as embodying the higher degree of reality of the invisible, angels reminding human beings how remote they are from human destiny or providing what Rilke called the 'direction' of his heart.[5] Saints, devils, and angels. People must touch that which is above the human so that God might instruct and lead them.

There is, however, another path: 'We mortal human beings can find no other ladder whereby to ascend unto God but by the works of God', wrote Robert Bellarmine, distinguishing the ascent of the mind from the rapture of the spirit and representing an intellectualistic tradition that he himself would trace back to Bonaventure's *Itinerarium mentis in Deum*.[6] A person progresses towards union with God by comprehending the real nature of things; these are divine products and 'the efficient cause may be known by the effects, and the example by the image'.[7] Conversely, the possession of God works a new union between the knowledge of God and all things in Jacob Boehme: 'In this light my spirit directly saw through all things, and knew God in and by all creatures, even in herbs and grass.'[8] There is a significant shift here from an arcane, magical immersion in the preternatural to a rational ascent made through graded orders of being. So this tradition often speaks of a ladder or of a journey of the mind to God, as Plato found a continuity of the developing intellect ranging through all studies and arts to its final contemplation of that which is best in existence.[9] The end is attained in ecstasy and vision, but the path and the guidance to this fulfilment is the dispassionate use of the mind, years of serious human thought. For still another tradition, neither the transcendence of the preternatural nor the elaborations of reasoning and vision offer an approach to the divine. 'The heart has its reason, which reason does not know' is often cited to justify this path.[10] Human beings are carried into the divine by affectivity and the surge of emotion. One is touched by God. So William James criticizes Cardinal Newman for his failure to realize that 'feeling is the deeper source of religion',[11] and all intellectual operations are 'interpretative and inductive operations, operations after the fact, consequent upon religious feeling, not co-ordinate with it, not independent of what it ascertains'.[12] The *Imitation of Christ* teaches that it is far more important to feel contrition; the only function of intellect, implicitly stated, would be the secondary contribution of knowing its definition.[13] John Wesley's *Journals* record 'righteousness, peace and joy in the Holy Ghost. These must be *felt*, or they have no being'. And again: 'How do you know whether you love me? Why, as you know whether you are hot or cold. You *feel* this moment that you do or do not love me. And I *feel* at this moment that I do not love God, which therefore I know because I *feel* it.'[14] Feelings can offer a more profound threshold of consciousness which catches up the whole person in the intensity of experience, and allows experience to indicate conversion, justification, progressive sanctification, co-operation with providence, and the promise of salvation. But feelings can also live in the far more modest statement of the *Theologia Germanica*: 'So this love so makes a man one with God, that he can never be separated from him.'[15]

Preternatural influences, process of intellection, attractions of affectivity – these have constituted the several ways in which human beings have attempted to receive the guidance of God, and their distinction and their interplay continue the complicated history of religious experience. Seldom does one predominate to the total exclusion of the other two. Often two will exist at various moments as the same movement towards God, sometimes even existing together in collaboration and in opposition to the third: affectivity can join with the preternatural to war against reason, or reason can find support in human emotions for its rejections of angels, emanations and stars.

It was not the genius of Ignatius of Loyola that he counted all three factors as critical within religious experience. This he did, but so did other major figures of his time such as Teresa of Jesus, John of the Cross, Peter of Alcántara, etc. What Ignatius provided was a structure within which each of these finds a significant place; none is dismissed out of hand. A co-ordination among them is established so that they reach an integrity of effect, and one is taught how to recognize and reply to each. This, perhaps more than any other contribution, comprises the unique value of his Rules for the Discernment of Spirits. They formalize insights and responses which have arisen and justified themselves in Ignatius's own religious practice, though they can trace a patristic heritage back to Hermas and Origen, and a location with the history of spirituality back to Athanasius's *Life of Antony*, the *Conferences* of Cassian, and Diadochus of Photike's *De perfectione spirituali capita centum*.[16] The Middle Ages continued this tradition in Bernard of Clairvaux, Henry of Friemar, Bernadine of Siena, Denis the Carthusian, and Gerson.[17] But Ignatius's work, though situated within this ecclesiastical tradition, seems strangely unaware of much of it. The origin of these Rules is much more to be sought in his unfolding *Autobiography* than in his readings of the fathers and doctors of the Church. What is unique about Ignatian discernment is its schematization. No author either before or after has offered such a concise codification; in this internal structure more than any other place should be sought the uniqueness of his vision. It is this argument which emerges from the actual text of his Rules.

RULES: FIRST WEEK

The initial rule sets up a structure which unites the various approaches to religious experience into a co-ordinate and causal matrix. Preternatural influences become either the good spirit or 'the enemy'; thoughts and intentionality become either the conscience with the self-accusations of reason or the imaginations of sensual pleasure; affectivity and emotion become either remorse or sensual pleasures which draw towards or maintain a state of sin. These three levels of influence are intrinsically and causally connected: the enemy through the imagination causes sensual attraction; the good spirit through the reason and conscience causes remorse. And the relationship between the two causal lines is contradiction on every level: the enemy *versus* the good spirit; imaginations of sensual pleasures *versus* the self-accusations of reason; sensual pleasures drawing towards sin *versus* remorse. What Ignatius has erected here is a tripartite division distributed into two contradictory columns. This matrix will serve as a general scheme for the rest of his elaboration of discernment.[18]

What is enormously important to notice is that the vectors in religious experience, the causal lines, can either move down, as they do in this first rule from preternatural influences through human imagination and rational intentionality into affective states, or they can move up, as they do in the fourth and fifth rules. Certain affective-conditions, consolation and desolation, can spontaneously generate commensurate thought: 'The thoughts that spring from consolation *(que salen de la consolación)* are contrary to the thoughts which spring from desolation *(que salen de la desolación)*.'[19] Irrespective of how one comes into a state of desolation, for example, whether by an accident of the day or by temperament or by external influences, there will be thoughts and perspectives which correspond to this state of affectivity. The line of causality now moves up from affectivity to thoughts. The fifth rule warns against being determined by these thoughts, because they almost mechanically place one under the influence of the evil spirit: 'As in consolation the good spirit rather leads and directs us by his counsel, so in desolation does the evil spirit.'[20] The schematization of religious experience allows one to move either under angelic inspiration through a quality of thoughts down to moods and sets of feeling, or contrariwise from moods and sets of feeling (irrespective of their origins) through a corresponding quality of thought to a location under angelic or diabolical influences.

This prior specification of the matrix, in the first rule, is geared to a particular state of religious disposition, for those whose lives are dominated by the capital sins, the roots of whose actions are found in pride, covetousness, lust, anger, etc.: that is, those who live religiously unconverted lives.[21] The mode of their temptation is pleasure, operating instinctively and almost automatically on the pleasure-pain axis. But the First Week also takes account of a more developed subject, one whose conscience is progressing through a period of purification, possibly even preparatory to a higher degree of union with God. For a person moving through purification, the modes of temptation are dialectically reversed, and the instrumentality of evil is no longer imagination but thought. A higher level of human development is presupposed: a person no longer dominated by imagination and sensual pleasures but operating by reason and insight. Here the evil spirit through false reasoning brings about pain and sadness and a sense of futility, the reasoning devolving upon obstacles to a continuation of the process of conversion. The good spirit moves in conjunction with the developmental effort of the person; and the effect of this influence upon human affectivity is courage and strength, consolation, tears, inspirations and calmness. Temptations still run on the pleasure-pain axis, but now they appeal to pain, the cost of discipleship.[22]

The first and second rules set up the initial schematization of the three levels of religious influence, a matrix whose variables are affectivity, imagination or intellectual intentionality, and preternatural personal influences. With one kind of subject, these variables achieve a particular kind of value; with another kind of subject, they are concretized differently. Ignatius can further unify the multiform realities of affectivity in terms of two critically important concepts: consolation and desolation. Neither is an influence external to a person, nor is either of them a quality of rational intentionality. They are states of affectivity, 'an interior motion' defined by the direction of the movement. Consolation is any interior movement of emotionality, feeling, or sensibility whose term is God – a person is drawn or driven to God. The primary instance of such an experience is that of love, but it can also include the tears of remorse, any sensible increase of faith, hope, charity, and a joy whose effect is quiet and peace in God. Desolation is precisely the opposite, that is, any movement of emotionality or sensibility whose term is evil, whether that affectivity be painful as a troubled mind or comfortably cynical as a movement to distrust.[23]

Consolation and desolation do not identify necessarily with pleasure and pain. The sting of conscience, for those 'going from mortal sin to mortal sin' is genuine consolation, for Ignatius, as is the 'shame and confusion' when one compares the fate of the damned with one's own history of sin, as in the First Exercise of the First Week. Both may be painful experiences of coming out of illusions.[24] On the other hand, men with their arms locked, singing

225

bawdy songs on their way to the local whorehouse, are in desolation for Ignatius: '*any movement to base and earthly things*'. Consolation and desolation, then, must be critically distinguished both from Freud's description of instinctual satisfaction and from the use of these terms in other spiritual authors. In no sense does consolation simply merge with pleasure and desolation with pain. They are obvious states of affectivity, but they are not denoted by their sensible or even spiritual enjoyment, but by their direction, by their terminus. As motives, then, for prayer, neither is posited except in its orientation towards God, a catching up of the feelings and sensibility of a human being in the orientation of all things to God. Consolation is any interior movement of human sensibility – irrespective of the cause – whose direction is God, whether that movement be one of exuberant emotion or quiet peace, even whether its presence is experientially pleasant or not. And the initial 'instantiation' of this experience is the finest description Ignatius gives of indifference: 'The soul begins to be on fire with the love of her Creator and Lord, and consequently, she can love no created thing on the face of the earth in itself, but only in the Creator of them all.'[25]

Once this schematization is established in the initial rules of these directions, the structure of the whole falls into an obvious unity. Advice is offered how each level of religious influence is to be handled when its movement is towards evil: Rules five and six, how to act directly against *desolation* itself; Rules seven to eleven, how to act directly against the *thoughts* that arise from desolation; Rules twelve to fourteen, how to act directly against the sphere of the *evil spirit*. The purpose of this essay would be dissipated by an extended gloss on each rule; its aim is to establish the synthetic nature of the Rules for Discernment of Spirits. But to substantiate these structural comments a brief comment is in order.

To act directly against *desolation*, since it places one within the guidance of evil, no change should occur in the direction toward which the desolation would organically point; one is to remain faithful to previous commitments and inspiration. On the contrary, since the contradictory of evil is good, one should take the clue from this pointing of desolation and tend towards the opposite way.[26]

Further, to move directly against the *thoughts* which proceed from desolation is not so much a question of action as of meditation and rational focus. One is to consider *(considere)* the nature of the process itself, that God is purifying one's radically human powers, and so has moved beyond sensibility as a newness in growth, and that grace in this developmental stage is insensibly present.[27] A person is to consider *(piense)* that consolation is part of his or her future.[28] Further, one must understand the three causes, reasons for this state of desolation.[29] One must prepare for desolation by thoughtful planning *(piense)* while in consolation.[30] Lastly, the subjects of reflection *(pensando)* during consolation and desolation are dialectical opposites: in the latter one meditates on the strength gained from grace, in the former one recognizes the weakness without such grace.[31]

Thirdly, when countering directly the pervasive influence of the *evil spirit* within human life, the focus is neither immediate choice nor a concentration of rational intentionality; it is three pivotal life stances, suggested through these three similes: the angry woman, the false lover, and the captain of an army. Through the first image, an initial courage and determination are demanded, an orientation whose origins come from confidence in God.[32] Through the second image, an openness with a confessor or with a spiritual director, an orientation whose origins comes from inter-personal, even ecclesial guidance.[33] Through the third image, an abiding and perceptive self-knowledge is indicated, an orientation whose origins bespeaks one's own self-appropriation.[34] These three similes indicate a response to the pervasive influence of evil within human life in terms of one's attitude towards God, towards others, and towards oneself.

In these fourteen rules, a matrix emerges for synthesizing religious experience on three different levels: ultra-human, rational and affective. This matrix provides both for the causal inter-relationship among the three, and the contradictory antitheses between the evil and the good. Established through these inter-connected variables, the structure is variously and flexibly realized differently by different kinds of subjects. Once this internal unity is asserted, serious but laconic directives are offered for responding to each kind of religious influence which would lead a human being into evil, whether through pleasure or through pain - whether the appeal is made to sensibility and feeling, to imaginative and rational intentionality, or through the perverse influence of powers that are beyond the human. The elaboration of discernment in the First

Week is geared to people tempted by obvious evil. Now the much more difficult question obtains: how to respond to religious influences when the matter is much more subtle, when evil draws under the appearance of good? The First Week saw temptation as unified both as phenomenon and as real; evil appeared to be what it is. The Second Week takes up the disjunction between the two: when the phenomenon is good but the reality is actually evil.

SECOND WEEK

The general matrix initially elaborated for the First Week is restated for the Second Week in its first rule: the enemy through specious reasoning effects sadness and perturbation, while spiritual joy comes from the influence of God and the angels. Once more, the antithetical relationships are established between the two groups of influences, and the causal vectors within each are set. A necessary level of rational intentionality is not placed immediately under the influence of God and the angels as something of invariant constancy: and this, because there will occur a kind of consolation that does not arise with commensurate thoughts.[35]

Another dimension of equal importance will be now added to this matrix: the temporal. The causality of the First Week, represented by single vertical lines, will be explained by the historical dimension. One must attend to the contrary historical ends to which moments of consolation will lead: ends which indicate whether this seeming moment of grace actually comprises a hidden temptation.[36] The introduction of evil into good is subtle and slow, carried on over a gradual devolution.[37] For this reason, one must attend to the process itself as well as to the first moment of consolation. It is no longer enough to know how to deal with attractions towards obvious evil: one must attend to one's attractions towards the good by analysis of the entire beginning, middle, and end of the experience.[38] These temporal divisions - so similar to the partition of the action of an Aristotelian drama - serve not only to indicate the possibilities of an ingress of evil into human activity, but to situate moments at which such an ingress can be discerned. Initially, one can determine the deceptive nature of this consolation by the term to which it has led.[39] Next, as one becomes more subtle, one can disentangle it from the course of the process itself, noting how the disintegrative process gradually became dominant.[40] Lastly, even the initial moment of first consolation can itself serve its own criteria for determining this falsity, antecedent to the development of this moment into a process.[41] The temporal, historical dimension given to the matrix of discernment in the Second Week is telling even in the last directive: one should distinguish the first moment of *consolación sin causa* from the second period which follows upon it.[42]

The addition of the temporal dimension is critically important for two more reasons: it indicates a different subject for whom these rules are more appropriate, and it allows for a more fundamental distinction between the kinds of consolation.

The rules for the First Week are geared for those whose motivation functions within the pleasure/pain polarities; they are tempted by apparent pleasures or by projected pain.[43] The rules for the Second Week are oriented towards those who are far more humanly developed and for whom instinctual satisfaction does not constitute the goal. Those who have passed through the First Week have appropriated with gratitude the saving love with which God has graced their personal histories and move through the mysteries of the life of Jesus to discover the direction that God would give their lives. Such persons are tempted more under the appearance of good. This embodies one of the most significant insights of Ignatian discernment: the good person is not so much tempted by the obviously evil whether satisfying or painful, as tempted under the appearance of the moral good *(de especie de bien)*.[44] Not obvious moral compromise, but the deceitful good will destroy such a person. Thus there is no discussion of desolation within these rules: desolation is a movement of affectivity away from God in some sort of evident manner – the phenomenon in the First Week bespoke the reality of the religious influence. Here it is quite different. The phenomenon is good, obviously good, and it is far more destructive than the evil. What is at issue here is the discrimination between that movement of affectivity which is genuinely and organically towards God, and that which is deceptive.[45]

Both the temporal dimensions of this new structure and the differentiation of the subject allow for a third, crucial distinction, one that works out of the relationship between rational intentionality and affectivity: consolation without and with a cause. *Consolación sin causa*, as Karl Rahner has pointed out, is characterized neither by its suddenness nor by its engulfing qualities, but rather by the absence of any antecedent intentionality proportional to the drawing of affectivity into God.[46] One is deeply drawn affectively towards God as subject without any prior grasp of an attribute through which affectivity might be moved. Very simply this kind of experience occurs when a person finds herself or himself deeply loving God, being drawn totally to God in love, without being aware of how one came to this. There could be a note of suddenness about it or surprise, but neither is particularly necessary. It is rather the total movement of affectivity and sensibility towards God without any proportional influence of imaginative or rational intentionality prior to the experience – whether this priority is conceived temporally or naturally. The fifteenth Annotation suggests such a consolation as pivotal: 'God works with the soul embracing her to his love and praise and so disposing her for the way in which she can better and hereafter serve him.'[47] For Ignatius this moment is self-authenticating, a movement of total affectivity and feeling towards God, a 'yes' which alone in our history contains no experience of 'no', which can have neither the level of intellectual intentionality as commensurate object nor the level of preternatural influence as an agent.[48]

In any other kind of consolation, of being drawn towards God, this is not true. When imaginative or rational intentionality either precedes affectivity or is commensurate with it, as thoughts spring out of consolation, the consolation is an equivocal experience. This *consolación con causa* can be either divine or angelic or diabolic, and the quality of its commensurate thoughts do not remove this ambiguity. Thus the distinctions among consolations allow the directives of the rules of the Second Week to form around each, emphasizing the second because of ambivalence of its direction and giving structure to the entire complex of these directives. While the initial rule laid down the basic matrix, and the second rule treated *consolación sin causa*, rules three to eight deal with *consolación con causa*, and the last combines both kinds of consolation into a single directive.

It is particularly in the *consolación con causa* that the temporal or historical dimension tells upon the operation and application of the original schematization. In this consolation, both good and evil can console the soul, but they engage it in a process whose end is either development or destruction. Here one is not dealing with a single moment or a period, but with an entire process, and the failure in the source will eventuate as a disintegration of the process. While the initial, atomic moment may well have contained nothing but obvious insights and attractions, little by little the process deteriorates, and the prior evil influence becomes more obviously in appearance what it primordially was in reality. These descriptive statements stand as presupposed in Ignatius's prescription for the reception and analysis of such consolation.[49]

The temporal distinctions within the process not only allow for a functional division of the internal structure, but the structure itself indicates a pattern of progressive maturity in assimilating this kind of discernment. Three directives correspond to these three moments. Initially, at the end of a process one can recognize that one has been 'taken in', by an examination of either level: of rational intentionality or affectivity. If the thoughts of the person are 'evil or distracting or less good than what the soul had previously proposed to herself to do', disintegration has taken place. Further, if sensibility or the complex of human feelings has been weakened or made restless or so troubled that a previous peace and tranquillity have been lost, then the process has either been corrupted at its beginning or been lost during its development. Notice that neither affection nor rational intentionality is self-justifying; it is their unity which must obtain and in which one level is critically judgemental of the other.[50] The second moment of the learning of discernment, given in the next rule, is within the process itself and resembles nothing so much as Ignatius's own experience at Loyola and Manresa: having found herself or himself 'taken in', a person retraces in memory and in retrospect the steps which led to the present situation, notices how evil was gradually introduced into the development, 'so that by such experience, observed and noted down, he may be on his guard in the future against his (the Enemy's) customary machinations'. Experience eventually gives a person control over the process itself, making him or her sensitive to the introduction of the lesser good, as the evaluation of the initial consolation continues.[51] Finally, it is subtly possible, even at the initiation of the consolation, to discern the true from the false: the true consolation will enter a person given over to the Lord, almost imperceptibly, in silence, as a drop of water enters a sponge. On the contrary, that which is not of God will enter with the violence and perceptibility of a drop of water hitting a rock. The condition of affectivity indicates the authenticity of the consolation long before any discriminations are elaborated on the worth of the ideas which spontaneously spring from this consolation.[52]

It is for this reason that the ninth Annotation warns seriously against giving the rules of the Second Week for those in the First Week.[53] The criteria in each are almost the opposite. In the First Week, affectivity was judged by its obvious direction, and distinguished as consolation and desolation; it was the moral worth of the attraction which qualified and denominated the sensibility. In the Second Week, the apparent moral worth of what is proposed is – at its beginning – beyond cavil; but its real worth is judged by affectivity, by one's feelings of peace and joy. Mix these up, and you have a monster on your hands. The one who feels at peace in cruelty is sick, or the religious who experiences joy in infidelity is pathological. Affectivity is not the criterion in the First Week; it is the criterion in the second. And between these two moments lies the conversion and reorientation of human sensibility worked through the purifications and completions of the First Week. Only when and to the degree that affectivity is ordered can it in turn become the clue to the direction in which one should go within the myriad good options which surround one's life.

This differentiation of religious experience into three levels, and the introduction of the temporal factors, allows Ignatius to draw the times of election into some parallels with the various levels in the discernment of spirits. The first time corresponds in some way to God's moving a person deliberately without the interplay of thoughts and affectivity, a movement in which, as with the *consolación sin causa*, there is no possibility of doubt.[54] The second time corresponds to the movements of affectivity which demand the full work of discernment; here affectivity is made the criterion of the divine call.[55] The third time emphasizes the processes of thoughts moving through the nature of options, but demanding confirmation in affectivity.[56] As in the Rules, more time is spent on the use of conscious reflection, but its integration with sensibility and emotion is cardinal to the judgment of its soundness.[57]

Thus it is important to notice a certain completion in these Rules for Discernment. They are geared to choice, to the discovery of the divine guidance in that which attracts me; one set is oriented to the situation when the attractions around me are obviously towards evil, another when the attractions which surround me are towards an apparent good. Both of them allow for the careful interplay of preternatural influences, thought and affectivity with the history of a human pursuit of salvation.

CONCLUSION

What Ignatius has accomplished through these few Rules for Discernment of Spirits is a schematization which goes far beyond the needs of a single individual attempting to choose among the manifold options within his or her life, or beyond the exigencies of a religious community moving to determine the direction which God would have it take. Ignatius has provided a flexible matrix, whose variables can be so divergently given their values that the entire structure can incorporate religious experiences of the most diverse inspiration. He has done so, not by opting for one of these divergent approaches over its competitors, but precisely by allowing each a critically important influence upon human choice and by uniting all of them through a complex causal structure. That the elements are there and that they are united, is crucial. Angelic influences without reason and affectivity become superstition and terror. Reason without affectivity would become rationalistic and abstract, a deism in which God does not interact with this world. Affectivity without reason would degenerate into its own sectarian varieties of enthusiasm. In any case, they are here – as they have been and are present within human religious traditions – and they are conjoined, so that one mutually supports and interprets the others. It is not so much their presence as their inter-relationship which is of pivotal importance, so that no area of religious experience be unattended to, and that no single one be allowed to become cancerous, so extended beyond its natural and organic location, that it subsumes the operation of the whole.

The effect of this structure so uniting these influences within an operative synthesis should be to open one not only to the various and marvellous ways in which God can be manifested within one's personal history, or even within the history of the Church, but to the myriad ways in which God can and has affected human history and religious consciousness. These Rules, studied and assimilated in depth, could well provide one of the instrumentalities with which the Church comes to grips with traditions with whom it has held too long a polemic, and to whose peculiar religious genius it has too long been hostile and resistant. Without hesitation and arrogance and also without a naive syncretism, the vocation of the contemporary Church is to discover the presence of the liberating Spirit of God within the most radical diverse religious forms and expressions. And for this urgent task, the Ignatian family should be able to present greater depth in understanding the Rules for Discernment of Spirits.

NOTES

1. For the early commentaries and elaborations of the 'Rules for Discernment of Spirits', cf. Joseph de Guibert, *The Jesuits: their spiritual doctrine and practice* (trans. William J. Young, Chicago, 1964), pp. 213, 257, 417. For a further discussion of the commentators, cf. Edward Malatesta (ed.), *Discernment of Spirits* - a translation of the article 'Discernement des Esprits', in *Dictionnaire de Spiritualité*, by Jacques Guillet, Gustave Bardy, François Vandenbroucke, Joseph Pegon, Henri Martin (Collegeville 1957), pp. 79ff.

2. Witness, for example, the extended and penetrating analysis conducted by Karl Rahner on the rules dealing with *consolación sin causa* - 'The Logic of Concrete Individual Knowledge in Ignatius Loyola', in *The Dynamic Element in the Church* (trans. W.J. O'Hara, New York, 1964), pp. 84-169. Another customary approach is to comment upon each rule without indicating the unity of the whole: for example, W.H. Longridge, *The Spiritual Exercises of Saint Ignatius of Loyola* (London 1919), pp. 184ff. Sometimes a pastiche of citations is formed into a single picture with an occasional comment: e.g., William A.M. Peters, *The Spiritual Exercises of Saint Ignatius: exposition and interpretation* (Jersey City 1968), pp. 117-18.

3. For the importance of internal structure in literary criticism, cf. Richard P. McKeon, 'The Philosophic Bases of Art and Criticism', in *Critics and Criticism: ancient and modern* (ed. R.S. Crane, Chicago, 1952), pp. 533ff.

4. Thus Bernard Lonergan SJ would agree with Friedrich Heiler, 'The History of Religions as Preparation for the Co-operation of Religions', in *The History of Religions* (ed. M. Eliade and J. Kitagawa, Chicago, 1959), pp. 142-153. Lonergan points out that there are at least six areas common to such world religions as Christianity, - Judaism, Islam, Mazdaism, Hinduism, Buddhism, Taoism: '. . . that there is a transcendent reality; that he is immanent in human hearts; that he is supreme beauty, truth,

righteousness, goodness; that he is love, mercy, compassion; that the way to him is repentance, self-denial, prayer; that the way is love of one's neighbour, even of one's enemies; that the way is love of God, so that bliss is conceived as knowledge of God, union with him, or dissolution into him', *Method in Theology* (New York 1972), p. 109.

5. Cf. Rainer Maria Rilke, *Duino Elegies* (trans. with commentary J.B. Leishman and Stephen Spender, New York, 1950), pp. 87-88.

6. Robert Bellarmine, *The Ascent of the Mind to God by a Ladder of Things Created*, trans. B. Gent (London 1928), pp. xxi-xxii. cf. Bonaventure, *Itinerarium Mentis in Deum*, trans. P. Boehner (New York 1956).

7. Bellarmine, op. cit., p. xxii.

8. Jacob Boehme, *The Aurora*, trans. John Sparrow (London 1960), xix, 13. p. 488.

9. Plato, *Republic*, vii 532-4, in *Plato: The Collected Dialogues Including the Letters*, (eds. Edith Hamilton and Huntington Cairns (New York 1961), pp. 764-6.

10. Pascal, *Pensées*, trans. W.F. Trotter (Chicago 1952), Section IV, 277, p. 222.

11. William James, *The Varieties of Religious Experience* (New York 1911), p. 431.

12. ibid., p. 433.

13. *The Imitation of Christ*, Bk i, ch. I.

14. John Wesley, *Journal*, quoted in Ronald Knox, *Enthusiasm* (New York 1961), p. 537.

15. *Theologia Germanica*, trans. Susanna Winkworth (London 1950), xii, p. 192.

16. For the patristic development of the discernment of spirits and its coincidence with the doctrine of Ignatius, cf. Hugo Rahner SJ, *Ignatius the Theologian*, trans. Michael Barry (New York 1968), pp. 165-80. cf. *Discernment of Spirits*, pp. 55-65.

17. *Discernment of Spirits*, pp. 65-78.

18. First rule, First Week (314). Diagrammatically, such a schema with its vectors of influence would read:

Good Spirit	Evil Spirit	(Preternatural)
↓	↓	
Judgment of Reason	Imagination	('Thoughts')
↓	↓	
Remorse	Sensual Pleasure	(Affectivity)

235

19. Exx 317: fourth rule, First Week.
20. Exx 318: fifth rule, First Week. Diagrammatically, such a schema with its vectors of influence would read:

Good Spirit	Evil Spirit	(Preternatural)
↑	↑	
Thoughts	Thoughts	('Thoughts')
↑	↑	
Consolation	Desolation	(Affectivity)

21. Exx 314: first rule, First Week.
22. Exx 315: second rule, First Week.
23. Exx 316-17: third and fourth rules, First Week.
24. Exx 314 & 48.
25. Exx 316: third rule, First Week.
26. Exx 318-19: fifth and sixth rules, First Week.
27. Exx 320: seventh rule, First Week.
28. Exx 321: eighth rule, First Week.
29. Exx 322: ninth rule, First Week.
30. Exx 323: tenth rule, First Week.
31. Exx 324: eleventh rule, First Week.
32. Exx 325: twelfth rule, First Week.
33. Exx 326: thirteenth rule, First Week.
34. Exx 327: fourteenth rule, First Week.
35. Exx 329: first rule, Second Week.
36. Exx 331: third rule, Second Week.
37. Exx 332, fourth rule, Second Week.
38. Exx 333: fifth rule, Second Week.
39. ibid.
40. Exx 334, sixth rule, Second Week.
41. Exx 335, seventh rule, Second Week.
42. Exx 336, eighth rule, Second Week.
43. Exx 314-15; 9: first and second rules, First Week; ninth Annotation.
44. Exx 10: tenth Annotation.
45. Exx 331-2: third and fourth rules, Second Week.

46. Karl Rahner, op. cit., pp. 129–156.

47. Exx 15: fifteenth Annotation.

48. Exx 330: second rule, Second Week.

49. Exx 331–2: third and fourth rules, Second Week.

50. Exx 333: fifth rule, Second Week.

51. Exx 334: sixth rule, Second Week.

52. Exx 335: seventh rule, Second Week.

53. Exx 9: ninth Annotation.

54. Exx 175: *El primer tiempo.*

55. Exx 176: *El secundo.*

56. Exx 177: *El tercero tiempo.*

57. Thus the cardinal importance of the 'confirmation' in the third time. cf. the sixth point of the first mode of making an election in the third time and the concluding remarks at the end of the second mode (Exx 183, 188).

CHAPTER NINETEEN

The Eighteenth Annotation and the Early Directories

Michael Ivens

In the giving of the Exercises, as in other fields of ministry currently under re-appraisal, return to the sources is both indispensable and potentially hazardous. The hazards – the real danger of absolutizing the past with the consequent neglect of new needs and possibilities – must be kept clearly in mind; the more so since unreflective literalism is an occupational temptation of practitioners of the Exercises. Nevertheless, the fact remains that we give the Exercises on the basis of a tradition. Behind us stand not only Ignatius's text but substantial evidence of the use and interpretation of the book in the first decades of Jesuit history. Reflection on the past must therefore be expected to have something to contribute towards dealing with the questions we ask about the present. In the following review of approaches to the Exercises during the time of the Directories (1540-99), I want to look at two questions in particular. First, how far did the early Jesuits, in practice, carry the principle, enunciated in the eighteenth Annotation, that the Exercises should be adapted in accordance with the health, education and spiritual dispositions of the individual? And secondly, how far, if at all, did the early Jesuits work with the categories so familiar today of individual and group retreats, preached and personally directed retreats?

Any discussion of forms of the Exercises, whether in Ignatius's or any other age, must take as axiomatic the quite distinctive character of the 'full and integral' Exercises, and their privileged status as 'the first and most efficacious ministry of the Society' (Nadal). At the same time, it was a ministry which the early Jesuits exercised with a definite though not extreme restraint. The insistence of the *Constitutions* that the full Exercises should be given only to 'a few outstanding persons'[1] must be interpreted in the light of the thousand-odd known instances of the full Exercises in the lifetime of

Ignatius.[2] Moreover, it is legitimate to suppose that Ignatius's cautious attitude was partly prompted by concern for his heavily taxed work-force and that he might have given the Exercises more freely than he did had there been time for 'every good enterprise'.[3] Nevertheless, practical considerations apart, Ignatius considered that the full Exercises called for education, maturity and more than common generosity, and that no benefit would accrue to individuals if making them became a fashion.

But in early Jesuit usage, the term 'making the Exercises' had a fluidity that has since been lost. Modern distinctions between 'Ignatian retreats' and the Exercises, between 'the thirty days' and 'adaptations' are absent from their terminology; and 'the Exercises' may refer either to the full Exercises or to the whole gamut of ways in which elements of the doctrine and methodology of Ignatius's book could be put to use. And when we ask who were the people who might make the Exercises in this wide sense, the answer we get from the Directories is impressively all-embracing. Virtually no age-group, no social or religious category, no level of spiritual or educational attainment seems excluded on principle from the sometimes laboured classifications of the Directories. The humblest class of exercitant is the *rudis* – the person lacking intellectual subtlety, reflective capacity and quite possibly literacy.[4] Proceeding up the scale we find mention of 'the slightly more gifted',[5] the gifted who seek only to purge their conscience;[6] people with both the mental and spiritual aptitude for the full Exercises but who have neither the time to make them nor a compelling need. In various forms the Exercises were given to ecclesiastics. Among laypeople, 'people of rank', 'judges', 'those holding public office' are singled out for mention. Religious, especially 'novice-masters, superiors, baccalaureates and preachers' are particularly apt candidates 'since the fruit produced will not remain in them alone but will generally flow to others'.[7] Suitably adapted, the Exercises might contribute to the catechesis of Jews, pagans and Protestants (Nadal). Confessors of schoolboys are recommended to give the Exercises to their charges by the fourth Jesuit General, Everard Mercurian (with the interesting admonition that boys are more effectively moved by the thought of paradise than hell).[8] And in view of the preponderance of masculine pronouns in Jesuit sources it may be worth noting that the early Jesuit ministry of the Exercises – like Ignatius's own

239

ministry at Manresa - knew no limit of sex, though Ignatius stipulated that women should come to the church for their meditations.[9] The masculine pronouns have been retained in references to these sources.

When we turn to the question of how the Exercises were 'adapted' to the variegated categories of people who made them, we must bear in mind that adaptation is essential to the methodology of the Exercises and not a concession permissible in some forms of retreat while out of place in others. From the book of the Exercises as well as the Directories, it is clear that even in the full Exercises, personal criteria must to some extent determine the structure and content of the Exercises as actually made. In the Exercises, food and the use of penance are left entirely to the discretion and devotion of the individual, and one of the earliest Directories (derived from Ignatius's own directions) elaborates on this point. In the matter of food, the retreatant is to tell the server what he wants for the next meal; and 'if he asks for a chicken or a trifle' they are to be given.[10] As for penance he is simply to be told what the Exercises say about them and given an instrument of penance if he asks for one.[11] Other modifications of régime are allowed for, which the text of the Exercises does not explicitly envisage. Thus, while silence is normally absolute, situations might arise in 'which the director or some mature and discreet person appointed by him might remain with the exercitant after dinner or supper for suitable recreation'.[12] Similarly, the server in charge of the retreatant's material needs might occasionally be a personal friend to whom, with the director's permission, he might 'open his heart'.[13]

More important, even in the full Exercises, the personal criterion must govern the very presentation of the Ignatian material. Points are to be given in writing or dictated. If possible, the director should not come with these points ready-made, and while he should have studied his material beforehand he should not come armed with the book.[14] Indeed, the absence of the book - only afterwards, if at all, would the sixteenth-century retreatant get his hands on a copy - is one of the more striking differences between the procedures of Ignatius's time and ours. In the sixteenth century the book of the Exercises was regarded primarily as a director's guide, secondly as a devotional aid to those who had already made the Exercises, and not at all as a retreatant's manual.[15] The material of the Exercises came in the form of a personal communication from a director who knew the Exercises and knew the retreatant.

But if adaptation belongs to the Exercises as such, it is carried to its furthest extent in the ministry of the Exercises in the wide sense, where we find evidence of a whole spectrum of devotional activity, all derived from the book of the Exercises, all designated as 'making the Exercises' yet differing in various degrees from the full Exercises. First, and cutting across other variations, there is the distinction of situation corresponding to the nineteenth and twentieth Annotations. The ideal conditions, certainly, were held to be those available in a Jesuit college or novitiate: silence, privacy, freedom from immediate concerns. On the other hand a sizeable proportion of those who made the Exercises did so at home. The régime they followed was such as to demand real commitment: an hour to an hour and a half of daily meditation and fidelity to such observances as the director should judge suitable;[16] but all this was far from the daily intensity of the twentieth Annotation retreat. Yet it was one of the ways the Directories envisage the full Exercises being made.

Secondly, variations of personal capacity and opportunity lead to retreats of varying lengths and to widely differing programmes of prayer. On the question of length, we find references in the Directories to retreats of eight days,[17] eight to ten days,[18] ten to twelve days,[19] fifteen days or more.[20] Similarly, individual needs must determine the use of time during retreat, a point developed at some length by the German Paul Hoffaeus whose *Instructiones Magistro Exercitantium* (*c.* 1575-80) contain detailed information on the kinds of *horaria* that sixteenth-century retreatants might be required to follow in the course of a 'closed retreat'. Of those with scant capacity for sustained prayer he demands two periods of half an hour only, in addition to which the programme included repetition of the morning prayer with the director; instruction on Christian doctrine, the rosary and the manner of hearing mass; attendance at three masses at intervals during the morning and vespers in the evening; reading, writing, manual work.[21] The 'more capable' were to make two hours of prayer.[22] For every other category of retreatant up to those making the Exercises in their entirety Hoffaeus allows individuals to adopt the number of hours of prayer they wish (*de horis transigendum est quot velint*),[23] with the cautious proviso that German layfolk (*externi germani*) should not usually exceed three hours.[24] He also proposes a way of covering the full programme of the Exercises on the basis of three hours prayer a day.[25]

Thirdly, individual variety is reflected in the variety of content that we find included under the Exercises in the wide sense. This meant in practice that for many, perhaps the majority, of those who made the Exercises, the basic stress was on the laying of foundations. Repeatedly the Directories emphasize what is spelt out in the eighteenth Annotation: the First Week meditations, the examens, the first method of prayer, basic moral instruction, preparation for a regular sacramental life, in short the whole programme of practical asceticism which the early Jesuits saw as the pre-condition for progress. Such was the programme to which Faber and Laynez introduced the townsfolk of Parma in 1540, and which Ignatius commends to Jesuit superiors in a circular letter in 1554:

> About the Spiritual Exercises our father has commissioned me to say there should be a record in every group of what you thought right to adopt with men and also women (but let the women come to the church to make the Exercises). He means the Exercises of the First Week, leaving them some method of praying according to their capacity, and this is not meant to be with any restriction of persons, provided they take a few hours in the day for that effect. In this way, the utility of the Exercises can be extended to many, up to the General Confession and some method of prayer as has been said.[26]

But while the early Jesuits had their feet on the ground and did not believe in teaching people to run before they could walk, it would be false to assume that the contents of the later exercises had no place in the case of those not making the full course. The popular ministry of the Exercises included meditation on the life of Christ. Mercurian proposes meditation on the mysteries of the rosary for the *rudes et illiterati*, while the infancy and passion gospels figure in his programme for schoolboys.[27] The *Contemplatio ad amorem*, whose precise significance in the Exercises is variously interpreted, is included by Hoffaeus in his recommendations for 'those wishing to purge their consciences by a general confession'.[28] And although material relevant to the Election is to be used sparingly outside the thirty days, even this could be given to people willing to devote at least fifteen days to the Exercises.[29] So while the First Week was specially suitable for the ordinary Christian, the evidence of the Directories forbids us to divide the ministry of the Exercises into a simple division between First Week and thirty days. They suggest rather that the potential of the Exercises to meet the needs of individuals could be realized only if the practice of the Exercises ranged across the multiple gradations of a spectrum.

The Exercises, whatever their form, were 'personal', then, in the sense that they consisted in a programme and content adapted to the needs and circumstances of the individual. Furthermore, it is beyond question that they were normally personal in the sense that they were conducted on a person-to-person basis and that making the Exercises in a group was regarded by the early Jesuits as a *pis aller* to be avoided if possible. From the practical viewpoint, of course, the person to person approach has obvious disadvantages, and the practical merits of the group were recognized from the beginning. Ignatius conceded that a convent community which wanted to make the Exercises *might* do them as a group, but he goes on to say that in that event 'they would certainly receive less fruit'.[30] By the time of Aquaviva's generalate, we find a novice master, pressured by numbers, gathering his charges together for points and common reflection; the experiment was stopped by Aquaviva on the grounds that the Exercises must be conducted on the basis of the 'agitations in the exercitant's soul'.[31] Hoffaeus envisages the possibility of retreats where points might be given in common and a copy posted on the notice board – but again such measures were to be adopted only under force of circumstances.[32] The general principle, however, is clear. Whatever the exceptions might have been – and there seems no coercive evidence that in Ignatius's lifetime the Exercises were ever given except person-to-person – the normal basis on which the Exercises were made was the personal relationship between 'the one who gives' and 'the one who makes'.

As far as the full Exercises are concerned, this claim obviously poses no difficulty. The full Exercises were given on a sufficiently limited scale for personal direction to fall within the scope of Jesuit resources. But how, it may be asked, in terms of sheer human possibility, could the Exercises have been given one-to-one in every case, even in situations, as at Parma, when they were given to whole neighbourhoods? The answer lies in the principle that not only exercitants but also givers of the Exercises fall into many 'grades' and hence it will often be a sufficient qualification for giving the Exercises simply to have made them oneself. A key figure in the early history of the Exercises is the neophyte retreat giver. Sometimes he might be a Jesuit novice; giving the Exercises under the guidance of an experienced practitioner in cases 'where less is risked'.[33] Sometimes he might be a religious – indeed the effects of the Exercises on religious communities appear to have been achieved largely by religious giving the Exercises to one another. He might be a parish priest passing on the Exercises to his 'subjects', or he might be a lay person, like the schoolmasters whom Faber describes as giving the Exercises to their apter pupils,[34] or a certain Julia Zerbini, confined to her bed by continual sickness, 'who had discovered the sweetness of the Exercises and began imparting them to the ladies who visited her'.[35] It was at Parma, where hundreds are reported to have made the Exercises at a single time, that the principle of the neophyte director was exploited to the utmost. The occasion was clearly something of a *tour de force* and it seemed natural to a later generation to suppose that what happened was on the lines of the mission-type retreats pioneered a century later in Brittany. In fact what happened was a massive enlistment of local resources:

> The Exercises grow from day to day. Many of those who have made them give them to others, one to ten another to fourteen. And so as soon as one nestful is completed another begins, so we see our children's children to the third and fourth generation. And altogether there is such a change in the life and customs of all, that it is something to praise God for.[36]

Clearly, we have to do here with something quite different from the full Exercises which Ignatius and the early Jesuits always refused to popularize. It is also clear that the wider reach of the Exercises did not require the experienced and skilled direction called for in the full Exercises – indeed 'direction' might be too inflated a term to use of a role which consisted presumably in the simplest kind of exposition. Given this, however, it is clear that the early Jesuits regarded the Exercises as a resource to be used in a variety of ways to help a wide variety of people. If the desire were there – if only the desire for a certain 'peace of soul' (Exx 18) – then somehow the opportunity could be found to use appropriate elements of the Exercises to meet people at their point of need. Moreover the early Jesuits recognized that just as there was something in the Exercises that ordinary people could benefit from, so there was something that ordinary people, having first received it themselves, could pass on to others.

NOTES

1. *Constitutions*, 409.

2. Ignacio Iparraguire SJ, *Práctica de los Ejercicios de san Ignacio de Loyola en vida de su autor* (Bilbao/Rome 1946), Appendix 1.

3. 'In the end you act. Your reverence must take into account the time you have, and your occupations, and the fruit of service to God, always putting in the first place the good which is greatest, most obligatory, and most appropriate to your own office and those entrusted to you, since it is impossible to take up all good enterprises.' Letter of Ignatius to a Jesuit engaged in giving the Exercises individually to members of a convent community (*Ep. Ig.*, ix, 220); quoted in de Guibert, *The Jesuits: their spiritual doctrine and practice* (Chicago 1964), p. 125.

4. MHSJ 76, p. 220.

5. ibid.

6. ibid., 76, p. 221.

7. 1599 Directory, ch. ix, MHSJ 76, p. 613; translated in W.H. Longridge, *The Spiritual Exercises of St Ignatius of Loyola*, 5th ed. (London 1955), p. 293.

8. MHSJ 76, pp. 254-5.

9. On the subject of women exercitants, the 1599 Directory contains the following sagacious paragraph: 'The same method therefore should be followed with them as with persons of little education, unless one or other among them should be of such good judgment and capacity for spiritual things, and should have so much leisure at home as shall enable her to make all the Exercises fully, or the greater part of them, in which case there is no reason why she should not do so. Prudence, however, requires that women should come to our Church to receive the meditations, and every caution should be taken that there may be no room for any suspicion or scandal. For which reason it may be best that the meditations should not be given in writing, but by word of mouth, lest men should think that some of them

were letters. But if writing must be used, let it be done with great discretion.' MHSJ 76, p. 616, translated Longridge, op. cit., p. 295.

10. MHSJ 76, p. 79, translated in *Autograph Directories of St Ignatius Loyola*, Program to Adapt the Spiritual Exercises (New Jersey), p. 14.

11. ibid., p. 80.

12. 1599 directory, ch. vi. MHSJ 76, p. 603, translated Longridge, p. 288.

13. ibid., ch. iv, MHSJ 76, p. 595, Longridge, p. 284.

14. MHSJ 76, pp. 74-5, translated in *Autograph Directories of St Ignatius Loyola*, p. 9.

15. In 1555, Ignatius wrote to a friend who had requested a copy of the book of the Exercises: 'I am sending you a book of the Exercises, that it may be useful to you. . . . The fact is that the force and energy of the Exercises consists in practice and activity, as their very name makes clear; and yet I did not find myself able to refuse your request. However, if possible, the book should be given only after the Exercises have been made.' *Ep. Ig.*, ix, 701. cf. George E. Ganss SJ, 'The authentic Spiritual Exercises of Ignatius: some facts of history and terminology', in *Studies in the Spirituality of Jesuits* (November 1969), vol. 1, no. 2, p. 12.

16. Exx 19, MHSJ 76, p. 234.

17. MHSJ 76, p. 137.

18. ibid., p. 281.

19. ibid., p. 224.

20. ibid., p. 137.

21. ibid., pp. 230-3.

22. ibid., p. 220.

23. ibid., p. 220.

24. ibid., p. 224.

25. ibid., pp. 235-40.

26. ibid., p. 106.

27. ibid., pp. 249, 255.

28. ibid., p. 221.

29. ibid., p. 224.

30. Letter of Ignatius, cf. n. 3 above.

31. G.A. Hugh SJ, 'The Exercises for Individuals and for Groups', Program to Adapt the Spiritual Exercises, p. 133.

32. MHSJ 76, p. 230.

33. *Constitutions*, 408-9.

34. Hugh, p. 144.

35. Hugh, p. 140.

36. Letter of Laynez, cf. Hugh, p. 141.

CHAPTER TWENTY

Ignatian Prayer or Jesuit Spirituality

Joseph Veale

Spiritualities are affected by the cultures they live through. To see Ignatian prayer as it was in the beginning, it is necessary to understand something of the shifts of culture and consciousness that have occurred since the sixteenth century. William Blake saw the cause of all the ills of his day in the 'two-horned heresy', the heresiarchs being Bacon, Locke and Newton. Somehow people had become more at odds with their world and at odds with themselves, the head in disharmony with the heart, the cerebral with the affective. 'Imagination' would put them together again and re-unite them with the world. T.S. Eliot coined the phrase 'dissociation of sensibility' to describe something similar.[1] Changes in the language of poets pointed to a shift in consciousness that occurred at some time in the seventeenth century. The sixteenth-century poets were able to incorporate 'their erudition into their sensibility: their mode of feeling was directly and freshly altered by their reading and thought'. 'There is a direct sensuous apprehension of thought, or a recreation of thought into feeling. . . . A thought to Donne was an experience; it modified his sensibility.' By the end of the seventeenth century, 'wit' and 'feeling' had been divorced; the poets 'thought and felt by fits, unbalanced'.

In many ways Ignatian prayer is like an old painting covered with layers of varnish and touched up by inferior hands. The art of removing varnish in order to disclose the living colours of the original is a relatively recent one. Similarly, it is only recently that the writings of Ignatius apart from his Exercises and Constitutions have been edited and to some extent studied. Future generations will see us to have had our proper biases and distortions. But we are in a better position to see what Ignatius was saying about apostolic contemplation than any generation since the death of the first companions. We have documents that they could not have had and we can see him more clearly in the current of the tradition that he reverenced, selected from and changed. In his teaching on prayer[2] he

248

was both more innovative and more traditional than has usually been realized. His immediate successors did not quite see how revolutionary he had been.

The charges made by sincere people against Jesuit spirituality are many. It is individualistic, rationalistic, voluntaristic, semi-Pelagian, introspective, moralistic, desiccating, a bully; it would force the free play of the spirit into a prison of methods. The Exercises were attacked at the beginning for opposite reasons. They were seen by sixteenth-century opponents like Melchior Cano and Thomas Pedroche as too mystical and affective, as insufficiently ascetical and rational, as giving a dangerous prominence to the interior illumination of the Holy Spirit.

It is ironical that the spirituality of many nineteenth- and twentieth-century Jesuits should have come to resemble the spirituality of Melchior Cano, the Society's ferocious opponent in its early years.[3] In his study of sixteenth-century spirituality in Spain, Emilio Colunga OP, calls men like Cano and Pedroche the 'intellectualists'.[4] The more contemplative Ignatian tradition always remained alive, sometimes more vigorous, sometimes less so. But unquestionably many were fearful of mysticism, suspicious of affectivity, sceptical about the probability of 'the Creator and Lord communicating himself to the devout soul in quest of his will',[5] and inclined to assume that discursive meditation remained for most the normal way of prayer.

Ignatius and the men who knew his mind best like Jerome Nadal were well aware how open the Exercises were to the charge of Illuminism. In the text of the Exercises, reference to the Holy Spirit is notably absent where you would expect it. In the Spain of the sixteenth century, it was not comfortable to be found guilty of Illuminism. Melchior Cano had his fellow-Dominican, Cardinal Carranza, imprisoned for sixteen years on the charge.[6]

The fear of being charged with Illuminism and later the fear of Illuminism itself, especially in the period between the Church's condemnation of quietism and the condemnation of Modernism,[7] helped to distort Jesuit understanding of Ignatius's teaching. Pedroche, the Spanish inquisitor, was accurate in pin-pointing those places in the Exercises that seemed to smack of Illuminism: Annotation 15;[8] the parts on indifference;[9] everything to do with Election;[10] the description of spiritual consolation.[11] Those parts, if

249

you add the remaining guidelines on discernment,[12] are the heart of the Exercises and of Ignatian teaching on apostolic life. When they are given small importance, Ignatian spirituality easily becomes an asceticism only.

The dangers of Illuminism, the well-founded fear of the early Jesuit Generals that some Spanish Jesuits would turn the new order from its apostolic calling and make it purely contemplative: these reasons largely explain the reserve of Borgia, Mercurian and Vitelleschi[13] towards certain Jesuit contemplatives. Largely, but not entirely: something else was at work that does not emerge explicitly in the documents of the time.

St Francis Borgia, himself a mystic, ordered Antonio Cordeses, one of the Spanish Provincials, to stop teaching his subjects a simple affective prayer in terms that are surprising:

> I understand that your reverence requires your subjects to make acts of love in their daily prayer, and that you desire to lead them all by this way. I praise your zeal and your good desires, for it is quite true that that is the best and loftiest spiritual exercise. But I warn you, my father, that not all are developed enough for this exercise, and that not all understand it or are capable of it. To teach them how to pray, the Lord has given us a good guide in the Spiritual Exercises of the Society. Later, some will continue in this manner of praying, others in another. . . . For the movements of the Holy Spirit are different, and different the characters and minds of men.[14]

Borgia's successor, Everard Mercurian, went further. He was a Fleming, formed in a climate of anti-Protestant polemic and fear of Illuminism, with a liking for what was logically coherent and systematic in spirituality.[15] He forbade Jesuits to read Tauler, Ruysbroeck, Mombaer, Herp, Raymond Lull, Gertrude, Mechtilde of Magdeburg and 'others like them'.[16] It was by his authority that the saintly director of St Teresa, Balthasar Alvarez, was ordered to stop praying contemplatively and to bring back those he was directing to safer ways.[17]

The incident helps us to understand the climate in which the definitive 1599 Directory could say:

> Applying the senses is different from meditation, since meditation is more intellectual and consists more in reasoning. Meditation is

altogether higher, since it reasons concerning the causes and effects of those mysteries. . . .[18]

The president of the commission which completed the Directory was Gil Gonzales Davila, one of the first to be alarmed by Balthasar Alvarez's way of prayer. The observation on meditation did not go unchallenged, and was ignored in practice by men like Gagliardi, La Palma, La Puente, Alvarez de Paz and Francis Suarez.[19] For the moment, however, the men wary of contemplation had prevailed. In the nineteenth century, in a Church even less favourable to contemplation, the authority of the Directory was to carry more weight than the Spanish writers.

The correspondence connected with the affair of Cordeses and Alvarez demonstrates how soon on both sides the characteristic language and attitudes of St Ignatius had been weakened. If, for convenience we label one side the 'ascetics' and the other the 'mystics', the 'ascetics' constantly stress the importance of prayer; the 'mystics' are equally concerned with the importance of the apostolate. Both are zealous to preserve the authentic tradition of the order. The 'mystics' appeal to the authority of the Exercises, especially the fourth Addition: 'I will remain . . . where I have found what I desire, without any eagerness to go on until I have been satisfied.'[20] But neither side argues from a close examination of the text of the Exercises, nor from the experience of making or giving them. Neither side appeals to the Ignatian phrase 'to find God in all things', nor to Nadal's *contemplativus in actione*. The 'ascetics' see prayer as being either discursive meditation, which they take to be suitable for beginners, or as mystical prayer in the sense of an extraordinary gift; they see it as being possible for active apostles, though unusual.[21] The 'mystics' were convinced that the degree of abnegation pointed to by the Ignatian Exercises and Constitutions must lead almost infallibly to the gift of contemplation.[22]

Jesuit folklore tends to cast John Roothaan, the General who re-established the Society after its restoration in 1814, in the role of the man who influenced Jesuit spirituality along an excessively rationalist path. The truth is not so simple. A man who wanted, in the midst of the labours of government, to edit and publish Gagliardi's commentaries on the Exercises, was certainly familiar with the contemplative Jesuit tradition.[23] It is true that Jesuits in the nineteenth century interpreted the Exercises in a rigid and literalist way. But it is more accurate to say that their lack of flexibility

is due less to a single man or a single doctrine than to institutional forces: the formation of scholastics (with numerous borrowings from Sulpician seminary practice), the long years when young men, just emerging from adolescence, were daily exposed to the care of men whose specialism was formation and isolated from the normal life of the Society.[24]

Thus Jesuits came to be accused of a rationalism in spirituality that is opposed to what Ignatius taught about apostolic prayer.

The Exercises are essentially a point of departure. It is surprising to find Borgia and Mercurian so soon after Ignatius's death confining the prayer of Jesuits to the surface meaning of the Exercises and, as far as one can judge, to the type of meditation recommended in the First Week. To understand the contemplation that finds God equally in the midst of action as in time of formal prayer needs, besides the text of the Exercises and reflection on the experience of making them, an acquaintance with the Ignatian Constitutions and reflection on the experience of trying to live them.

When we remember how careful Ignatius was in selecting and preparing people for making the full Exercises and in selecting those he allowed to give them, we begin to realize how essential is the function of 'the one giving them', and how central to the whole pedagogy of spiritual growth is the discerning relationship between one 'maker' and one 'giver'.

It is possible to read the text in an excessively quietist or in an excessively Pelagian way. Ignatius gave those he trained to give the Exercises no theory of prayer or spirituality. He apprenticed them to the art, and they acquired it in a living tradition. He would have wanted them to be neither anti-mystical nor anti-ascetical, but capable flexibly of guiding a particular person 'according to the measure of God's grace' given at any particular time, away from inert passivity or anxious activity.

The theoretical distinctions we are familiar with – 'ordinary', 'extraordinary', 'acquired contemplation', 'infused contemplation' – are all tools of the seventeenth century. Had he known them, Ignatius might still have refused to use them. They can be of some use to directors but more questionable for learners. It is clear that Ignatius was well aware of the dangers of a certain kind of chat about 'mysticism'.[25] Yet, had he lived in the aftermath of the quietist rumpus or in the bleak aftertaste of the Age of Reason, he might well have been trenchant in his comments on those who, like Bossuet, insisted on the great rarity of 'more visitations' and the dogged expectation of 'fewer'.[26]

The main question concerns the effects a particular style of pedagogy may have on limiting or expanding the expectations and preconceptions of those who embark on a life of prayer. Ignatius would keep his counsel. He would place the responsibility for encouragement or deflation where it belongs, on the director.

The evils that Jesuit spirituality has sometimes committed would have been avoidable if succeeding generations had taken Ignatius's directives seriously. When the Exercises are given a Pelagian interpretation, and when the role of individual direction is diminished or precluded, manipulation is a danger and the invasion of the Spirit's freedom is to some extent inevitable.

Ignatius valued freedom. 'Our Father wanted us, in all our activities, as far as possible, to be free, at ease in ourselves, and obedient to the light given particularly to each one.'[27] This is only the extension of the clear directives of the text of the Exercises and of the autograph Directories. The one giving the Exercises 'should not influence him to adopt one state or another. . . . That is against the directives of the Exercises and the spirit of the Company, which desires that men should be led to enter the Company freely and only by God's movement. . . . To do the contrary is to introduce the sickle into the harvest field of our Lord God.'[29]

It is possible to find a purely ascetical meaning in the Exercises. It would be possible, though not so easy, to give an excessive mystical reading to the text. A logician coming innocent to the text might possibly be puzzled by the incompatibility of the active and passive verbs: 'their purpose is to conquer self and to regulate one's life'; 'I call it consolation when an interior movement is aroused in the soul'; 'every way of preparing and disposing the soul to rid itself of all inordinate affections'; 'it is better that the Creator and Lord in person . . . himself dispose the soul.' The words need to be placed in the context of an experience of growth: 'The *more* the soul is in solitude (the more it co-operates as best it can to dispose itself), the *more* fit it renders itself to approach and be united with its Creator and Lord. The *more* closely it is united with him, the more it is disposed to receive . . . gifts. . . .'[29] All growth towards God is, from the beginning, at the same time both passive and active.

Nadal, faithful to Ignatius's mind, demonstrates the same refusal to close doors that is implicit in the Exercises, and that Ignatius trusted to the good sense and discernment of the people he trained to give them:

> We are sure that the privilege given to Fr Ignatius is granted to the whole Company; the same grace of contemplation is meant for all of us and is given along with our vocation. Superiors and prefects of prayer are to show that good sense that we know to have been native to him. When they judge in the Lord that someone is growing in prayer and led by the good Spirit, they are to avoid interfering. They should rather give him heart and confidence, so that he may grow with ease and strength in the Lord (*in Domino suaviter quidem et fortiter*).[30]

The Exercises are a point of departure.

But towards what destination? We know that at the beginning some found, through making the Exercises, Carthusian or Dominican vocations. Many were led into the new purely apostolic vocation. It seems evident that even the second generation of Jesuits did not altogether grasp the originality of a life in which everything, including prayer, was to be determined by the overriding claims of the needs of people. But Nadal was sure that the apostolic vocation, if faithfully lived, would mean a participation, in however modest a degree, in the privilege given to Ignatius. He describes it as a contemplative gift:

> To *contemplate* and to *savour affectively* the things of the spirit and God present in all things, in all activities and relationships.[31]

We know that Ignatius's own prayer was eucharistic and trinitarian. But that of itself would not indicate any difference from the tradition of monastic prayer. The account we have of his prayer in the diary fragment of 1544-5 reveals the highest mystical graces.[32] It is not a prayer that abstracts from the world of creatures. It is absorbed in God and focused on the concrete and the particular. We find sense, sensibility, imagination, will and intelligence, the whole person concerned with a practical decision, with finding what God wants in the matter of poverty in the new order.

The great bulk of the western writings on mysticism belongs to the tradition that goes back from John of the Cross, through the Rhenish mystics, to pseudo-Denis. It does not follow that most of those called to contemplative intimacy were of that kind; we simply do not know. But so great is the authority of that tradition that some writers, including Jesuits, assume that 'mysticism' is of one kind.

Such an assumption has practical consequences. A spiritual director may take it that everyone who is drawn to prayer must follow the same road. And those who want to pray may similarly assume that the contemplative path described by John of the Cross is the only 'real' one. If they are also called to consecrated apostolic life, they may become bewildered and lose their way, or give up and turn to 'activism'. Or they may become 'Carmelites in action'. But it may not be what God was drawing them to, to the possible detriment of apostolic effectiveness. It is many years since Joseph de Guibert's authoritative study of Ignatius's mysticism was published.[33] In the English-speaking world, at least, not much reflection has been made on its implications for the prayer of those who are called to the Ignatian grace of 'finding God in all things'.

Michael Wadding of Waterford – the only Irish Jesuit who has given a small classic to the literature of spiritual theology – in his *Practica de la theologia mistica* (1681), used a terminology that goes back to pseudo-Denis to distinguish different kinds of contemplative gifts: the 'seraphic' and the 'cherubic'. Auguste Saudreau added a third kind, the 'angelic'. De Guibert accepts the rough categories and finds from his analysis of Ignatius's letters, from the autobiography and from a close examination of the diary, that he belongs like St Paul to the third kind.[34]

The terms conveniently describe 'three main currents of Catholic mysticism'. St Francis of Assisi is an instance of the first; in him affective love is dominant; the direct effect of grace falls chiefly on the will. St John of the Cross is an example of the second; grace chiefly affects the intelligence. In the third kind the infused gifts more directly affect the memory and imagination, the faculties that look to the concrete and to action.[35]

We do not find any trace of ideas or words (in Ignatius) influenced by pseudo-Denis. The part played by imagination, by the sensibility, by tears, as much as the direction of his mysticism, not to contemplative union seen as centre and summit, but towards the service of God, placed him outside the current of intellectual and 'speculative' contemplation. . . . Service of God is not, of course, lacking in either the cherubic or the seraphic kind of mystic. But in Ignatius service is not simply the sequel or consequence of the infused light. It is the very object towards which all his infused gifts tend and upon which they centre.[36]

The Holy Spirit is not confined by human categories, no matter how rough or refined. No adequate study, to my knowledge, has yet been made of the common ground and the important difference between monastic, mixed and apostolic contemplation. It is misleading simply to equate John of the Cross's *nada* with Ignatian 'indifference'. It can be unhelpful to assume that Carmelite prayer is the way for all. What is inescapable in any way is an experience of purification and illumination, whether the image of night or darkness be used or not. Maurice Giuliani is convincing in finding the apostle's purification and illumination in the radical contemplative abnegation of faith-full obedience.[37] The frustrations of apostolic life are a part of that obedience.

Which brings us back at last to the curious fact of Borgia's reserve towards Cordeses, of Mercurian's towards Alvarez, of Vitelleschi's towards Lallemant.[38] It was not, as has sometimes been suggested, a simple alignment of ascetics against mystics. In a sense both sides were right and both were wrong. The Generals were right in seeing that not all that the mystics were saying was according to Ignatius's mind. The 'mystics' were right in seeing that Jesuit spirituality is not a pure asceticism. But Cordeses and Alvarez, like all the Spaniards of that time who took prayer seriously, and Lallemant later, were influenced by Herp. When Ignatius's good friends, the Carthusians of Cologne, dedicated an edition of Herp to him, his reply was a classic of courteous embarrassment.[39] There was something in Herp, whose work dominated sixteenth-century Spanish spirituality, as there was in Tauler, that Ignatius found unacceptable. But he had found himself immediately at home in the tradition he discovered in Ludolph and Cisneros.

These are not just battles long ago that have nothing to do with us. The only way to dissolve false traditions is by trying, as best we can, to get at the real ones. We are now in a position to discard a false impression, common at one time, that writers like La Puente and de Paz were marginal and out of step, that the ascetic tradition was the central and authentic one in Jesuit spirituality. We can see, too, that we have somewhat less to learn from the French mystical writers of the seventeenth century than we have from Gregory the Great, Bernard, Aquinas, Bonaventure, and the great Carthusians and Cistercians. The words Ignatius received from them and transposed, especially key words like *sentir y gustar*, *affectus*, *devotio*, begin to be understood as soon as they are seen in the tradition of monastic theology and contemplation.[40]

Besides, there are present trends in spirituality and Christian living that we need to look at. There is the possibility of a new Illuminism in the charismatic movement. There is the constant danger of subjectivism in theology. Ignatius left us, in his art of discernment, if we can use it, a way of avoiding the pitfalls of subjectivism and objectivism. In the tenth part of the Constitutions he has also left us his balanced sense of the relationship between the human and the divine. We need that, if we are to avoid the extremes of neglecting the human and neglecting the divine. There is a new devout humanism in the air, less elegant than the seventeenth-century kind, that can be so concerned with the development of human potentialities as to soften the gospel's point and pain. We must hope, too, that we are not in for a new version of the mutual incomprehension of the 'mystics' and the 'ascetics', with the possibility of an *ascéticisme* coming from the world of psychology. A new Pelagianism might tend, as Thomas Pedroche did, to say of the fifteenth Annotation, 'There is no such experience'. In the work of the Exercises we need all the help we can get, since 'human means ought to be sought with diligence . . . and the art of dealing and conversing with men'.[41] But it is 'the love which will descend from the Divine Goodness,[42] "the interior gifts"[43] that alone will make . . . the exterior means effective'.

It would be failure indeed to fail to help those whose vocation it is to labour in the world to find a way towards a contemplation that goes with work and transforms it, so that eventually by God's gift the world of work and the world of prayer compenetrate. Karl Rahner once committed himself to saying: 'I dare to think that Ignatius belongs to the future, not to the age now coming to an end.' But he added the observation: 'It remains to be seen whether those who historically call themselves his disciples and pupils will be the ones who really represent this spirit in the future.'[44]

NOTES

1. cf. T.S. Eliot, 'The Metaphysical Poets', *Selected Prose* (London 1953), pp. 111ff.

2. MHSJ, *Ep. Ign.* II, letter 466; ibid. XII, Appendix VI, letter 3. cf. Gonçalves da Camara, *Memorial* (Paris 1966), no. 256.

3. I. Iparraguire, 'Fuentes y estudios de la espiritualidad ignaciana', in *Manresa* 28 (1956), p. 22.

4. E. Colunga OP, 'Intelectualistas y misticos en la teologia española en el siglo XVI', in *Ciencia Tomista* 9 and 10 (1914), cited in Iparraguirre, *Práctica de los ejercicios de san Ignatio de Loyola en vida de su autor* (Rome 1946), pp. 92-9. According to Iparraguirre, theologians like Melchior Cano were concerned for the purity of the faith, opposed religious publications in the vernacular, were afraid of urging laymen to the spiritual life lest the distinction between religious and lay be weakened, were suspicious of anything affective in prayer, and were inclined to scent Illuminism in any writing that strayed from the language of the schools.

5. Exx 15.

6. L. Cognet, *La Spiritualité Moderne, I, l'essor: 1500-1650* (Paris 1966), p. 149.

7. That is, 1687 to 1907.

8. Exx 15. Here is Pedroche's comment on Annotation fifteen: 'These words manifest and clearly contain and affirm and teach a proposition and assertion that is temerarious and scandalous and heretical. . . . Preaching has no place, nor a preacher, to persuade (the exercitant) which particular choice among many goods he ought to make. . . . It is clear to me that this doctrine belongs to the *dejados* and *alumbrados*; the written work is left aside, with all the teaching and doctrine which good and wise men have given. These men give themselves over to what the spirit and God tells them there in the recesses of the soul.' MHSJ, *Historia Soc. Jesu* (Polanco), III, 509-10.

9. Exx 23, 46, 157, 170, 179. The word 'indifference' is not found in the text of the Exercises.

10. Exx 135, 169-89.

11. Exx 316. cf. Iparraguire, *Práctica de los ejercicios* p. 99.

12. Exx 313-36.

13. Generals of the Society of Jesus: Borgia, 3rd General 1565-72; Mercurian 1573-80; Aquaviva 1581-1615; Vitelleschi 1615-45.

14. P. Dudon, 'Les idées du P. Antonio Cordeses sur l'oraison', in *Revue d'ascétique et de mystique* (RAM), 12 (1931), pp. 97ff. cf. J. de Guibert, *The Jesuits: their spiritual doctrine and practice* (St Louis 1972), p. 198.

15. I. Iparraguirre, 'Élaboration de la spiritualité de la compagnie 1556-1606', in *Dictionnaire de spiritualité* (Paris 1937-) Cited as DS, VIII, col. 975. All articles in DS VIII under *Jésuites* are published separately as *Les Jésuites* (Paris 1974).

16. '*et alia huiusmodi*'.

17. P. Dudon, 'Les leçons d'oraison du P. Balthasar Alvarez 1573-1578', in RAM 2 (1921), pp. 36ff.

18. MHSJ, *Directoria*, 681, Cap. 20.

19. ibid., p. 301, no. 116.

20. Exx 76.

21. cf. de Guibert, pp. 468-70.

22. cf. P. Dudon, *Les leçons*, p. 45.

23. H. Bernard-Maître, 'Le Pere Jean-Philippe Roothaan et la Vulgata latine des Exercises de saint Ignace', in RAM 37 (1961), p. 199.

24. P. Vallin, 'La compagnie rétablie en France 1814-1950', in DS VIII, col. 1047. Also in *Les Jésuites*, p. 165.

25. da Camara: op. cit., nos 195, 196.

26. cf. *Constitutions*, 260.

27. da Camara, op. cit., no. 357.

28. MHSJ, *Directoria*, Doc. 4. p. 95.

29. Exx 20.

30. MHSJ, *Epist. Nadal*, 'In examen annotationes', p. 652.

31. ibid., p. 651. *In omnibus rebus, actionibus, colloquiis. . . . Dei praesentiam rerumque spiritualium affectum sentiret atque contemplaretur.*

32. 'We are in the company of a soul that is being led by God in ways of infused contemplation *to the same degree, though not in the same manner*, as a St Francis of Assisi or a St John of the Cross'; de Guibert, op. cit., p. 44.

33. 'Mystique Ignatienne', in RAM 19 (1938), pp. 1-22, 113-40.

34. ibid., p. 136. All this section is, of course, based on de Guibert's study.

35. ibid., p. 135.

36. ibid., p. 137.

37. M. Giuliani, 'Nuit et Lumière de l'obéissance', in *Christus* (1955), pp. 349ff.

38. Vitelleschi, the successor of Aquaviva, wrote on 5 April 1629 that he was disquieted to hear that Lallemant, whom he had recently appointed instructor of tertians, was *totus mysticus*. cf. Michel de Certeau, 'Crise sociale et réformisme spirituel au début du XVIIe siècle: Une "nouvelle spiritualité" chez les Jésuites français', in RAM 41 (1965), pp. 339ff.

39. MHSJ, X, p. 349.

40. cf. Jean Leclercq, 'Théologie et prière', in *Chances de la spiritualité occidentale* (Paris 1966), p. 209.

41. *Constitutions* 814.

42. ibid., 671.

43. ibid., 813.

44. K. Rahner, *Mission and Grace III* (London 1966), p. 185.

Selected Further Reading

TEXTS

Autobiography

Among more recent English versions are:
William Yeomans (trans.), *Inigo: original testament* (London, Inigo Enterprises, 1985).
William J. Young (trans.), *St Ignatius' Own Story* (Chicago, Loyola University Press, 1980 edition).

The Spiritual Exercises

The most commonly used text in English is that edited by Louis J. Puhl (Chicago, Loyola University Press, 1950).

A modern non-literal interpretation of the text is David L. Fleming, *The Spiritual Exercises of St Ignatius: a literal translation and a contemporary reading* (St Louis, Institute of Jesuit Sources, 1979).
See also George E. Ganss, ed., *Ignatius of Loyola: The Spiritual Exercises and Selected Works*, Classics of Western Spirituality series (New York, Paulist Press, 1991).

IGNATIUS OF LOYOLA

Recent accounts of his life include:
Philip Caraman, *Ignatius of Loyola* (London, Collins, 1990).
Candido de Dalmases, *Ignatius of Loyola, founder of the Jesuits, his life and work* (ET. St Louis, Institute of Jesuit Sources, 1985).

A brief but useful essay is that by Imhof in:
Karl Rahner and Paul Imhof, *Ignatius of Loyola* (ET. London, Collins, 1979).

A more specific perspective is provided by:
André Ravier, *Ignatius of Loyola and the Founding of the Society of Jesus* (ET. San Francisco, Ignatius Press, 1987).

IGNATIAN SPIRITUALITY: GENERAL

The best general introduction to Ignatian spirituality is the recently published:

261

Selected Further Reading

David Lonsdale, *Eyes to See, Ears to Hear: an introduction to Ignatian spirituality* (London, Darton, Longman & Todd, 1990).

A useful account of Ignatian prayer is provided by: Margaret Hebblethwaite, *Finding God in All Things* (London, Collins, 1987).

A classic and detailed, though dated, account is:
Joseph de Guibert, *The Jesuits: their spiritual doctrine and practice* (ET. St Louis, Institute of Jesuit Sources, 1972).

Two provocative essays on contemporary historical and theological problems of interpretation are:
Philip Endean, 'Who do you say Ignatius is? Jesuit fundamentalism and beyond', *Studies in the Spirituality of Jesuits* 19, 5 (November 1987).

Roger Haight, 'Foundational issues in Jesuit spirituality', *Studies in the Spirituality of Jesuits* 19, 4 (September 1987).

THE SPIRITUAL EXERCISES: GENERAL STUDIES

A classic but controversial study is:
William A.M. Peters, *The Spiritual Exercises of St Ignatius: exposition and interpretation* (Rome, Centrum Ignatianum Spiritualitatis, 1978 edition).

A critical study from the perspective of liberation theology is:
Juan Luis Segundo, *The Christ of the Ignatian Exercises* (ET. London, Sheed & Ward, 1988).

Gilles Cusson, *Biblical Theology and the Spiritual Exercises*, translated by Mary Angela Roduit and George E. Ganss (St Louis, Institute of Jesuit Sources, 1988). This is an authorized translation of Cusson's *Pédagogie de l'expérience spirituelle personelle: Bible et Exercices Spirituels*.

Other recent short studies and essays include:
Brian McDermott, 'With him, in him: the graces of the Spiritual Exercises', *Studies in the Spirituality of Jesuits* 19, 4 (September 1986).

John Padberg, 'Personal experience and the Spiritual Exercises: the example of St Ignatius', *Studies in the Spirituality of Jesuits* 10, 5 (November 1978).

Peter Schinneller, 'The new approaches to Christology and their use in the Spiritual Exercises', *Studies in the Spirituality of Jesuits* 12, 4-5 (September/November 1980).

John Sobrino, 'The Christ of the Ignatian Exercises', Appendix in *Christology at the Crossroads* (ET. London, SCM, 1978).

Although dated, a useful bibliography of works in English prior to 1981 is:
Paul Begheyn, 'A bibliography of St Ignatius' Spiritual Exercises', *Studies in the Spirituality of Jesuits* 13, 2 (March 1981). This bibliography is updated to 1991 by Paul Begheyn and Kenneth Bogart in *Studies in the Spirituality of Jesuits* 23, 3 (May 1991).

PRESENTING THE SPIRITUAL EXERCISES

Three of the best-known general aids for retreat directors are:
Marian Cowan and John Futrell, *The Spiritual Exercises of St Ignatius of Loyola: a handbook for direction* (Denver, Ministry Training Services, 1981).
John English, *Spiritual Freedom* (Guelph, Loyola House, 1982).
David L. Fleming (ed.), *Notes on the Spiritual Exercises of St Ignatius of Loyola* (St Louis, Review for Religious, 1981).

On presenting the 'Exercises in daily life' see:
Maurice Giuliani, *The Exercises in Daily Life*, English edition of *Progressio*, Supplement 18-19, November 1981 (Christian Life Communities, Rome).
John Veltri, *Orientations*, volumes 1 & 2 (Guelph, Loyola House, 1979 & 1981).
Joseph Tetlow, *Choosing Christ in the World* (St Louis, Institute of Jesuit Sources, 1989).
Gilles Cusson, *The Spiritual Exercises Made in Everyday Life: A Method and a Biblical Interpretation*, translated by Mary Angela Roduit and George E. Ganss (St Louis Institute of Jesuit Sources, 1989). This is an authorized translation of Cusson's *Conduis-moi sur le chemin d'éternité*.

Also essays in:
'The Spiritual Exercises in daily life', *The Way Supplement* 49 (Spring 1984).

THE SPIRITUAL EXERCISES: SPECIFIC ELEMENTS

See the essays in Fleming, *Notes*, above. What follows is a selection of useful sources to complement the present volume:

Overall dynamic
Alexander Lefrank, 'The Spiritual Exercises as a way of liberation: the social dimension' in *The Way Supplement* 46 (Spring 1983).
Joseph Veale, 'The Dynamic of the Exercises' in *The Way Supplement* 52 (Spring 1985).

Principle and Foundation
Andrew Hamilton, 'The right use of creatures' in *The Way* 26, 3 (July 1986).
Philip Sheldrake, 'The Principle and Foundation and images of God' in *The Way Supplement* 48 (Autumn 1983).
Joseph Tetlow, 'The fundamentum: creation in the Principle and Foundation', *Studies in the Spirituality of Jesuits* 21, 4 (September 1989).

Selected Further Reading

First Week
Other essays in 'Presenting the First Week', *The Way Supplement* 48 (Autumn 1983).
And:
Joseph Hitter, 'The First Week and the love of God' in *The Way Supplement* 34 (Autumn 1978).
Gerard W. Hughes, 'The First Week and the formation of conscience' in *The Way Supplement* 24 (Spring 1975).
Seamus Murphy, 'The mission to justice and giving the Exercises' in *The Way Supplement* 55 (Spring 1986).

The Kingdom
Robert L. Schmitt, 'The Christ-experience and relationship fostered in the Spiritual Exercises of St Ignatius of Loyola', *Studies in the Spirituality of Jesuits* 6, 5 (October 1974).
Robert L. Schmitt, 'Presenting the Call of the King' in *The Way Supplement* 52 (Spring 1985).

Second Week
Other essays in 'Aspects of the Second Week', *The Way Supplement* 52 (Spring 1985).

The Two Standards
Dean Brackley, 'Downward mobility: social implications of St Ignatius' Two Standards', *Studies in the Spirituality of Jesuits* 20, 1 (January 1988).
Dermot Mansfield, 'Presenting the Two Standards' in *The Way Supplement* 55 (Spring 1986).
James McPolin, 'The Two Standards in Scripture' in *The Way Supplement* 55 (Spring 1986).
Aloysius Pieris, 'To be poor as Jesus was poor?' in *The Way* 24, 3 (July 1984).

Third and Fourth Weeks
Other essays in 'The Spiritual Exercises: Weeks Three and Four' *The Way Supplement* 58 (Spring 1987).
And:
Peter Fennessey, 'The Third Week of the Exercises' in *The Way Supplement* 34 (Autumn 1978).
Brian McNamara, 'Prayer in Gethsemane' in *The Way Supplement* 27 (Spring 1976).

The Contemplatio
Michael Buckley, 'The Contemplation to Attain Love' in *The Way Supplement* 24 (Spring 1975).

Olga Warnke, 'The Contemplation to Attain Love' in *The Way Supplement* 58 (Spring 1987).

Prayer in the Exercises
Other essays in 'Prayer in the Spiritual Exercises', *The Way Supplement* 27 (Spring 1976).
And:
George Aschenbrenner, 'Becoming whom we contemplate' in *The Way Supplement* 52 (Spring 1985).
George Aschenbrenner, 'Consciousness Examen' in *Review for Religious* 31 (1972), pp. 14-21.
John Ashton, 'The Imitation of Christ' in *The Way Supplement* 16 (Summer 1972).
Philip Sheldrake, 'Imagination and prayer', Ch. 8 in *Images of Holiness* (Darton, Longman & Todd, London/Ave Maria, Notre Dame, 1987).
David Townsend, 'The Examen and the Exercises: a reappraisal' in *The Way Supplement* 52 (Spring 1985).

Discernment, Election and Choice
The most comprehensive contemporary study is:
Jules J. Toner, *A commentary on St Ignatius' Rules for the Discernment of Spirits* (Institute of Jesuit Sources, St Louis, 1981).
Toner's latest work on the subject of discernment is *Discerning God's Will: Ignatius of Loyola's Teaching on Christian Decision Making* (Institute of Jesuit Sources, St Louis, 1991).
A recent attempt to reassess the origins of the Rules for Discernment is:
Philip Endean, 'Discerning behind the Rules: Ignatius' first letter to Teresa Rejadell' in *The Way Supplement* 64 (Spring 1989).
A readable introduction is:
Thomas Green, *Weeds among the Wheat* (Ave Maria, Notre Dame, 1983).
Other useful essays include:
Lavinia Byrne, 'Asking for the grace' in *The Way Supplement* 64 (Spring 1989).
Nicholas King, 'Ignatius Loyola and decision-making' in *The Way Supplement* 24 (Spring 1975).
Michael Kyne, 'Discernment of spirits and Christian growth' in *The Way Supplement* 6 (May 1968).
Laurence Murphy, 'Psychological problems of Christian choice' in *The Way Supplement* 24 (Spring 1975).
Michael O'Sullivan, 'Trust your feelings but use your head: Discernment and the psychology of decision making', *Studies in the Spirituality of Jesuits* 22, 4 (September 1990).

Selected Further Reading

Spiritual Direction and the Exercises
Paul Begheyn, 'Soul friend: the director in the Spiritual Exercises of Ignatius of Loyola' in *The Way* 29, 2 (April 1989).

Philip Sheldrake, 'St Ignatius Loyola and spiritual direction', in Lavinia Byrne (ed), *Traditions of Spiritual Guidance* (London, Geoffrey Chapman, 1990).

David Townsend, 'The counsellor, the director and the Annotations' in *The Way Supplement* 42 (Autumn 1981).

Index

267

imagination 24, 47-8, 52 n10, 60, 78, 145, 170, 193
indifference 53, 55-6, 249, 258 n9

Jesuits *see* Society of Jesus
Jesus 18-19, 24, 25-6, 73-5, 77-81, 86-7, 89, 92, 95, 110, 117, 119-27, 139, 146, 152, 167, 173-4, 194

Kingdom of Christ, Contemplation on 4, 25, 81, 137, 162

Letters of Ignatius 101, 165, 242, 245 n3, 246 n15
love 34, 116, 154, 161, 170, 171, 192-4

Mary 88, 111, 112-13, 115-16, 134-5
mysteries of the life of Christ 78, 90, 92-3, 104, 110-12, 128-9, 145-7, 150, 152, 157-8, 242
mysticism 92, 94-5, 109

penance 44, 50-1
poverty 45, 78-9, 82-4, 132, 167, 189, 203
Prayer, Ignatian 89, 103, 105, 136, 146, 151, 197-8, 248-57
general 23, 26, 45, 64, 88, 96, 104, 117-18, 133, 135, 139, 153, 169-71, 181-2, 191-2 three methods of 106-110 preparation for 45, 47, 48, 53-4, 146 review of, *see* review of prayer
Presupposition, the 19, 51 n8
Principle and Foundation, First 26, 43, 54, 56, 58, 61, 63, 70, 86, 137, 138, 156-7, 160, 162, 174

relationship with God 42, 106-7, 138, 146, 153, 156, 189, 193, 196, 220, 230
repetition 23, 117, 151

retreatant 5-6, 19-20, 22, 33-7, 42-44, 53, 59, 129, 136, 138, 140, 180-9, 240-1, 252
retreats 5-6, 22-5, 28-9, 37, 140, 153, 179, 191, 203-4, 241
review of prayer 23, 54, 139, 151

Scripture 17, 21, 22, 47, 59, 60, 78, 99, 115, 119-27, 134, 136-7, 187-8, 197
Second Week 19, 25, 46, 63, 70, 77-8, 81, 83, 84-5, 86-95, 98, 101, 103-11, 112, 117, 138, 158, 159, 228-32
service 63, 69, 71, 75, 77, 81-5, 90-1, 92, 95, 100, 118, 154, 161, 162-3, 167, 199, 214
sin; meditations on 58-9, 160-1 social 66-76, 160 personal 22, 45, 57-8, 59, 60-2, 67, 69, 105, 137, 138, 157, 159-60 cosmic/ original 80, 86, 91, 111, 223
social justice 4, 32, 77-85, 100-1, 111, 145, 152-3, 188-9, 203-4, 214
Society of Jesus 12 n6, 20, 31, 36-7, 50, 154, 238-40, 242-5, 249-57
spiritual direction 133, 166, 168-74, 185-6, 191, 196-7, 203-14, 244

Thinking with the Church, Rules for 3, 4, 21
Third Week 19, 64, 103-13, 138, 161
Three Classes of Men, meditation on 4, 25, 70, 81, 82, 94, 138, 159, 162
Three Kinds of Humility 25, 75, 83, 88, 104, 110, 138, 159, 162
Two Standards, meditation on the 4, 70, 75, 81, 88, 90-2, 94, 96-102, 104, 105, 110, 138, 157, 159, 162

will of God 42, 62, 78, 87, 92, 159, 167, 199

Index of References to
The Spiritual Exercises

Numbers refer to standard paragraphing of modern texts